The Drama of the American Short Story, 1800–1865

The Drama of the American Short Story, 1800–1865

Michael J. Collins

University of Michigan Press
Ann Arbor

Copyright © 2016 by Michael J. Collins
All rights reserved

This book may not be reproduced, in whole or in part, including illustrations, in any form (beyond that copying permitted by Sections 107 and 108 of the U.S. Copyright Law and except by reviewers for the public press), without written permission from the publisher.

Published in the United States of America by the
University of Michigan Press
Manufactured in the United States of America
⊛ Printed on acid-free paper

2019   2018   2017   2016   4   3   2   1

A CIP catalog record for this book is available from the British Library.

Library of Congress Cataloging-in-Publication Data

Names: Collins, Michael J. (Michael James), 1984– author.
Title: The drama of the American short story, 1800–1865 / Michael J. Collins.
Description: Ann Arbor : University of Michigan Press, 2016. | Includes bibliographical references and index.
Identifiers: LCCN 2016007481| ISBN 9780472130030 (hardcover : alk. paper) | ISBN 9780472122165 (e-book)
Subjects: LCSH: Short stories, American—History and criticism. | American fiction—19th century—History and criticism. | Performance in literature. | Performing arts in literature. | Theater in literature. | Ritual in literature. | America—In literature. | National characteristics, American, in literature.
Classification: LCC PS374.S5 C55   2016 | DDC 813/.010903—dc23
LC record available at https://lccn.loc.gov/2016007481

Acknowledgments

This book is the work of many years, many readers, much patience, and much love. Any list of my debts of gratitude will always be woefully insufficient. Traditionally, acknowledgments end with the author's relatives, but I wish to take a different approach. Throughout this long process, my family have been the first people to whom I have turned to test out ideas, ask for support, and seek out encouragement—even when it was inappropriate, needy, or plain irritating to do so. As such, they deserve to be right at the top. Form should follow function. While writing this book I fell deeply in love with the beautiful, wonderful, intelligent, and tolerant Rebecca, who is a terribly good sport in loving this distracted, frequently distant man back. This book was written as I married you and became a father to the miraculous Samuel—whose sweet, toddling invasions of my office were never as unwelcome as I, regrettably, sometimes made them seem. As I write these acknowledgments, I await the imminent arrival of another, as yet unnamed, addition to our little family. I hope to give you all the attention you deserve. You may never understand how much inspiration your forthcoming birth was to finally finish writing. My parents and my sisters are also owed much. In my parents' case, this is financial as well as emotional. Unending thanks.

I would like to thank Judie Newman, Graham Thompson, Celeste-Marie Bernier, and all the staff in the Centre for American Studies at the University of Nottingham for all the support they offered me in the initial stages of this project. I owe huge thanks to my colleagues at the various universities in the UK who saw fit to employ me and keep me solvent as I wrote this book: Martin Halliwell at Leicester and Dick Ellis at Birmingham especially. My colleagues and friends in the English Department at the University of Kent—Will Norman, Stella Bolaki, David Herd, David Stirrup, Sara Lyons—are a source of unending inspiration and motivation.

All my students at Kent who have endured my anecdotes about the bizarre world of nineteenth-century theatre culture deserve praise for their endurance. Fellow British-based nineteenth-century Americanists Emily Coit, Tom Wright, Peter Riley, Andrew Lawson, Matthew Pethers, and everyone in BAAS and BRANCA helped give courage, conviction, and coherence to this work. Sue Currell has been a major supporter of me and my work and I thank her gushingly.

In the USA I would like to extend my profound gratitude to Don Pease and Eric Lott, whose seminars at UCD Dublin and in Dartmouth were unforgettable formative experiences for me as a scholar. Conversations with Nancy Bentley, Meredith McGill, and Brad Evans had more effect than they may have realized. Such kindness needs to be acknowledged. I also want to thank the librarians at the Library Company of Philadelphia, the Bobst Library at NYU, the British Library, the Templeman Library at the University of Kent, and the Hallward Library at the University of Nottingham for tracking down some truly weird stuff.

Funding for this project came via the University of Nottingham, the AHRC, and the Leverhulme Trust. I would also like to thank the Fulbright Commission for sending me to New York in 2010 and everyone at NYU Steinhardt.

A very early version of chapter 1 appeared in *US Studies Online* as "The Knickerbocker Atlantic: Ritual and the Federalist Tradition in Washington Irving's *Sketch-Book*" (no. 16, Spring 2010). A version of chapter 2 appeared in *Symbiosis: A Journal of Anglo-American Literary Relations* as "Republicanism and the Masonic Imagination in Edgar Allan Poe's 'The Cask of Amontillado'" (vol. 12, no. 2, October 2008). Sections from chapter 3 appeared in *Comparative American Studies* as "The Rule of Men Entirely Great: Republicanism, Ritual, and *Richelieu* in Melville's 'The Two Temples'" (vol. 10, no. 4, December 2012). A section from chapter 4 appeared in *Journal of American Studies* as "The Master-Key of Our Theme: Master Betty and the Politics of Theatricality in Herman Melville's 'The Fiddler'" (vol. 47, no. 3, 2013). I am thankful to all the peer reviewers and readers for these publications and especially to Tom Dwyer, LeAnn Fields, and the two anonymous readers for the University of Michigan Press, whose suggestions for improvement were spot on in every case—even when I didn't follow them to the letter. Any overreaching of logic herein is purely my own. The successes I owe to them.

Finally, I would like to thank Rebecca and Sam again. Honestly, thank you. There are no words. Rebecca, I am taking you to dinner. Sam, I am buying you a rabbit / guinea pig.

Contents

Introduction: The Irving Brothers at the
Park Theatre, 1802   1

1 "No Garden of Thought, nor Elysium of Fancy":
Washington Irving's *The Sketch-Book of Geoffrey
Crayon, Gent.*   33

2 The Rites of Pure Brotherhood: Fraternalism and
Performance in Poe and Lippard   77

3 "The Rule of Men Entirely Great": *Richelieu*, Ritual, and
Republicanism in Melville's Diptychs   117

4 The "Child of Nature," or the "Wonder of the Age":
Melville's Child Prodigies   153

5 "Contending for an Empire": Performing Sincerity
in Hawthorne's New England   191

Epilogue: Louisa May Alcott's Theatrical Realism   227

Notes   245

Bibliography   251

Index   265

Introduction

The Irving Brothers at the Park Theatre, 1802

On November 15, 1802, a nineteen-year-old Washington Irving published the first in a series of nine fictional letters in the *Morning Chronicle*, a New York newspaper edited by his brother Peter that was closely aligned to Aaron Burr's wing of the Democratic-Republican Party. The narrator was an "odd old fellow" (Irving, *History, Tales, and Sketches*, 5), bachelor, "uninterested spectator" (5), and thinly disguised Federalist named Jonathan Oldstyle, who offered the reader his curmudgeonly observations upon the "strange and preposterous" (7) customs, fashions, and manners of the rising post-Revolutionary generation. The letters consisted of meditations on diverse topics such as the changing landscape of modern marriage, the decline of the "chivalric" tradition of duelling, and the purpose of "bowing . . . scraping . . . [and] complimenting" in ballroom etiquette. However, the greatest body of Oldstyle's missives (Letters III to VIII) were reserved for meditations upon theatre culture: from the behavior of actors and audiences to the roles played by critics, scenery, politics, and architecture in shaping the performance. In the hands of a teenaged Washington Irving the theatre became a synecdoche for almost all of the performances of identity, personal or ritualized, that characterized the social life of early nineteenth-century New York. Irving's letters, though, remain something of an anomaly in American literary history, barely accounted for by the critical record save as juvenilia that look forward to his aesthetically more accomplished future developments.

It is a well-established critical insight that Oldstyle's dispatches to the *Morning Chronicle* were partly intended as a pastiche of earlier English precedents, particularly the work of the eighteenth-century Whig writers Joseph Addison and Richard Steele.[1] Irving borrowed from Addison and

Steele a sense that acts of spectatorship—the observation of social behaviors, rituals, and performances—were important to understanding the residual, dominant, and emergent politics of the modern populace. Like Addison and Steele, theatre for Oldstyle was not just a means of entertainment but also an organizing principle of modern life. Over one hundred years after Irving's Oldstyle letters, Walter Benjamin would make a similar point in his famous essay on Baudelaire. For Benjamin, newspapers (whether Addison's *Spectator*, Peter Irving's *Chronicle*, or the *feuilletons* of 1830s Paris) attempted to find pleasure and meaning in the oftentimes inscrutable, chaotic, and threatening actions of modern urban crowds and so transformed the experience of modern everyday life into a series of dramas comprising of "individual genre scenes" (*Illuminations*, 169). These "genre scenes" framed events in such a way that particular attention might be paid to the effects of gesture and social theatre, which, Benjamin suggested, drew print into the orbit of theatre and allowed spectators to consider how the lives and actions of embodied individuals were both shaped by, and occasionally resisted, ideologically inflected interpretations of historical progress.[2]

Irving lived in a postimperial, circum-Atlantic world that was being molded culturally by the influence of various European, African, and indigenous diasporas. In this new, uncertain world, performative characteristics of style, gesture, posture, and decorum were important vectors of personal, political, economic, and national identity, as well as being procedures often required in order to facilitate access to various public spheres of speech and print. Oldstyle may have been a figure of fun for a youthful Irving and his readers, a decaying soul whose commitments to the "grand—*days of old*" (10) were radically out of keeping with the progressive mores of young America, but he also spoke certain truths about the character of the new nation. Like Addison's spectator, Oldstyle did not just attend the theatre but looked upon everyday life "as if it were a theater" (Brand, 34) and in so doing drew attention to the important, frequently unacknowledged cultural work undertaken by the performing bodies of the new American people.

Irving did not just copy Addison's style; he also innovated within the form of the literary sketch. What made Irving's narrator radically distinct from the persona of the classical Addisonian spectator was the manner in which he drew attention to the social effects of his own corporeality. Through his descriptions of an injury he sustained "aside of [his] head with a rotten pippin" thrown from the "gods" upon the "honest folks in the pit" (Letter IV, 14) and various comments about the humorous effects of his dress and posture, Oldstyle reflected upon his condition as what would in a later age of formalized ethnographic research be labelled a "participant-observer." In the traditional English version of the spectatorial essay or sketch, the author did not dwell on the particularities of the narrator's character beyond their bachelorhood and superabundance of free time. In fact, the narrator was usually little more than a conduit: remaining relatively passive, detached, and free from normal "social, familial or economic obligations" (Brand, 28) that beset all genuine historical actors. This disregard for the psychological and emotional life of the character would leave the reader free to insert themselves into the world the narrator described. In the Oldstyle letters though, Irving deployed his command of older English literary styles in order to respond directly to the immediate social changes that were shaping his own postcolonial American society. The claim implicit in Irving's decision to adopt the style of English spectatorial essay, that life resembles theatre, was made at a moment in which theatregoing, spectatorship, and an association with English cultural traditions such as the theatre were anything but apolitical, passive, or detached. They were, rather, becoming increasingly charged with the utmost political and national significance.

In *The Drama of the American Short Story, 1800–1865* I describe how the short story genre in American letters holds a special relationship with performance. I argue that without the influence of performance culture of various diverse kinds (religious ritual, stage melodramas, folk culture, oratory) the short story may not have come into meaningful existence or would have emerged with a distinctly different character. In so doing, I suggest that in order to fully understand how the short story form operated in early to mid-nineteenth-century American society, one must consider three elements in conjunction: the printed context in which the work appeared, the performance and expressive culture surrounding that work, and the role played by the story within a transnational framework of memory, exchange, and cultural borrowing. To begin, I will explore some of the contexts surrounding Washington Irving's first dabbles in New York newspaper writing.

Like a great many young New Yorkers of his era, Washington Irving knew the theatre very well indeed. In his *Life and Letters*, Irving's nephew and biographer Pierre Irving would paint his uncle as if he were a comedic type in one of his own satirical essays. Pierre Irving remarked that as a child his uncle would flout the Scottish Presbyterian "parental interdict" against the stage and "go early and see [a] play—then hurry home to prayers . . . then get slyly out of the window on to a woodshed. . . . to steal back to see the after-piece" (*Life and Letters, Vol. 1*, 35). Additionally, in writing the Oldstyle sketches, the young author drew upon his own experience as a member of an influential and well-connected group of journalists that, like the "cluster of young fellows" (Letter IV, 15) and dandies Oldstyle lampooned in his letters, lay at the vanguard of a now nearly forgotten New York literary and political scene: Dr. Peter Irving, Charles Adams (son of President John Adams), and the Quaker abolitionist Elias Hicks.[3] According to the first major historian of the American theatre, William Dunlap, these politically engaged young men were some of America's first major critics and "were regular frequenters of the New York theatre . . . [who] put down their remarks on the play of the evening, meeting next evening to criticise the critique, and give it passport to the press" (195). The Oldstyle letters were composed in this space between daily work and evening theatregoing. Given Irving's own relationship with the theatre, it is not, perhaps, a surprise that the central character of one his first forays into the short story was as theatre critic (of sorts). Indeed, in selecting this figure Irving was writing himself into the literary tradition of the Enlightenment spectatorial essay: a form with a long and prestigious pedigree in British letters. Irving's essays serve as a useful starting point for this book because in addition to being generalized examples of short narrative style before the advent of the "tale" or short story proper, a development Irving would himself be significant in making, they also emerged within the context of a very specific early national history that serves as an archetype for many of the concerns that would shape the short story throughout the first half of the nineteenth century. Telling this story involves returning to the specific site and context in which Irving first began to write professionally in short form: New York in 1802. Still more specifically, it means resurrecting life at William Dunlap's elite Park Theatre, which first opened its doors in 1798.

During the time at which Irving published the Oldstyle letters, conflict raged across the United States between two dominant, competing conceptions of the role of drama in civic life. According to David Waldstreicher, in order to aid their treatment of the new nation as a coherent and stable whole that was unflinchingly committed to the newly minted Constitution, the politically conservative Federalists often emphasized the consensus-building function of drama, while also arguing that it was able (where other genres were unable) to express the necessity of cultural ties to Europe.[4] For Federalists, the theatre was often a site of moral instruction and civic participation, a synecdoche of their larger republican dream of communitarian government by "assent of a unified populace" (51) that at least appeared spontaneous even if it was in fact regulated by (to borrow Herman Melville's rather apt metaphor) politically elite "stage managers" (*Moby-Dick*, 7). On the other hand,

Democratic-Republicans would come to regard the stage as a dynamic site of dissent that offered spectators a lens upon the rapidly changing everyday feelings and attitudes of an increasingly diverse citizenry. More than this though, a hangover from Constitutional debates between Federalists and antifederalists in the 1780s had bequeathed to Democratic-Republicans in many of the larger cities of the United States a taint of the antitheatricalism that had been a strong strain in American Protestant culture. Theatre, it had been argued by many antifederalists, was a British institution, and so was an uneasy presence in the new democratic landscape that needed to be developed along liberal principles.[5]

In New York though, the story was far more complicated than just being about Federalists and Democratic-Republicans, or theatricalism and antitheatricalism. In the post-Revolutionary period New York theatre was as much defined by the experience of class as it was by political allegiances, since as a city New York had traditionally exhibited higher levels of enthusiasm for performance across party lines. As Heather Nathans has shown, while Puritan Boston and Quaker Philadelphia had "experienced major shifts in political and cultural power during the Revolution" (*Early American Theatre from the Revolution to Thomas Jefferson*, 123) that had seen the rise of an ideological agenda of "republican simplicity" and a drive to use the stage to promote moral decency and civic pride, New York City was much less committed to this "common-sense," populist style of politics. Instead, what dominated the New York scene was the culture of the marketplace—the financial incentives that came from a functioning theatre culture and a strong tradition of public display of class and position. From a purely nationalist perspective Irving was a strange case: a Democratic-Republican with affection for Federalist posturing, theatricality, and the stage, and an Anglophile who idolized Aaron Burr (yet came to loathe the president he served under, Thomas Jefferson). Yet, within the context of New York City his attention to theatre and performance was perhaps less surprising, since without the dominance of a strong tradition of "republican simplicity" one could more successfully be both a dandyish "young buck" and Democrat; such divisions were not so mutually exclusive as in Boston or Philadelphia.

Returning to the Park Theatre will help me illustrate my argument. The Park was designed in part to provide the Federalist financial elites of the city a space free from the class and political wranglings that had disturbed the "sanctity" of the older John Street Theatre in the last two decades of the eighteenth century. The 1790s had seen the emergence of a new power base and political machine among the Federalists' Democratic-Republican rivals, organized around a network of allegiances to the artisan fraternity known as the Tammany Society and to George Clinton (then-governor of New York State) and his acolytes. These Tammany Democrats had launched a campaign to destabilize the traditional Federalist mercantile elites of the city—a group known colloquially as the Tontines for their relationship to a coffeehouse of that name—from their position of dominance over city politics. As Nathans has shown, the Tammany Society's policy of publically disrupting performances at the John Street Theatre had "by the summer of 1794 . . . made the theater inhospitable to its wealthier patrons" (137), leading the Tontines to search for a new site through which to generate wealth and display their cultural capital in the city, unimpeded by the agitation and disruption of their artisan and state Democratic rivals.

As known supporters of the Democrats and personal friends of Aaron Burr, the Irving brothers' very presence at the Park Theatre was a deliberate and public gesture of defiance that was made all the more piquant by Washington Irving's own literary performances in the Oldstyle letters, which were much discussed across party lines within the city. The Oldstyle letters were loaded with references that pointed to the same contemporary concerns that Peter Irving discussed in the pages of the *Chronicle*: the relationship between Anglophilia and class, young Americans and old, Federalists and Democrats, and rugged country people and urban cosmopolites. Appearing in a partisan newspaper dedicated to advancing the cause of the Democratic-Republican Party in the new nation, the *Morning Chronicle* letters also highlighted the centrality of theatre, performance, and ritual to the culture and politics of print in this era. Yet in so doing, they also staked out a middle space for Irving's own emergent literary style, which took the form of an affectionate burlesque of both the "rough" artisans of Tammany Hall and the "Old-Style" Federalists of the Tontine Coffeehouse. Crucially, the short sketches were not direct, confrontational performances of political sensibilities of the kind that proved so controversial during the conflicts over the John Street Theatre, and neither were they essays that staked out clear political positions in print—a common mode in an era of a highly partisan publication industry. At the core of Irving's short narrative style was an appeal to a version of consensus organized around the theatre as a site of potential cross-cultural mixing that moved beyond local debates to engage with something like a "national" culture. Across this book, I will show how rather than being an anomaly, Irving's New York style, and his liminal position within national debates, can be seen as the archetype for the American short story writer in the first half of the nineteenth century, which would come to fuller fruition in the work of writers such as Melville, Hawthorne, and Poe, whose work was beginning to be directed towards burgeoning national markets during the antebellum era. Like Irving, these writers held largely democratic views but were prone to pronounced moments of class snobbery, they were Anglophiles with grudges against Britain, and, most importantly, they were thinkers whose insistence upon the performative nature of identity set them at odds with the emergent essentialism of much antebellum nationalism, transnational "romantic" culture, and the fixity of party lines.

The Irving brothers were far from the first in the Revolutionary era and early republic to utilize a newspaper aesthetic that limned the boundaries of drama and print to comment on the social and political conditions of the emerging national scene. Washington Irving's clearest progenitor was Mercy Otis Warren, whose work for the *Massachusetts Spy* and the *Boston Gazette* between 1772 and 1775 also couched political critique in the language of theatre and social ritual. As Sandra J. Sarkela has noted, Warren's short "dramatic sketches" from *The Adulateur* and *The Defeat* that appeared in these newspapers were released to coincide with the evolving news of Governor of Massachusetts Thomas Hutchinson's ongoing political battles with the burgeoning patriot movement. Warren's "dramatic sketches" were not intended to be fully autonomous theatrical texts, or initially even to be staged, but were instead excerpts from fictional performances in Boston that commented satirically on the reports contained within the paper. Sarkela notes:

> Rather than falling for the ruse that there actually was, or should have been, a complete literary text from which the sketches were excerpted, we realize that Warren's creation of a fictional theatrical performance blurred the line between fact and fiction. Not complete didactic dramas in a conventional sense, Warren's sketches are made up of one or two speeches or brief dialogues between fictional but easily recognizable real-life figures. On the surface, readers were presented with excerpts from a tragedy that bore a superficial resemblance to other plays they may have known or imagined. ("Freedom's Call," 545)

By writing about localized political disputes in the form of tragic high drama, Warren was able to extend regional matters into a discussion of wider national concerns about freedom and liberty in the New World. This allowed her to generate a version of Boston that placed it at the vanguard of American patriot republicanism. In much the same way, Irving's "Oldstyle" letters spoke to regional debates (John Street Playhouse, the Park, Clinton versus Hamilton) yet reworked that material to engage with the wider national and transnational concerns of the Jeffersonian era.

As a New Yorker of the post-Revolutionary generation it is not clear whether Irving had encountered Warren's work, yet the artful combination of drama and print constituted an important eighteenth-century precedent for what I describe across this book as the developing form of the short story. Warren's mixture of fact and fiction, ritual, drama, theatre, and the essay is an important precursor to the development of the short story in American literature, which drew together these generic influences in an especially effective way in the succeeding antebellum era. Perhaps more significantly though is how the new early national scene that Dunlap described, and in which the Irving brothers participated actively, was in some respects more overtly gendered as male than the one in which Warren wrote and worked. This is to say that the reopening of the theatres following the Revolution regendered the public sphere in a way that was often hostile to female writers and thinkers who chose, like Warren (and her fellow Massachusetts-based playwright, journalist, and essayist Judith Sargent Murray), to engage directly in politics. Indeed, an important argument in this book is that the rise of the theatre in the United States came at a time when national political debate was becoming increasingly gendered according to the pernicious logic of separate spheres as a masculine pursuit, with the demands of Jeffersonian-era liberalism often calling for women who engaged in politics to do so through the lens of domesticity and not, as Warren had, through the avowedly public discourse of theatre.

Washington Irving's first forays into public life and fiction looked forward to an important shift in the cultural landscape of New York, and America more generally, in which performance—frequently subjected to censure in the northern colonies on religious grounds and once banned by the Continental Congress—became a newly resurgent element of post-Revolutionary social and political life. In the early national and antebellum eras critics and essayists increasingly looked to various forms of drama as a measure of the changing political landscape. The most famous and astute foreign observer of US democracy, Alexis de Tocqueville, would even suggest that changes in theatre and expressive culture were the earliest markers of a new democratic landscape: "when the Revolution that has changed the social and political state of an aristocratic people begins to penetrate their literature it generally first manifests itself in the drama" (*Democracy in America*, 358). As the work of Jeffrey Richards and others has shown, throughout the 1790s and the first decade of the 1800s, Revolutionary-era local and state prohibitions against theatrical performances were beginning to be lifted, occasioning a significant rise in the number of registered American theatres, professional acting troupes, playtexts in manuscript and print circulation, and, of course, critics. Nineteenth-century America was becoming "theatrical" in previously inconceivable ways—following the precedent set by a New York culture of display. "After a decade of confusion and hesitancy following the Revolution," writes Richards, "theater in America gained sufficient momentum to be accepted as a professional entertainment in most cities of size in the United States" (in Gustafson, *Cultural Narratives*, 73). In addition, various other theatrical or expressive forms (Masonic rituals, parlor theatricals, circuses, folk revivals) began to appear on the American scene that were as likely to aid as to hamper progress towards the establishment of a new, modern, national culture.

What made drama different from other genres of cultural expression in the era was how readily apparent it made the tense relationships between the differing needs of the artist and the audience. Lawrence Levine has argued that before a more fixed or immutable "hierarchy of culture" (*Highbrow/ Lowbrow*, 7) developed in the later nineteenth century, effectively neutering the bawdy back and forth between the stage and the audience that had traditionally defined the British theatregoing experience, playhouses were important sites of social, political, and class admixture and interaction— even if this took the form of direct confrontation, as in the case of the Tammany invasion of the John Street Playhouse. For Levine, as the bourgeois playgoers of the antebellum era began to advocate an approach to drama that emphasized the quality of the actors' performances and the interpretation of the text, the working classes began to be exiled to theatres that had been designed specifically with them in mind. In New York, where class was among the most dominant forms of identity, this process was already well underway by the first decades of the nineteenth century. Levine's influential argument also registered the rise of the wholly ironic concept of cultural autonomy in the arts as a consequence of the bifurcation of class—so-called "good" art became that of the financial elites. The short story though would remain skeptical of the notion of an autonomous sphere of artistic production that was elevated from the culture of the market in the nineteenth century. If, as I argue here, the short story reflected the theatre, it never fully bought into the elite reification of cultural autonomy that would shape the stage in the closing decades of the century, and would retain the "burlesque" sensibility of Irving's early republic.[6]

Irving may have moved in Aaron Burr's rather upper-crust Democratic-

Republican circle during the first decade of the nineteenth century, but he was actually not financially that secure and took evident pleasure in the slightly anarchic quality of the post-Revolutionary theatre, which in the New York of the late eighteenth and early nineteenth centuries was always threatening to break out into class war. As I show in chapter 1, this desire to move through different registers of experience would often lead Irving to playfully mock or burlesque claims to the authority of text and its potential as a means of objectively expressing that most elusive of romantic beasts, "the general will" of the people (Rousseau, *The Social Contract*, 150). This "general will," as Irving knew from his experiences at the Park, was little but a dream in the United States. New York especially was engaged in near-constant battles for supremacy between various interest groups. As time wore on the nation continued to be a place of dispute and uncertainty as local Federalist/Democrat rivalries gave way to further antagonisms based on national concerns of gender, class, region, race, and slavery.

This period of growing "theatricality" would also see the passage (and then rapid expiration) of the controversial Sedition Act of 1798. Signed into federal law by President John Adams, the act was a classic piece of Federalist legislation designed to control the pernicious influence of French Jacobinism in the new nation by preventing any individual from "writing, printing, uttering or publishing any false, scandalous and malicious writing or writings against the government of the United States" (*United States Statutes at Large*, US Congress, 1845). Although it reached into all areas of literary production in early America, it was the theatre that was most affected by the sedition laws. This was because in asking the citizenry that they remain vigilant and police culture for the sake of the new nation, the Sedition Act effectively transformed "passive" acts of spectatorship and literary consumption into politicized performances of civic engagement. Additionally, unlike prose, theatre ran the risk of being hit twice by the laws since drama exists as both text and as performance. This was to have huge effects in the development of competing political styles in the early republican United States, which became organized around an assumption that had been held by Federalists since the Revolution: that one "performed" their patriotism externally rather than merely held it as a passionate private conviction. Furthermore, by dissolving the distinction between the practices of "writing," "printing," "uttering," and "publishing," the Sedition Act blurred the traditional line in British Common Law of defamation between the oratorical act of slander and the textual act of libel, rendering all production and circulation of text or speech in the early republic effectively a performative act in the public sphere and closing the gap not just between prose and performance but between a pervasive eighteenth-century transatlantic culture of display and nineteenth-century national politics. The sedition laws, then, were of a piece with a growing culture of display. Their central argument about national identity being expressive was made at a time when theatre itself was gaining an institutional foothold in America. They suggested that the culture of display now extended into the emerging "culture industry," accepting both the rise of the theatre as inevitable and as something that would need to be policed to ensure that this flowering of expressive culture did not precipitate a backsliding of the nation into political anarchy.

In *Absence and Memory in Colonial American Theatre* (2006) Odai Johnson suggests that in all but a few cases there was limited prohibition against the writing of plays in America before the Revolution, and by corollary before the Sedition Act, even among those that objected on religious or cultural grounds to the very idea of an individual publically playing at different identities. Contrary to some of the more pervasive cultural myths in American literary history concerning the large-scale antitheatricalism of US literary culture, Johnson has noted that there had been little prohibition against playtexts being written or circulated in the United States prior to the Revolution. Motivated primarily by localized disputes, the primary concern for conservatives from the colonial era onwards had been theatre *in performance*, not as text, something that it is much harder for historians to locate and trace than the extensive, preserved, legal records testifying to cases carried out against the stage. Johnson states, "for material and ideologic reasons, the ephemera of theatrical production has not found repository in the cultural memory in the same way, or with the same weight as the legal records have" (4). Indeed, "a hegemony of preservation has played across the field, favoring the rich memory of the judicial record [a record dominated by antitheatrical elites] over the ephemera of performance" (8). The argument follows that this attention to preserved texts has engendered a narrative of antitheatricalism in American criticism more broadly, which actually belies the endemic, if fleeting, nature of all sorts of performance throughout American history.[7] The reality was that American versions of plays were often mangled, heterogeneous affairs in which characters and incidents from other shows that had proved to be crowd-pleasers were recycled with shameless impunity and little regard for realism or authorial consistency. The result is that the ephemeral nature of performance in America, where references and meanings are rendered highly contingent upon the contemporary moment of their performance, has led to the perception that it was (a) bad art from the perspective of a national tradition and (b) less culturally significant than the extensive prohibitions against it, which twentieth-century critics have often argued "proves" how the story of American national literature is one of poetry and prose primarily, and not of performance. New York was somewhat different, however, because of the history of class display and performance that had always defined its culture, even at times when there was no formal theatrical presence in the city.

What was exceptional about the moment of the Alien and Sedition Acts was that performance and text were beginning to be drawn together. At a moment when prose and performance were both subject to considerable surveillance on party-political grounds, Irving used short fiction to negotiate a space for the expression of political and social concerns that could not easily find an outlet in the traditional partisan press as either newspaper articles or political tracts, or in the actual theatre, which was also a highly partisan space. It is no coincidence that it is in this context that Irving develops the short story as a highly performative style of textual narrative to comment upon an era in which cultural production was so very politicized. This condition of being in between performance and written language would constitute a tradition in short story narrative after him. I would argue that Irving's earliest work in the short-form prose is important for two reasons of literary history and cultural memory. First, the Oldstyle letters testify to the fact that performance was debated politically in the early republic beyond a traditionally bifurcated narrative that mapped pro- and antitheatrical advocacy onto a party-political divide between Federalists and Democrats respectively. The letters present a narrative in which neither Oldstyle, nor the "young fellows" he attacks, nor his Democrat friend Quoz are "antitheatrical" in the slightest, even if they debate various aspects of local theatre culture. Second, through the very act of placing performance into words through the short story—the techniques of ekphrasis that characterize many of the Oldstyle dispatches—Irving bridged between a text-based understanding of American literary history that was dominated by an antitheatrical legacy and a performance history whose lack of material record has made it hard for historians and literary critics to resurrect or accurately represent.

Irving's short story style was shaped by his experiences at the Park, where he could see firsthand just how implicated seemingly small gestures and behaviors could be in many of fiercest political and class disputes of the age. During the time that Irving was frequently attending performances at the Park, Dunlap wrote and staged one of the most controversial plays of the era, *André: A Tragedy*. In the play Dunlap shows sympathy for a well-known

English soldier that had been executed in 1780 for the part he had played in the mutiny of the loathed American General Benedict Arnold. At a key moment in the first performance of the play an American solider named Bland performed a gesture that infuriated the New York crowd. Dunlap writes,

> The tragedy of "André" was performed for the first time on the 30th March, 1798. The receipts were $817, a temporary relief. The play was received with warm applause, until Mr. Cooper, in the character of a young American officer, who had been treated as a brother by André, when a prisoner with the British, in his zeal and gratitude, having pleaded for the life of the spy in vain, *tears the American cockade from his casque, and throws it from him.* This was not, perhaps could not be, understood by a mixed company; they thought the country and its defenders insulted, and a hiss ensued—it was soon quieted, and the play ended with applause. But the feeling excited by the incident was propagated out of doors. (Dunlap, 226)

As Caleb Crain notes in *American Sympathy: Men, Friendship, and Literature in the New Nation*, to many Americans the execution of John André had been a profound test of the limits of sentimental affiliation in their emerging nation. André embodied many of the values that were often associated with the ideal citizen of the new republic that was under construction, while regrettably also being a loyal subject of the British crown. He was a handsome man of great cultivation, taste, and deportment who represented a version of "Englishness" that many in America feared was in danger of being hastily devoured in the scramble for a new, exceptional national culture. For Crain, André embodied "a principle higher and more appealing than nationality, an ideal to which America as a nation aspired—the disinterested fraternity of men" (Crain, 2). The sentimental ideals of "fraternity" and "disinterest" were central to the project of American literature because they enacted the complex balancing act of "bind[ing] men without curtailing their liberty" (5). As I explore more in chapter 2, this paradoxical negotiation of affective bonds and individual liberty was a central concern for early nationalists, yet continued throughout the century as the battle between "aristocrat" and "democrat" and took on a new class politics in the market revolution as a conflict between bourgeois and mechanic. The forms of "fraternity" that had developed under the British imperial system were necessary for the development and maintenance of the new national political unity but always existed in tension with more entropic forms of liberal self-reliance. That the audience at the Park Theatre were more aggrieved by the breach of decorum elicited by a physical action than the principle of the piece as a whole—Adam Smith's Enlightenment, cosmopolitan suggestion that sympathy was possible, even desirable, across national, cultural, and military borders—speaks to how concerns about national culture found voice in the sensitive politics of the body in the early republic. When placed in the context of 1798 New York though, the controversy around this performance goes deeper than merely being an expression of an ongoing tension between Anglophiles and radical republicans. In tearing off the cockade, Dunlap seemed committed to offending almost everyone in the theatre, especially his largely Federalist Tontine subscribers. Nationalists of both parties would have seen a traitorous gesture that defamed the beloved American military (George Washington's army wore black cockades) conducted in the context of a play actually about traitors and at a moment when the Sedition Act was coming into play in the state, but the Federalist elites would also have seen a more localized slight. In response to international tensions with France (where Jacobins had begun to wear red, white, and blue cockades), Federalists in New York had taken controversially to the wearing of black cockades as a mark of their anti-Jacobinism. Since we can assume that Bland as a member of the Continental Army was wearing a black cockade, the tearing off of the badge would have had local, national, and international implications. Dunlap's reference to the "mixed company" of the Park Theatre resonates at the complex intersection of transatlantic, national, and local concerns that characterized much of the political culture of the early republic, vectoring a not-too-subtle reference to New York Federalist elites through a larger history of Anglo-American and Franco-American conflict. In speaking of the country's "defenders" the playwright and historian was being arch—referring simultaneously to the American military and to Federalists who considered themselves protectors of US national sovereignty against the spread of European mobocracy. Dunlap misread his brief at the Tontine-sponsored Park Theatre in assuming that the relatively comfortable status of much of his audience would afford him more creative license than at more rowdy theatres. In response to this outcry Dunlap rewrote the piece, removing the offensive gesture while barely altering some of its more audaciously cosmopolitan claims. The play was transformed from a potentially seditious piece of transatlantic republican theatre into a popular, nationalist pageant, *The Glory of Columbia; Her Yeomanry*, that became a major text in the Park's repertoire in the more nationalist era of Jackson's presidency.

Dunlap's response to the audience's discontent shows how much weight performance and gesture carried in the period and how important it is for us as critics to pay attention to concerns that seem ephemeral. However, the affair of the cockade also highlights another feature of performance in America at this time that would later become crucial to its meaning in short fiction. In Europe (particularly Britain and France) state-appointed censors such as the Lord Chamberlain regulated dramatic representation and shaped the character of the stage to a remarkable degree. However, in the United States participants and audiences played the censorial role. This made drama of every kind an extraordinarily unpredictable exercise that was largely dependent on the whims and caprices of what in the early republic were largely localized tastes and preferences and in the antebellum era became the ever-growing free market. Riots, assaults upon actors, public slanders of patriotism or morality, and hideous reversals of fortune were common features of the public culture of nineteenth-century America. Without censors or traditions of official endorsement like Britain to "pre-vet" material before it reached the stage and log copies within official repositories, the actual performance on the night was everything and could make or break a play. William Dunlap frequently bemoaned the fact that a lack of elite federal laws and regulations governing performance in the United States stunted the drama as "Brute force lorded it over intellect and the arts [whose] professors were considered servile" (2). What early American and antebellum defenders of states' rights regarded as their democratic privilege to choose the character of their entertainments, playhouse owners often saw as an example of what Alexis de Tocqueville famously referred to as "the tyranny of the majority." The driving force behind performance in the United States was not usually aesthetic accomplishment—a quality that would come to be valorized in the era of romanticism in terms of the cult of artistic autonomy—as much as the audience's desire for abundance, choice, and to not be left lagging behind the artistic and theatrical culture of Europe. Coupled with this was as an illicit thrill in reworking scenes from European performance culture into a bastardized American idiom that at once paid deference to the Old World and burlesqued it. This urge for abundance, choice, and play was supported by a system of unregulated trade in printed playtexts as well as a lack of official control over plagiarism until the very end of the nineteenth century. In fact, as Jeffrey Richards has suggested, the lack of regulation for both print and performance allowed these categories to be mutually reinforcing cultural entities in the early to mid-nineteenth-century United States, when performance culture was seeking to establish the firm foothold that it would have by the end of this period: "the pirating of plays increased substantially after 1790, tied largely to the restoration and expansion of legal theater" ("Print, Manuscript, and Stage Performance" in *Cultural Narratives*, ed. Gustafson, 75). Oldstyle comments on this tradition of messy, unbounded, unregulated performance in Letter V from December 11, 1802, in which he describes

> [A] fault that prevails among our performers . . . dressing for the same piece in the fashions of different ages and countries, so that while one actor is strutting about the stage in the cuirass and helmet of Alexander, another dressed up in a gold-laced coat and a bag-wig, with a chapeau de bras under his arm, is taking snuff in the fashion of one or two centuries back, and perhaps a third figuring with Suwarrow boots, in the true style of modern buckism. (Irving, 21)

Resurrecting the ephemeral moments of nineteenth-century performance history is one of the primary aims of this book, as doing so assists in the project of rethinking what the short story was attempting to achieve as a form of narrative frequently invested in performance as a political strategy. As such, this book is not so much about references to the texts of specific plays in the short stories of the period, although this is extremely important at points in the argument (especially chapter 3), as it is about performance culture: the gestures, self-consciously "theatrical" behaviors, symbolic acts, and anecdotes of which the theatre *as an institution* is an especially rich repository. Critics such as Lawrence Levine and Charles Olson have already done much to demonstrate the ubiquity of knowledge about the work of playwrights such as Shakespeare or Sheridan in nineteenth-century America. Merely noting references and intertexts is therefore not my object here. When I speak of theatre in this book, it is generally meant to reference a style and its institutional history separate from manuscripts and literary sources— the history of Anglo-American performance—rather more than the various dramatic texts that were drawn upon to produce those performances, which were, at least in the earlier period, commonly rewritten versions of foreign dramas. In other words, I am interested in what people *did*, not just what they had *read*. How was reading a short story informed by the performance history surrounding it? Where does the short story lie on a scale of public art that places the novel on one side and theatre on the other?

The American tradition of producing cheap, reprinted editions of foreign plays, or else stealing them on the sly, did little to cultivate a national drama but did allow playhouses to quickly stage performances of works that already had a proven record of success internationally. Despite his protestations concerning the intellectually barren American theatrical landscape, Dunlap himself made a good living from unofficial stage adaptations and translations of French and German folk melodramas, tragedies, and novels, which constituted a good deal of the dramatic fare consumed by early American playgoers. By midcentury this process did not just involve the adaptation of foreign material. The expansion of print culture from the 1820s onwards also allowed playwrights to draw on the growing body of successful works by their own countrymen. Sarah Meer has demonstrated exhaustively the important role played by Harriet Beecher Stowe's *Uncle Tom's Cabin* on the antebellum stage, but there were also adaptations of other popular works, such as James Fenimore Cooper's *Leatherstocking Tales*, George Lippard's *The Quaker City*, and Irving's own "Rip Van Winkle."

The relationship of print to the stage was not just a one-way process through which successful printed texts underwent dramatization. By midcentury printed versions of plays were often appended as extras with journals, periodicals, and mammoth weekly papers like *New World* and *Brother Jonathan* or could be bought from outside the theatre for reading or staging at home. Dion Boucicault would dramatize this process in his melodrama *The Poor of New York* (1857), which included a clownish character called Badger whose job is to sell copies of plays to patrons and passersby who have not been able to experience the performance firsthand. Badger's insistence that his "Book of the opera" is "the only authorized edition" (*The Poor of New York*, 29) is a knowing nod by Boucicault to the widespread unofficial practice of the reprinting and plagiarism of plays that had yet to finish their runs on the stage. In fact, a great deal of the drama consumed by Americans at the time was not first experienced in the theatre. As Isabelle Lehuu has suggested, "by the nineteenth-century, plays were read or recited, revealing practices of oral reading at a time when reading was becoming a more private and silent activity. These popular publications of tragedy and melodrama [including works by Victorian luminaries like Benjamin Disraeli, Edward Bulwer-Lytton, and Sheridan Knowles] confirmed a common cultural configuration between reading, theatregoing, and even acting" (74).

While the theatre itself was increasingly becoming gendered as a male-only space, it was this rise in print culture that made it possible for most white middle-class women to participate in this American performance culture. Considered in this way, Jo March's famous parlor theatricals and "Pickwick Club" performances from L. M. Alcott's *Little Women* represented an important tradition of nineteenth-century interaction between performance and print, the embodiment of beloved fictional characters by children and adults in a domestic setting. For women in particular, who by tradition or certain expectations of "decency" were cautioned against attendance at the theatre, parlor theatricals were by the middle of the century a crucial means of bringing the public culture of the stage into what was coded by many thinkers as their "separate sphere." In the epilogue to this book, I show how what started as a largely male tradition of exploring the relationship between the short story and performance paved the way in the later century for the development of new styles of female-authored narrative, in which the interaction between print and performance served as a means to critique the increasingly solidified gender roles and expectations of the period, especially those that pitted the "essential" nature of female domestic duty and subservience against a definition of masculinity as adventurous, public, and performative.

In Irving's earlier world of bachelors and dandies, attendance at the theatre was a symbolic act through which one defined their political, social, and gender identity and an exercise in democratic engagement. Indeed, as Andrew Quoz, another of Irving's fictional personae and Oldstyle's Democratic foil would observe, in the new century "the theatre . . . begins to answer all the purposes of a coffee-house" (23). In choosing to explore a connection between the coffeehouses of Addison's eighteenth-century London and the New York theatre in his Oldstyle letters, Irving made an important claim about the symbiotic relationship between the performance and print publics of his own time. As Jürgen Habermas and others have noted, the coffeehouses of eighteenth-century Europe had an important role to play in the development of the new bourgeois public sphere of print, which was in turn a shaping influence in the democratization of formerly aristocratic national cultures. "The bourgeois public sphere took root," writes Harold Mah, "in different social institutions in eighteenth-century Europe. In England, it found a base in coffeehouses and in journals such as *The Tatler*; in France, it first appeared in Parisian salons after mid-century; and in Germany, it assumed a more modest form in reading clubs" (157). These early citizens would circulate printed materials and engage in debates about their content and message. Coffeehouses allowed individuals to envision themselves as participating in the shaping of what Benedict Anderson referred to as the "imagined community" of the nation through the act of debating printed culture.

Theatres would have served very similar purposes to the coffeehouses—especially in the era before talking through the performance became taboo in elite playhouses—but did so with two interrelated qualifications. Unlike a public sphere organized exclusively around a printed text that foregrounded ideas and imagination, and in which the sympathy required for nation building operated between two largely disembodied intellects (reader and writer), attendance at the theatre asked of citizens that they pay attention both to the gestures and actions on the stage and each other's conduct and behavior, conceiving of political engagement as an embodied state reliant upon performative, often ritualized, codes of action. Additionally, to his contemporary readers the "coffeehouse" to which Quoz referred may have resonated as a subtle reference to the Tontine Coffeehouse—an institution whose dominance of New York City politics was increasingly being challenged by the expressive dissent and political "street theatre" of Tammany Hall. In writing back to the Federalist Oldstyle, Quoz is engaged in a witty play of his own, gently mocking his friend's increasingly outdated political vision.

When considering the role played by embodied sentiment and sympathy in the early United States it is useful to take note of Erving Goffman's observation that at the point of exchange with another person or culture "the self" usually takes on the status of a sacred "ritual object." For Goffman, "it is important to see that the self is in part a ceremonial thing, a sacred object which must be treated with proper ritual care and in turn must be presented in a proper light to others" (30). Since social ritual must articulate itself in response to preexisting gestural precedents (witnessing an entirely new performative manner of being in the world would, after all, be an extraordinarily confusing or alienating experience), performance culture demonstrates how a public sphere that accounted for the actions of the body in the shaping of an emergent political culture could never be either wholly nationalistic or wholly original. As Joseph Roach has remarked, "expressive movements" (the regime of drama and performance) are "mnemonic reserves . . . remembered by bodies" (*Cities of the Dead*, 26) across vast swathes of historical time. Whether it be an innocuous handshake or some more loaded gesture of deference such as a bow, preexisting behaviors patterned into the reserves of muscle memory by association with over two hundred years of European rule died hard in early America. For young American men—for, as Richard Busch has noted, theatre in the early nineteenth century was largely "a male club" ("Bowery B'Hoys," 374)—the American theatre was a site in which lively political dispute over the new nation was mediated through self-conscious public displays that inevitably recalled the old.

By focusing on print alone, critics have often missed the role served by performance as a parallel medium that worked in tandem with text during the nineteenth century in establishing a writer's public persona, often in unconventional or unauthorized ways. By the middle of the nineteenth century, authorial work, especially in the emergent world of magazine and periodical writing, was involved in a complex feedback loop. Often, fiction, poetry, and essays would publicize the writer's talents and interests in advance of fee-paying lectures and readings, at which events subscriptions were sought for the very magazines in which these texts appeared. These lectures and readings often took place in the growing number of spaces designated for performance, making authors as much a part of the culture of the stage as actors or musicians. Consequently, various forms of performance—so often regarded as the preceding text in a long-established *telos* of media development—expanded along with print in this era. For a writer in an age in which the cylinder printing press was making it increasingly possible for a consumer to procure such a dizzying abundance of printed materials that critics had begun to claim that the marketplace for print was becoming saturated, a talent of self-promotion and theatricality became an essential tool for survival.[8] Whereas literature in the eighteenth century often made a virtue of anonymity as a means to bolster the notion that the producer of a text spoke in a disinterested manner for the national benefit, the commodification of writing in the early republic and antebellum eras, as well as the entrance of new class identities into the public sphere, occasioned the return of the physical body into the discourse of print. This, in turn, resulted in a heightened interest in theatricality as a means to describe the new literary marketplace. As Isabelle Lehuu has suggested, print in the nineteenth century, with its ebullient forms of typography, richly drawn illustrations, and jaunty design, is often best understood as performative in itself, both a reflection of a burgeoning "theatrical" and ritualized social world and a shaping component of it. As I show in this book, the world of print and the world of the stage are brought productively into dialogue in the short story through the various ways the genre and the media in which it first appeared dramatized abundance, choice, and aesthetic play.

I have begun this study of the short story form with Irving's fictional theatre critic because it helps to highlight the growing importance of theatre and performance in nineteenth-century social and political life, a fact that critics have been slow to attribute any major significance in shaping early American and antebellum literary culture. This oversight can be accounted for by a long tradition of Americanist literary criticism informed by romantic myths of the United States' essential uniqueness. Theatre and theatre culture did not fare well critically in the era of nationalist literary canon building, when scholars were looking inwardly for signs of the indigenous "Americanness of American Literature" (*"Anna Karenina" and Other Essays*, F. R. Leavis). While the early American playwrights that might have filled the perceived need for a national drama (Royall Tyler, William Dunlap, John Howard Payne, Mercy Otis Warren) were firmly committed to the political objective of nationhood, because they often looked to Europe for their aesthetic models, their version of the American theatre did not serve the needs of many twentieth-century Americanist scholars who would for the most part choose to emphasize the more revolutionary stylistic interventions of later antebellum prose writers like Emerson and Thoreau. In a post–World War II moment punctuated by classic "myth and symbol" texts such as Leo Marx's *The Machine in the Garden* (1964), F. O. Matthiessen's *American Renaissance* (1941), and Henry Nash Smith's *Virgin Land* (1950), there was a pronounced tendency to look especially to literature conceived of as a written text as the main wellspring of information about a national culture that was frequently defined according to the tenets of Cold War criticism as liberal—that is, invested in discourses of individual natural rights. For these critics, American romanticism, whether it took the form of poetry, the essay, or the novel, called for a focused attention upon the work of text in order to posit a direct and intimate communication between writer and reader, unmediated by the process of labor, the rituals of republican civic culture, the vagaries of the market, or the pen of the critic. What Melville referred to in "Hawthorne and His Mosses" as "truth-telling" was, therefore, far from a neutral, depoliticized act. Instead, it was an integral aesthetic component of the claims of liberal American Renaissance writers to "enjoy an original relation to the universe" (Emerson, *Nature*, 35) and a precondition for nationalist self-invention. But such an unmediated relation between text and reader was also potentially dangerous, since the directness of this communication always raised, albeit obliquely, the threat of demagoguery, undue influence, and seduction.

Even though it was a profoundly reductive approach to cultural expression in the United States, the antiperformative faith in textual authority exhibited by "myth and symbol" criticism had a coherent logic. The body in performance, as opposed to the internal, mental spaces explored in myth and symbol's valorization of the romantic thinking subject, is a poor site to investigate if one's express wish is to locate a coherent, bounded, national identity. This is because, as Joseph Roach has remarked, performances "make publicly visible through symbolic action both the tangible existence of social boundaries and, at the same time . . . their anxiety-inducing instability"

(39). Put another way, performing subjects are what Victor Turner referred to as *liminars*, people "betwixt and between," in transition between orders of national and symbolic meaning, pulled in multiple directions, and (as seen in the confused utterances of Rip Van Winkle or the baffling silence of Bartleby) constantly prone to the threat of gross miscommunication. Unlike the "truth-telling" prose text, the performing self is a subject too wily to be pinned easily to a coherent national tradition.

The same claims to "inbetweenedness" might be made of the short story genre itself. According to most of our current genre theories, the nineteenth-century short story is placed somewhere on a spectrum between "romanticism" and "realism"—that is, between the collective logic of folklore and the expressions of "reality" that found their finest outlets in the modern novel. Taking "Young Goodman Brown" as his archetype, Charles May has suggested "the story manifests a compromise, between realism and allegorical romance, that characterizes the development of short fiction since Horace Walpole's eighteenth-century. . . . Gothic novella *The Castle of Otranto*" (*The Short Story: The Reality of Artifice*, 7). This is again why performance serves as an important lens through which to read short fiction. Even at its most "romantic," speculative, or fantastical, performance culture is still the work of bodies acting in a real, material space that is a site of tension, conflict, and friction. Performance theory challenges the nationalism that can only ever be a product of pure imagination separate from those bodies. Yet claims as to the nationalism of the short story form still exist. If the short story seems an especially "American" form of narrative it is because critics have successfully mapped this tension between realism and romanticism onto the conditions of the "American mind," suggesting that the clash of idealism with pragmatism that has shaped US political culture has its literary corollary in the form.

Recent critics such as Sandra Gustafson, Christopher Looby, Jay Fliegelman, Mary Kelley, and others have shown that a historic critical, disciplinary, and pedagogical division between performance studies and the history of the book has often resulted in a privileging of text as the primary repository of meaning for nineteenth-century literary studies, inadvertently perpetuating this romantic-nationalist mythology. Over time this has resulted in a tendency to overlook the symbiotic interactions between literacy and the embodied genres of performance that motivated works such as Irving's Oldstyle letters. Indeed, even in this age of transnational criticism Claire Sponsler has observed a marked tendency among "studies of transatlantic encounters . . . to valorize written representations over performance as the

key site of cultural contact and negotiation" (5). To offer new perspectives on American cultural practices, and because a singular focus upon text has been so historically tied to a national critical tradition, the exercise of the new transnational scholarship calls for an interdisciplinary approach that can bridge the divide between performance and print. To this end, my central claim in this book is that the short story form developed as a response to the complex intersections between histrionics and textuality that defined the early to midnineteenth-century transatlantic literary world. I show how the short story genre began in America as a means of capturing ekphrasitically how the politics and culture of the transnational nineteenth century were carried and expressed in the actions of embodied individuals as much, if not more, than the intellectual and disembodied spaces of concepts and ideologies encoded by a purely written language.[9] In doing this, I am expanding upon Christopher Looby's observation that Irving and others frequently satirized the political culture of early America as a hollow, overinflated "logocracy, or government of words" (2): a purely intellectual and speculative enterprise that paid little heed to what Victor Turner referred to as the social drama, "the many-levelled complexity . . . of human lives experienced first hand" (Turner, *From Ritual to Theatre*, 9). In addition to this I would add that Irving helped inaugurate a tradition of American short story writing that exhibited a marked discomfort with the power dynamics of written language. In place of the authority of text, I propose the short story form in this era would frequently empower nonlinguistic expressivity, rendering the gesturing body as a radical, parallel site of meaning.

In seeing the short story form as in constant negotiation with the formal logic that located certain forms of authority in written language I am contributing to a tradition. In *The Nineteenth-Century American Short Story: Language, Form, and Ideology* (1993), Douglas Tallack argued that the very brevity of the short story makes it "a form which contains, or seeks to contain, language" (vii). To write a short story is to express oneself creatively within the confines of a genre in which "there is less language and more form than in the novel . . . so that beginnings and endings seem to stand out" (vii). What I would add to this observation is how frequently the nineteenth-century short story's attention to various forms of expressive culture serve to extend the reach of the text beyond a formally closed model of beginnings and endings. In other words, the short story *gestures* outwards from the text towards a wider culture; it puts out feelers and its images latch on to other media. The claim implicit in Poe's "The Masque of the Red Death" that no amount of attention to hermetic formalism or language can contain the outside world indefinitely, might serve as a symbol of the especial porousness of the short story in a more general sense. In order to build a critical approach that takes adequate account of the nineteenth-century American short story's consideration of the role performance plays as a marker of all art's embeddedness within wider cultural and symbolic systems of meaning, I find it useful to read the form as a species of literature akin to Ngugi wa Thiong'o concept of "orature." Joseph Roach has helpfully summarized "orature" in the following way:

> [It] comprises a range of forms, which, though they may invest themselves variously in gesture, song, dance, processions, storytelling, proverbs, gossip, customs, rites, and rituals, are nevertheless produced alongside or within mediated literacies of various kinds and degrees. In other words, orature goes beyond a schematized opposition of literacy and orality as transcendent categories; rather, it acknowledges that these modes of communication have produced one another interactively over time and that their histrionic operations may be usefully examined under the rubric of performance. (Roach, 11–12)

In orature no aspect of cultural expression or communicative form is privileged over another, but is considered as a node within a wider network of meaning.

Considering the short story in this way, then, asks for a renewed attention to *form*, a move that has been somewhat controversial in literary criticism in recent years. Marjorie Levinson has noted that the rise of new historicism in criticism has often come with an attendant "denunciation of form as an ideological mystification" ("What Is New Formalism?" 559). Instead of concerning itself with formal elements, the argument proceeds, new historicist literary criticism has tended to focus upon a version of *representation* that characterizes the prerogative of critics as being the rewriting of a historical record marked by the significant elision of different cultural or subaltern groups. In this reasoning, too formal an analysis would be ideologically blind, even politically irresponsible. This raises a significant question when approaching the short story through historicist paradigms as I do in this book. If the short story is, as Tallack suggests, the most overtly *formal* of prose styles (in the sense of being deeply engaged with its own form), then must it also be always somewhat conservative, ideologically mystified, or unethical at the level of representation? I see the solution to this Gordian knot as lying in a renewed attention to performance in the short story. Not only does an interest in performance (which includes the work *form* and is first used to mean "to fashion" or "furnish forth") open up a text to various disciplinary and categorical influences, as Thiong'o notes, it also asks one to consider the relation of that text to its context—the pronounced aim of new historicism. By looking at performance culture therefore I wish to show how the short story can be both formal and embedded in its contextual history. In other words, it can be both representational and artfully abstract simultaneously.

Beginning with Irving, American short fiction in the nineteenth century would share a distinct relationship with performance.[10] Indeed, some forty-four years later in "The Philosophy of Composition" (a work that while nominally concerning the production of poetry has provided much of the critical nomenclature for subsequent short story theory) Poe (himself a noted theatre critic, onetime playwright, and child of actors) would utilize a surprisingly rich range of metaphors and references drawn from the world of the stage. The author denounced as frauds those that claimed to speak truth without the mediation of the body through a self-conscious, self-deprecating act in which he showed "the wheels and pinions—the tackle for scene-shifting—the step-ladders and demon-traps—the cock's feathers, the red paint and the black patches, which . . . constitute the properties of the literary *histrio*" (163). In this essay and another on Hawthorne's *Twice-Told Tales* Poe developed a critical vocabulary that has since become commonplace in interpretations of the short story genre: the notion that the primary aim of writing should be "unity of impression" (163), that "there is a distinct limit, as regards length, to all works of literary art—the limit of a single sitting" (164), and that the best magazine fiction operates through "circumscription of space" (166). Few scholars though have drawn attention to how much the meaning of "The Philosophy of Composition" pivoted on a relationship between writing and the stage. This is actually rather surprising, since Poe, Hawthorne, Melville, and Irving's short stories especially are often structured very overtly around moments of crisis and cultural performance: legal trials, Puritan religious practices, carnivals, masques, harvest festivals, etc. The short story's development as a distinct genre in the nineteenth century therefore paralleled changes in the American theatre, which, as Amy Hughes has argued, by the middle decades of the century had come to be organized increasingly around melodramatic moments, "situations, effects and tableaux" that point to the fact that "the coup de theatre" was beginning to "play [. . .] a role in American cultural production more generally" (*Spectacles of Reform*, 5). The "circumscription of space" that Poe had characterized as one of the essential elements of the nineteenth-century short story (what critics Winther, Lothe, and Skei have called the "Art of Brevity") produced a similar focus of attention upon the materiality of the body and its effects as Hughes has diagnosed on the stage. While Poe's own work provides the most obvious examples of this phenomenon, however, writers from Irving onwards had utilized the form as a means to engage with questions of social ritual, gesture, and embodiment—topics for which references to the stage often served as convenient shorthand.

Critics of the short story have often commented that a tendency to explain the form in the terms of other genres (poetry, the novel, etc.) is a consequence of its lack of a "significant tradition prior to the nineteenth century" (Tallack, 13) upon which one might draw. Edgar Allan Poe's attempts to define the formal qualities of the genre in particular have led readers to attempt to account for the short story in the terms of poetry, referring specifically to a "Romantic preference for intense lyric effects" (13). This grafting of the internality of a poetic, individualized, romantic consciousness onto generic theories of the short story has consistently produced readings that have emphasized the form's "visionary," "epiphanic," anticommunal, antitheatrical, even "antinomian" (Tallack) qualities as markers of the genre's peculiar national credentials, but this claim rests upon assumptions that are either anachronistic or excessively privilege a certain textual record over forms of ephemera that radically reconceptualize practices of reading. The romantic approach to the short story certainly proved useful in describing the short work of modernists such as Ernest Hemingway or Sherwood Anderson who deliberately structured their works to build towards "lyric moments" or epiphanies that allowed their heroes to momentarily transcend their grounded historical circumstances. However, this reading also had the effect of relegating the theatrical and expressive nature of the genre to the status of a residue left over from storytelling's primitive and ritualistic origins. The most popular tendency in short story theory still remains to follow the modernist Frank O'Connor, who suggested in *The Lonely Voice* (1963) that the short story "began, and continues to function, as a *private* [my italics] art intended to satisfy the standards of the individual, solitary, critical reader" (14). Indeed, O'Connor's preoccupation with the lyric has, over the years, come to standardize readings of the short story as a form committed to a model of authorship that posited an unmediated relationship between the solitary reader and the author's text. This vision of the short story as a solitary form for a single reader is loaded with problematic class assumptions. In identifying the form with a privatized, stable, and by implication bourgeois subject position, O'Connor belied the fact that its origins lie in an epoch punctuated by international industrial and political revolutions when identities were in a near-constant state of uncertainty and flux and large-scale crises developed around the misapprehension of the smallest of revealing, behavioral ticks.

Among other concerns, O'Connor's analysis has bequeathed short story criticism a distorted relationship to questions of a distinctive American national culture. In attempting to account for American literature's special pedigree in the short story, critics have often relied on O'Connor to argue that separation from major European publishing centers produced a form that was especially rich in instances of romantic alienation by which means outsider characters could become detached from the currents of history and able to reveal previously concealed truths. Hawthorne, Poe, Melville, and Irving, so the romantic argument proceeds, developed the short story as a national form that highlighted alienation, subjectivity, and an unmediated form of communication between reader and writer in order to reflect upon their peripheral position in relation to British imperial power. One also frequently encounters a specifically economic argument that often restates, albeit in an altered form, O'Connor's sense of the short story as the genre of choice for the political underdog. Charles May has offered a number of compelling modern arguments about the form over the years, but in *The Short Story: The Reality of Artifice* (1995) we hear echoes of O'Connor in the claim that

> short fiction's combination of the romantic and the realistic begins most vigorously in the United States . . . The reason was primarily economic; American writers stood little chance of competing against English novelists, whose works were cheaply and readily available in America because of lack of copyright control. (24)

May makes a specifically nationalist claim for the short story that takes little account of the *logic* of the genre—that is, what it can do, or what the authors might wish for it to do—beyond its position in competition with the British novel in the marketplace. I argue here that the periodical form did not merely provide a "vehicle for short fiction . . . in part to provide a means for American writers to publish their work" (24). The rise of the short story was not accidental in that way. Instead, I suggest that the form can do things that the novel cannot. It has a formal logic that is embedded in the specifics of its culture that far exceeds simple economics. Indeed, as Meredith McGill has noted, American writers were well aware of the lack of copyright and often used the easy reprinting it permitted to drive interest in their work. Some even published short fiction anonymously, fully aware of the potential copyright infringements so as to drive circulation.

Unlike the competing prose genre it closely resembles, the novel, which was influential in the development of the bourgeois private sphere and its reflective reading subjects in the sentimental imagination (organized around either individual or family reading), the early emergence of short stories within newspapers and periodicals meant that they were treated in a different manner and commonly circulated within a public space of exchange and debate that often criticized as arrogant fantasies the romantic notion of a sublime, transcendent, coherent intellect, author, or the sentimental characterization of the nation as a reified, impermeable family unit. If, as Elizabeth Barnes has convincingly shown, the novel in this period served to correlate personal liberalism with political nationalism by means of a focus "on private life in general and the family in particular" (23), then the short story was its unruly, sociable sibling. Surveying the landscape of the nineteenth-century short story, one sees a genre that frequently disrupts the public/private distinctions central to the Enlightenment project of nationalist development by assaulting the reader with depictions of theatrical rituals that blurred arbitrary disciplinary boundaries dividing the sacred and the profane, the ancient and modern, the European and American, and the redressive and celebratory.

Consequently, I argue here that the short story in its earliest phase was a very poor candidate for a stable, national literary form.[11] Almost from the start, its finest examples were playful with the boundaries of nations, classes, and cultures. By drawing attention to the importance of performance and ritual, which, as Joseph Roach has elegantly stated, is by its very nature always a product of a "circum-Atlantic interculture," the short story collapsed borders between the body and the text. In order to demonstrate the ways in which the short story bridges the divide between performance and print, I will be drawing upon the intellectual resources offered to literary studies by cultural anthropology and performance theory. I show how reading the short story alongside histories of theatre and performance, and with a focused attention on the cultural work done by gesture and social ritual, destabilizes a national critical tradition that locates the development of a coherent US culture within the auspices of a purely printed iteration of the public sphere. In so doing, I also highlight how theatre appears as a key structuring metaphor for the era's emergent periodical culture well into the antebellum era. Reading the short story alongside theatre therefore provides an important lens on the genre in its developmental phase. I also propose that in order to fully comprehend the cultural work of the short story in the American nineteenth century, readers must understand how the genre works both as performance in itself and as a medium that reflects upon the growing power of performance in nineteenth-century social life.[12]

In chapter 1, I show how Irving developed the short story proper in *The Sketch-Book* as a form invested in exploring the cultural and symbolic power of gesture and performance to express historical bonds of transatlantic fellowship and memory that were at risk of being cast aside by the development of a distinct American national culture. By reading *The Sketch-Book*'s meditations on history and textuality in this way I show how Irving's work negotiated a space between an emerging model of romantic authorship that emphasized the importance of newness, "nature," and inviolate selfhood, and one invested in the embodied responses of a performing subject.

Chapter 2 looks at the relationship between the short story and the ritual practices of transatlantic fraternal orders. In particular, I consider how the short stories of Edgar Allan Poe and George Lippard used fraternal rituals to comment on the importance of performed bonds to the identities of middle- and laboring-class men in mid-nineteenth-century America. Additionally, I read Lippard's serials in the *White Banner* (the paper of his own labor fraternity, the Brotherhood of the Union) as fictional prompts to the ritual practices of the order. I argue that by printing short stories that included the secret signs and symbols of the Brotherhood, Lippard collapsed a distinction between the printed word and ritual in an endeavor to bring men together in the historically meaningful bonds of union required for radical political action.

In chapters 3 and 4, I explore the various meanings attached to theatre and ritual in the short fiction of Herman Melville. In particular, I look at the role played by the Astor Place Riot in shaping Melville's work for *Harper's* and *Putnam's* magazines. Chapter 3 explores how Melville's reference in his diptychs to the British playwright Edward Bulwer-Lytton's work *Richelieu; or, The Conspiracy* is designed to offer a model of ideal republican leadership by which the nation might confront the threats to order posed by the increasingly sectarian and bifurcated politics of antebellum America. Chapter 4 continues this approach by offering new readings of "The Fiddler" and "Bartleby, the Scrivener" through the lens of performance and ritual theory. I argue that in these stories we see Melville confronting how status and class affect possibilities for speech and action within the increasingly performative and theatrical landscape of the modern American public sphere.

Chapter 5 considers the way that Nathaniel Hawthorne's short fiction is invested in the question of how to perform "sincerely" within the carnivalesque, potentially anonymous, spaces of the antebellum literary marketplace. I argue that for Hawthorne the answer came by means of an aesthetic interest in the powerful rituals of mourning that shaped antebellum middle-class culture. By publishing works that meditated upon the power of spectacle within a marketplace that often read short fiction as the textual analogue of theatre, I argue that Hawthorne effectively ironized traditions of New England antitheatricalism that had their origins in the intellectual culture of Calvinism.

In the epilogue, I turn briefly to the short work of Louisa May Alcott. In my readings of Alcott's short fiction I demonstrate how she developed a new approach to the dramatic tradition of the short story that navigates between the culture of performance explored in the early nineteenth-century short story and one informed by the rise of local color fiction and the emergent science of anthropology in the postbellum period. I argue that her interest in tableaux vivants and parlor theatricals should be considered as part of her wider project of using drama and performance to burlesque the claims made by many realists to the fixity of racialized, gendered, and classed categories.

In developing a new generic theory of the short story, I inevitably give shorter shrift than I might desire to major writers whose work developed within different traditions than the one I am describing. For example, the vast majority of the writers considered here are male. This is partly justified by the focus of my attention upon theatre, cultural performances that often had almost exclusively male audiences in the first half of the nineteenth century. It is no coincidence that as the theatre develops with a specific focus on the entertainment of male audiences that it begins to serve as an imaginative reserve for predominantly male writers. However, if there is anything we might say with confidence about the short story, it is that it is infinitely adaptable. Indeed, Kasia Boddy has recently argued that the genre is a peculiarly chameleonic form shaped as much, if not more, by paratext than authorial intent: "where we read the story shapes the expectations we bring to our reading of it, and thus the effect it has on us" (Boddy, 117). By beginning with the relationship between the post-Revolutionary New York theatre and the public sphere of print, I have also inevitably focused my inquiry down to the work of a formally educated, literate population working either in Britain or in the American Northeast. However, at all times I endeavor to consider the ways in which Irving, Poe, Melville, Hawthorne, and Alcott offered readers one particular approach to the short story genre among many. Where it was pertinent to outline a competing tradition (such as Poe's pillory of the gothic "Blackwood's Article," Hawthorne's send-up of the tradition of the "romantic fragment," and traditions of female-authored local color writing in "Main Street") I have done so. For the most part though, I argue that the very writers that critics have used to build a national canon would have likely considered their short work as having roots in a distinctly transatlantic history that sat uneasily within a purely nationalist cultural framework.

CHAPTER 1

"No Garden of Thought, nor Elysium of Fancy"

Washington Irving's *The Sketch-Book of Geoffrey Crayon, Gent.*

> Mr. Roscoe . . . has claimed none of the accorded privileges of talent. He has shut himself up in no garden of thought, nor elysium of fancy; but has gone forth into the highways and thoroughfares of life.
> —Washington Irving, "Roscoe"

> On entering the amphitheatre new objects of wonder presented themselves. On a level spot in the centre was a company of odd-looking personages playing at ninepins. They were dressed in a quaint outlandish fashion . . . yet they maintained the gravest faces, the most mysterious silence . . . Nothing interrupted the stillness of the scene . . .
> —Washington Irving, "Rip Van Winkle"

The central role played by Washington Irving's work in the development of the literary sketch as a distinct form in Anglo-American letters has long been established. Seen as a major exponent of the form in its early years, Irving's work in *The Sketch-Book* helped to establish a tradition of detached, often comic, first-person narration focused on the aesthetic potency of impressionistic and picturesque imagery. In addition to his sketches, in works that appeared alongside them in *The Sketch-Book*, "The Legend of Sleepy Hollow" and "Rip Van Winkle," Irving helped pioneer the "tale" or "short story proper" as a distinct genre in nineteenth-century literature. The disjointed structure of *The Sketch-Book* has often led critics to treat Irving's achievements in each form as separate and distinct, but this approach frequently misses how dependent the overall effect of the work is upon the sequential nature of its form when experienced in the manner that Irving initially intended, as a seven-part serial publication. Reading *The Sketch-Book* in sequence reveals Irving's self-conscious awareness of the formal limitations of the literary sketch and helps to reveal some of the motivations behind his development of the short story proper. By means of his clever use of Geoffrey Crayon as a performed persona that registers a conflicted allegiance between American newness and Old World historicism, Irving questions the political unconscious of the literary sketch itself, which he renders as an amnesiac form acutely unable to array the successive events of life into a meaningful historical continuity. Additionally, through Crayon Irving registers a challenge to an emergent romantic nationalism that imagined American identity as a radical ontological state made possible through text's capacity to imagine new conditions of perception. In order to criticize an emergent liberal, romantic tradition in American letters that valorized the individual consciousness over the collective and sacralized the transformative potential of newness, Irving created the short story as a form invested in the power of gesture and performance as the preferred media for the transmission of history as a lived experience.

Before coming to *The Sketch-Book* though, it is worth considering Irving's critical reputation, since to do so reveals many underlying ideological assumptions about his own work and American literary and political culture more generally. Despite the central positions occupied by Irving's creations within the history of the short story, his reputation has been unstable in relation to an American national canon. In *America's Sketchbook: The Cultural Life of a Nineteenth-Century Literary Genre* (1998), Kristie Hamilton summarizes a common critical approach to Irving's literary sketches when she writes, "[he] creates the sketch writer as doubly detached—above a scene . . . and purportedly independent of society's prejudices as Romantic poets sought to be" (21). Hamilton also states that "the claim of detachment allied elite educated, Euro-American males with an older, masculine European literary and philosophical tradition that had already been appropriated for the bourgeoisie by, among others, Joseph Addison and Samuel Johnson" (24). Hamilton's reading of Irving makes two key assumptions that I will attempt to debunk in the following chapter: the understanding that Irving's sketches create political and social detachment by utilizing text to establish a comparatively neutral space for romantic reflection, and his uncomfortable position as an "American" writer. Washington Irving's contribution to the

American short story is incalculable, but the fact remains that his work was a weak advertisement for the nation. A New Yorker first, a subject of British imperial history second, and only last an American, his cosmopolitanism is his true legacy, and it was carried in the form he developed in American letters. Irving's persistence in the canon is surprising, but all the more so is his development of the "short story proper," which as a genre might not have survived the 1820s vogue for nationalistic historical romance novels like John Neal's *Logan* or Lydia Maria Child's *Hobomok*, had it not been for Nathaniel Hawthorne and Edgar Allan Poe's renovations of the form in the 1830s.

By depicting social life through the form of the sketch, Addison, Johnson, and other British authors frequently sought to identify themselves as separate from the actions they described. In the hands of these classicists, the sketch was an elite form characterized by its critical, disinterested, and ironically detached personae. Indeed, as Jeffrey Rubin-Dorsky has remarked, Irving's deployment of this "English" style in *The Sketch-Book* has been called upon to indicate his poor candidacy for national canonization: "because Irving wrote as well as the eighteenth-century [British writers] (Addison, Goldsmith, Sterne) whose prose served as models for his unconvoluted style . . . his readers have imagined him a gentleman of letters in the stately English tradition" ("Sketches of Anxiety," 499). This association of the sketch with elitist detachment has led to Irving being compared unfavorably to the generation of writers that followed him in terms that have often confounded his literary aesthetics with his political allegiances. Furthermore, the cultivated refinement of his prose, so the argument goes, did not equip Irving for service to a national tradition that was increasingly read in terms of a logic of liberal, individualistic expression and self-fashioning. John Neal would famously make this point in the "Unpublished Preface to the North American Stories" of 1825, preempting Melville by some twenty-odd years in referring to Irving as the "American Addison."

A long tradition of seeing Irving's work as politically regressive within the context of an emergent American national culture began with Herman Melville's rejection of him during his early years of association with the "Young America" movement. As Paul Giles has remarked, "Melville . . . quickly wrote off Irving's literary persona Geoffrey Crayon, as an almost plagiaristic extrapolation from the work of Oliver Goldsmith" (*Transatlantic Insurrections*, 142). In addition to his claims of plagiarism, and in spite of the support the older writer gave to him in his early career, the young Herman Melville berated Irving because his upper-middle-class, mercantile, New York heritage tarred him by association with an elite, Anglophile Hamiltonian Federalism that had been largely superseded in the age of Andrew Jackson by a more bullish, liberal, and unrefined romantic nationalism. For the young Melville, Irving's Anglophilia in *The Sketch-Book* did not chime with Young America's celebration of newness and a largely Jeffersonian national imaginary characterized by faith in agrarianism, natural rights, and manifest destiny. Indeed, Christopher Looby has noted how this ideology was made possible by Jefferson's decision to imagine post-Revolutionary America in Lockean terms as a blank page awaiting a Promethean application of the written word. For Jefferson, the character of America's future depended upon the awesome power of text to reshape reality according to newly discovered or imagined truths. "Thomas Jefferson," writes Looby, "gave a linguistic turn to [the conception of American newness] when in 1824 he retrospectively claimed that 'our Revolution . . . presented us an album on which we were free to write what we pleased'" (*Voicing America*, 17). By contrast, Alexander Hamilton's Federalist vision represented America as an inheritor of an embodied history of transatlantic exchange. For Hamiltonian Federalists, national culture and national rights could not be created anew through mere language, since history was carried in the very bodies of the American citizenry.

Melville's brand of anti-Irving sentiment was picked up by such early texts of American Studies as D. H. Lawrence's *Studies in Classic American Literature* and F. O. Matthiessen's *American Renaissance: Art and Expression in the Age of Emerson and Whitman*, whose own readings of Melville's work have vicariously affected how scholars have engaged with Irving up to the present day. Lawrence and Matthiessen failed to include Irving in their picture of American literary history and in so doing contributed to a nationalist American studies' field imaginary that resisted Irving's cosmopolitanism and the republican political culture that underpinned it. Historically, scholars have rejected Irving's contribution to American letters as the product of an elite, conservative imagination seeking to distance itself from what was deemed unpleasant, uncomfortable, or unappealing in his national culture by reliance on the aesthetic conventions of the English literary sketch. As Dana Brand notes in *The Spectator and the City in Nineteenth-Century American Literature*, the tradition begun by figures such as Addison and Steele of "a spectatorial persona [that] enjoys a diversity without grossness, randomness without danger, amusing bustle of mild interest rather than terrifying chaos of profound fascination" (33) sought to make safe the increasing disorder of modern life for the emerging middle classes. For the British sketch writer the world became a theatre in which their vision corresponded to the central tower of Jeremy Bentham's panopticon. Addison and Steele's spectator could see all and yet remain respectively unseen because their position within the symbolic order—as white, wealthy males—was comparatively secure. As Michel Foucault famously argued, the dream of a truly objective vision is, after all, a political privilege afforded only to those whose political or social insiderhood might provide a screen against exposure.

In the hands of an outsider to British domestic life such as Washington Irving though, the literary sketch served a markedly different purpose. By deploying Geoffrey Crayon as a lens through which he could observe British manners and ritual forms, Irving was not registering his alienation from American culture so much as revealing that culture's embeddedness within a transatlantic history of performance and exchange. Whereas for Addison, Steele, Johnson, and others the sketch form displayed a desire for objectivity, to be "doubly detached—above a scene" (Hamilton, 21), for Irving it was a means of demonstrating his attachment to events and moreover the historical place of the American within British imperial circum-Atlantic history.

It is therefore precisely what many scholars have perceived as Irving's failings that make his short fiction important within the new landscape of transnational American studies. Irving's work, particularly *The Sketch-Book of Geoffrey Crayon* (1819) and *Bracebridge Hall, or The Humorists* (1822), does not uncritically venerate the picturesque qualities of British culture at the expense of "indigenous" American themes. Irving was, rather, interested in exploring how the self-evident fact that the heritage of the Old World was carried over in the manners and customs of the postcolonial American populace troubled the establishment of a unique, hermetic, and autochthonous US culture. It is certain that Irving, writing behind the mask of Geoffrey Crayon, finds much to admire of the British in *The Sketch-Book* and *Bracebridge Hall*, but this admiration takes the form of what Elisa Tamarkin has usefully called the art of "paying respects to the symbolic value of England" (*Anglophilia*, xxiii) as both the seedbed of American democratic manners and behaviors and a potential conduit through which he could register his opposition to many of the more insidious aspects of US national culture.

Yet, like many in the early republic, Irving doubted the validity of an American national character based upon essential, organicist principles that tied the "sublime" and "natural" rights of man to the conditions of the uncultivated American landscape.[1] These principles were often associated with Jefferson and his followers, who largely saw America's future in an ideology of agrarian individualism and romantic natural rights that spoke little to middle-class New Yorkers like Irving and his brothers. In spite of his early association with the Democrat Aaron Burr, a connection that Andrew Burstein has suggested was rooted more in Burr's powerful charisma and personal patronage than in his Democratic-Republican politics, Irving ultimately preferred "the Federalists' notion that good government did not require pandering to a mythic 'people'" (Burstein, 20) and favored the possibilities of a cosmopolitan culture that imagined authority to be a product less of natural rights than of civic virtue. Just as he had done before in *Salmagundi* and in the Oldstyle letters, Irving used his own local New York heritage as a means to reconsider larger national and transnational forces. The tradition of letters in which Irving was schooled was actually quite different from Addison and Steele's vision of aesthetic distance and detachment as the path to an objective truth. Unlike Addison or Steele, Irving did not think of print as providing an ideal, purportedly disinterested, space for objective, philosophical reflection or contemplative speculation. Indeed, in his earliest days as a writer Irving had made a name for himself by parodying the deep thinkers and *philosophes* of the Enlightenment age. Rather, as I suggested in the introduction, Irving's use of fiction was shaped by his long involvement with the cut and thrust of New York print culture, which possessed a more immersive relationship with events, as individuals staked out positions that corresponded to the day-to-day operations of the city's Democratic-Republican and Federalist power bases. Because New York inherited more fully from Britain the notion that one's right to power and influence was connected with one's hierarchical position within a republican culture of civic participation and display, in which all actions were meaningful only so far as they responded to preexisting social precedents, New York art often rejected the artificial, discreet, and hermetic textual framework favored by the romantic mind and posited a more open, adaptable, and ludic interplay between performance and print that, when read in directly national terms, more generally corresponded with conservative Federalist style than with that of the more liberal Democrats. Considering Irving's work in the terms of antebellum nationalism then, as Melville did, is to see his sketch work as essentially conservative, more precisely Federalist, in style, but this is ultimately misleading. Such an approach to the reading of literary culture had a precedent in earlier Constitutional ratification debates. As David Waldstreicher remarks in his study of the politics of national celebration in early republican America, *In the Midst of Perpetual Fetes*, Federalists often sought to distinguish themselves from their Democratic-Republican opponents by sanctioning

> a repeated move from performance to print and back [that] epitomized a profound, complex set of cultural forms in which traditional festivals were inverted into dirges and reinverted to become celebra-

tions, only to be improved upon in song, in dance, in the streets, in church, and, once again in print. (24)

According to Waldstreicher, Democratic-Republicans and their antifederalist forebears were often skeptical about celebrating a national culture that still included an influential upper-middle-class elite as part of its political landscape and used print as a means to register their dissent or detachment from the contrived world of civic ritual. By contrast, Federalists often favored a politics of national celebration that saw print as a participant in a performance of collective feeling. "Reports of celebrations," Waldstreicher asserts, "helped create the sense . . . [of] a national movement, an inevitable expression of the national popular will" (55). The public and private realms of performance and writing became mutually interdependent for Federalists in a way that was less true for Democrats, whose interests lay in the power of text to create an imaginative space of future potential. As Waldstreicher remarks, "the coherence of the process arose, not from the simple addition of celebrations and printed discourse, but from their natural reinforcement, so that it becomes hard to tell where the ritual or the reportage begins or ends" (27). For Federalists, rituals, performances, and festivals were simultaneously a way of displaying their elite power and presence within late eighteenth-century American politics and demonstrating the assent of the masses to that presence. Rather than praising the dissensus-building function of such things as elections and parades, Federalists tended to focus on how these events were ritualized expressions of republican ideals of civic participation.

This attitude can be seen early on in Irving's career in a letter to his friend Mary Fairlie of May 2, 1807. In the letter Irving describes how his search for "whim, character and absurdity" (*Life and Letters*, 187) have driven him to the spend three days of an election among "the mob" in a bar in New York's rowdy Seventh Ward. Irving writes,

> We have toiled through the purgatory of an election, and may the day stand for aye accursed on the Kalendar, for never were poor devils more intolerably beaten and discomfited than my forlorn brethren, the Federalists. What makes me the more outrageous is, that I got fairly drawn into the vortex, and before the third day was expired, I was as deep in the mud and politics as ever a moderate gentleman would wish to be; and I drank beer with the multitude; and I talked handbill-fashion with the demagogues, and I shook hands with the mob—whom my heart abhoreth. . . . My patriotism all at once blazed forth, and I determined to save my country! . . . Truly this saving

one's country is a naseauous piece of business . . ." (*Life and Letters*, 186–87)

Typically playful and exuberant, Irving's treatment of a real-life election day performs a fascinating act of burlesque reversal by coding an austere, modern act of patriotic duty (voting) in the formal terms of a festive, somewhat transgressive, ritualized, even medieval, carnival. In so doing, Irving renders a process through which individuals register their difference and dissent from the established order and from each other as a performance of collective, democratic feeling. Indeed, Irving confesses to his desire to be saved from the "vortex" of political action because his Federalist-leaning "heart abhoreth" the mob, but he ultimately accepts that both he and the wider populace share a common humanity and a common political future. Irving describes himself as a patriot not because he leans especially strongly in favor a particular party-political or nationalist agenda (he refers to a Federalist Party that he did not openly support as "brethren"), or because he has given considerable thought to his country's political future, but because he participates in the festivities that attend democratic culture. Once again, Irving's literary imagination responds to the immediate moment, the ephemeral acts of celebration and festivity around an election, as a means to access a wider historical purview that would conceptualize all Americans as part of a common humanity.

Unlike Jefferson's Democratic-Republicans, whose literature often adopted a dissenting, schismatic approach to politics that favored romantic assertions of essential laws, sublime truths, and the power of nature, Irving's New York City heritage led him to envision life as a social phenomenon structured around a series of performances and playful constructions of identity. Furthermore, the pro-urban, commercially speculative, and cosmopolitan sensibility of his mind engendered in him an understanding that people were incapable of self-reliant individualism, bound through ritual to a common, historical culture, and that one's qualification for political power did not lay in the richness of their imagination or the potency of their rhetoric but in republican codes of civic participation. For this logic to have any legitimacy individuals had to be seen in the public sphere, not remain unverifiable and critical as the aesthetic of the British literary sketch would have had it.

Republican Selfhood and *The Sketch-Book*

In the following section I read the first four chapters of *The Sketch-Book* alongside this tradition of republican civic culture in order to demonstrate how Geoffrey Crayon's narrative functions as a satire of romantic detachment. In order to accomplish this, one must first separate the persona of Geoffrey Crayon from Irving's own. While Diedrich Knickerbocker of the earlier *A History of New York* (1809) is usually treated as a comic, constructed character, Crayon has been more often read as a literal reflection of Irving himself. To do this requires the reader to pay close attention to the historical moment of *The Sketch-Book*'s composition, during which any literary performance of elite Anglophile detachment would have had especially potent political and social resonances: "Recovering the cultural and historical nuances of *The Sketch-Book*," writes Matthew Pethers, "first necessitates the removal of Irving's literary persona from its cosy nook by the antebellum hearth and its re-insertion into a public realm dominated by the War of 1812 and The Battle of Waterloo" (8).

Like *A History of New York*, *The Sketch-Book* is a work of metafiction and satire, in which Geoffrey Crayon is constantly fighting on two fronts to maintain control over his narrative and over the sketch form itself. In the first chapter of *The Sketch-Book*, "The Author's Account of Himself," Irving opens with an epigraph from John Lyly's *Eupheus*:

> I am of this mind with Homer, that as the snaile that crept out of her shel was turned eftsoones into a Toad, and thereby was forced to make a stoole to sit on; so the traveller that stragleth from his owne country is in a short time transformed into so monstrous a shape that he is faine to alter his mansion with his manners and to live where he can, not where he would. (743)

Thus, before Crayon has introduced himself in his own words Irving presents an epigraph that offers a comic vision of the traveller that alludes at once to the transformative potential of travel and the danger such a process poses to an easy nationalism. Lyly's epigraph suggests that the traveller becomes something unrecognizable or "monstrous" because of his experiences, a figure peculiarly at odds with the polite, "rambling" sentimentalist that Crayon imagines himself to be. Context, the epigraph suggests, is the crucial element shaping character, not one's internalized self-perception or "natural" inheritance.

From the offset, Irving develops a tension between the framing device of the epigraph and Geoffrey Crayon's own first-person narration. Crayon opens his interventions into *The Sketch-Book* with the statement "I was always fond of visiting new scenes and observing strange characters and manners" (743) before providing a potted history of his life in America that generates an image of constancy. Irving juxtaposes the metamorphic, dynamic, Renaissance vision of John Lyly with Crayon's own perception of a life marked by consistency and stasis—typified by phrases such as "I was always" and "this rambling propensity *strengthened* with my years" (743). In addition, the focus on observation, as opposed to a contact or relationship with history suggested by the epigraph, casts Crayon as a detached spectator attempting to offer the reader an impossibly objective account of his own mental and physical development. The disjunction between the epigraph and the text imposes an uncertainty upon Crayon's following narrative. Irving begins *The Sketch-Book* playfully by exposing the discontinuities that exist between the narrator's sense of himself and the transformative capacities engendered by a life of motion and experience.

"The Author's Account of Himself" functions to expose the performed nature of authorial identity. Geoffrey Crayon, like Diedrich Knickerbocker, William Wizard, Jonathan Oldstyle, and others of Irving's personae before him, is involved in a simultaneous process of depiction, explication, and self-fashioning. Crayon alludes to the tradition of spectatorship in which he seeks to establish himself in the final paragraph of the piece when he states, "I cannot say that I have studied [scenes from life] with the eye of a philosopher, but rather the sauntering gaze with which humble lovers of the picturesque stroll from the window of one print shop to another" (745). The reference to "the eye of a philosopher" follows another reference to philosophers in the previous paragraph, which slyly hints at Irving's own perception of the poor hold such thinkers have upon reality: "I was anxious to see the great men of Europe; for I had read in the works of various philosophers, that all animals degenerated in America, and man among them" (744). Crayon's desire to see England stems from his wish to "see the gigantic race from which I am degenerated" (744). Such a wish gives sanction to the ideas of the philosophers, yet in their second mention ("I cannot say that I have studied them with the eye of a philosopher") Crayon doubts his capacity to exert such philosophical authority upon the world. Instead, Crayon's gaze is fleeting, "caught sometimes by the delineations of beauty, sometimes by the distortions of caricature, and sometimes by the loveliness of landscape" (745). The incapacity of Crayon to maintain coherence in the face of experience casts doubt on the authority of his proceeding narrative and of text more generally. The tradition of spectatorship inaugurated by Addison and Steele, and in which Crayon seeks to place himself, is questioned through his inability to impose order upon events. As Martin Roth notes of Irving's earlier persona Diedrich Knickerbocker, he is "unable to order the story in his mind, unable to exert any control over the story he wishes to tell, unable to decide whether the story is fact, myth, actual or marvellous" (169). Applying such a reading to Crayon contradicts the suggestion that as a sketch writer, Irving sought to impose the same level of authority and control upon the world he views as did Johnson, Addison, or Steele. Instead of reflecting the romantic ideal of a neutral, unharassed space of individual contemplation in his sketches, Irving uses the form to engage in a playful and self-reflexive burlesque of romantic claims to objective vision.

In an earlier passage from "The Author's Account of Himself" Crayon alludes to his discontent with his current American scene:

> I visited various parts of my own country, and had I been merely a lover of fine scenery, I should have felt little desire to seek elsewhere its gratification for on no country have the charms of nature been more prodigiously lavished . . . no, never need an American look beyond his own country for the sublime and beautiful of natural scenery. (744)

For Crayon, the meaning of America has become inextricably tied to romantic conceptions of the sublimity of the New World landscape. Crayon feels little parity with the grandeur of American scenery, but his response to it is expressed in the tenor of a broader romanticism. Even as Crayon purports to reject the romantic worldview, he is subject to its influences, describing the landscape in terms that were already becoming outdated by 1819 through association with Jefferson's increasingly common and hackneyed declarations of America's future promise. "Her mighty lakes," Crayon states, "like oceans of liquid silver; her mountains with their bright aerial tints; her valleys teeming with wild fertility; her tremendous cataracts thundering in their solitudes" (744). No amount of impressive imagery or grand rhetoric can disguise that fact that the enthusiastic viewer of early nineteenth-century romanticism has come to resemble a bored, lone spectator longing for some new object to gratify him: "had I been merely a lover of fine scenery, I should have felt little desire to seek elsewhere its gratification" (743). As Albert von Frank remarks in *The Sacred Game* (1985), Crayon is a confused character in whose narrative it is "often difficult to distinguish between the literary nationalist, with his grudge against history, and the provincial Anglophile who wants nothing more than to have history reassert itself" (61). Irving plays out these tensions through the sketch form, which possesses at once a historical association with English literature and a formal propensity towards the disembodied consciousness that marked its place within the history of transatlantic romanticism.

The vast excess of Crayon's language in this passage runs counter to the "sauntering . . . humble . . . picturesque . . . delineations of beauty" (745) that he then claims to favor. Crayon's desire to see the world as "from the window of one print shop to another" (745) replaces the stultifying experience of the sublime landscape with an equally staid and detached series of tableaux that are really nothing more than a degraded form of romantic disinterest. As Brand notes of the sketch form, it often corresponds with a larger romantic attempt to free the individual from the pressures of an involvement with an emergent international market culture by exploring the possibilities of being "not a shopper, but a window shopper . . . maintaining an independence from commercial activity that corresponds to his independence from social and familial responsibilities" (37). Bored by expressions of the sublime in nature, yet unable to abandon his reliance upon the sketch form's inbuilt romantic sensibilities, Crayon presents himself as horribly conflicted. In this way, Irving satirizes the kinds of grand nationalist rhetoric often associated with Jefferson's Democratic-Republican Party as well as the more insidious manner by which the American mind is colonized and delimited by such rhetoric. From the opening few paragraphs the narrative of *The Sketch-Book* concerns Irving's attempt, through Crayon, to resist appropriation by a romantic sensibility increasingly becoming inseparable from Jefferson's cultural nationalism.

To do justice to the complexity of *The Sketch-Book* it is valuable to approach it as a sequential series of evolving, interconnected chapters rather than as a discontinuous narrative of detached, unrelated picturesque sketches. In any reading of *The Sketch-Book* it is important to account for why Irving chose to have these articles bound together rather than circulated separately in periodicals or as newspaper articles. One reason is certainly financial. In doing so, Irving was able to ensure greater returns from a work that would likely have been widely reprinted without his knowledge in a transatlantic marketplace that was unprotected by intellectual copyright laws. Equally as significant though are the aesthetic effects of such an approach. To present a series of sketches asks the reader to consider them sequentially and to observe how the authorial persona performs within different social and political contexts. It is a republican conception of selfhood, whereby the protagonist's subjectivity is rendered as more dynamic, public, and unstable than that of the more traditional British literary sketch. The first of these numbers comprised "The Author's Account of Himself," "The Voyage,"

"Roscoe," "The Wife," and "Rip Van Winkle." Rather than breaking up these sketches and publishing them in different magazines, Irving ensured that they were bound together and printed in a high-quality quarto. This suggests that Irving intended *The Sketch-Book* to be read sequentially—that they worked better as a continuous narrative than as discrete sketches. Additionally, the book not only explored the importance of sociality and republican civic culture in its text, it also performed these ideas in its material form. *The Sketch-Book* was light, small enough to be portable, and printed with a "large type and copious margin" (*Life and Letters*, 416) that implied it was to be either consumed on the move or shared around middle-class parlors as a spur to conversation or public reading.

Irving's challenge to the coherence of the romantic mode's egocentric subjectivism is continued in the second chapter of *The Sketch-Book*, "The Voyage." In this piece Crayon is consistently foiled in his attempts to envision the Atlantic in terms that corresponded with a broadly romantic ideal of an imaginative neutral space. Crayon remarks, "the vast space of waters, that separates the hemispheres is like a blank page in existence . . . From the moment you lose sight of the land you have left, all is vacancy until you step on the opposite shore . . ." (746). However, in the paragraph immediately following this assertion, Crayon undercuts himself by describing this sense of "vacancy" as at once liberating and troubling, providing the mind with a space for "meditation" and "reverie" as well as an object of profound fear and trepidation. Qualifying his assertions, Crayon remarks, "a wide sea voyage severs us at once . . . it makes us conscious of being cast loose from the secure anchorage of settled life and set adrift upon a doubtful world" (746).

Matthew Pethers has noted how Irving's view of the sublime frequently resembles Edmund Burke's theory of romantic aesthetics. For Irving, sublimity and terror share a common space in the imagination. Crayon wishes to find comfort in "the temporary absence of worldly scenes" (747) produced by the ocean, but instead finds an alienating sense of disconnection and solitude. In this way Irving emphasizes the equation of romantic amnesia with the genteel "sauntering gaze" of the sketch genre he first made in "The Author's Account of Himself." By suggesting that the blankness of the ocean and the "picturesque" qualities of the sketcher's tableaux share a common space in the imagination, Irving collapses the distinction that Crayon makes between the "sublime and beautiful of natural scenery" (744) and "the picturesque stroll from the window of one print shop to another" (745). Crayon's desire for aesthetic distance and objectivity is juxtaposed with a strange fear he has for the "vacancy" of the ocean. Rather than being a way of providing comfort and safety for middle-class readers as it had in the cases of Addison, Steele, and Johnson, a sense that the writer is always in some way in command of what he views, for Irving the aesthetic distance of the literary sketch is a source of a profound terror and anxiety about the annihilation of selfhood and denial of historical memory. When later reflecting on the awe associated with the ocean Crayon retracts his remarks about the "vacancy" of the sea. Instead, he suggests, "a sea voyage is full of subjects for meditation: but then they are wonders of the deep and of the air, and rather tend to abstract the mind from worldly themes" (747). Never failing to miss an opportunity to satirize his hapless narrator's tendency to fall into romantic reverie, Irving immediately places Crayon in a position in which he is forced to confront the "worldly themes" from which he often "tend[s] to abstract the mind" (747). After musing grandiloquently upon how a distant ship is "a glorious monument of human invention; which has triumphed over wind and wave; has brought the ends of the earth into communion" (747), Crayon's ship passes by a horrific wreck. Crayon writes:

> We one day spied some shapeless object drifting at a distance . . . It proved to be the mast of a ship that must have been completely wrecked; for there were the remains of handkerchiefs, by which some of the crew had fastened themselves to a spar to prevent their being washed off by the waves . . . But where, thought I, is the crew!—Their struggle has long been over—their bones lie whitening among the caverns of the deep. Silence—oblivion, like the waves, have closed over them . . . (748)

In his image of a shipwreck as the source of "silence" and "oblivion" Irving provides a bathetic counterpoint to Crayon's vision of Atlantic trade as a "monument to human invention" and the source of "communion." If, as Pethers suggests, Irving followed Edmund Burke in seeing the connections between a "sense of terror and the exercise of state power" (16) at the center of the sublime, then the implications of this image within a narrative of Anglo-American travel are intriguing. Crayon notes, "there was no trace by which the name of the ship could be ascertained . . . the wreck had evidently drifted about for many months . . . long sea weeds flaunted their sides" (748). In the context of the recent War of 1812 the image of a shipwreck and drowning sailors seems poignant. The sublime is tied in his mind to the annihilation of individual identity as the sea removes all prospects of identification and historical knowledge, creating a "vacancy." Crayon's vision of a ship that has "triumphed over wind and wave . . . diffus[ing] the light of knowledge and the charities of cultivated life, and has thus bound together those scattered portions of the human race" (748) is a romantic image that resembles Jefferson's famous declarations on the possibilities of national progress. In his first inaugural address of 1801 Jefferson had called America:

> A rising nation, spread over a wide and fruitful land, traversing all the seas with the rich productions of their industry, engaged in commerce with nations who feel power and forget right, advancing rapidly to destinies beyond the reach of mortal eye . . . (291)

By immediately presenting Crayon with this image's cruel inverse, Irving exposes the contradictions inherent in romantic-nationalist rhetoric. Jefferson's famed notion of an "Empire for Liberty" is exposed as a sham that belies a true history of violence. Burke's equation of the sublime with state power maps romantic thinking onto the kind of imperial consciousness that produced the War of 1812. For Irving, the assertions of national providence that were becoming associated with the Anglophobia of Jefferson's Democratic-Republicans were conditions of mere rhetoric, constructed through a textual imagination that obscured such horrors as Indian extermination (something he would later explore in "Traits of Indian Character," *A Tour of the Prairies*, and *Astoria*) and the triangular trade. Not only has the sea presumably killed all of the men aboard, but it has also annihilated all records of the ship's name. Read alongside Crayon's earlier suggestion that the sea produces a "vacancy," the erosion of the ship's name is Irving's poignant warning against unverifiability that is, in turn, a warning against the seductions of rhetoric and a critique of the sketch form's claims to aesthetic detachment. For Irving, bellicose nationalism, a position of aesthetic detachment, and romantic providentialism shared a common space in the early nineteenth-century Atlantic imaginary: the desire for the annihilation of history.

Suddenly afraid and aware of his solitude, Crayon seeks out the company of others. "As we sat round the dull lamp in the cabin," he writes, "every one had his tale of shipwreck or disaster" (748). What follows is another shipwreck tale, this time relayed by the captain. In addition to a context for the shipwreck that Crayon has just seen, the captain imposes an authority upon his narrative that forces him to "put an end to all my fine fancies" (749). The captain's tale of his vessel accidentally sinking a smaller one when she "struck her just a mid-ships" (749) in the dense fog "of Newfoundland" (748) highlights, for Crayon, his relative weakness against the sublime and fickle power of the sea. The captain's vessel is described as "a fine stout ship" (748) "going at a great rate through the water" (749), an image of vitality against which the "small schooner at anchor" (749) is powerless. The notion that the smaller ship is stationary is interesting in relation to Crayon's earlier characterization of himself as a writer disposed to see the world as static tableaux arranged purely for his own pleasure. The schooner, a metaphor for Crayon himself, goes unregarded by the captain's ship because she is anchored and idling. For Irving, the boat's absence of motion is coupled with a romantic imagination that conceptualizes the world as static and picturesque and removes one from the dynamic currents of history and incident.

The chapter concludes with Crayon's safe arrival at Liverpool. At this point his narrative changes its focus, jumping from Crayon's romantic reveries to the bodies and actions of his fellow passengers. As the ship approaches dock Crayon draws attention to the significance of gesture and nonlinguistic expression:

> I could distinguish the merchant to whom the ship was consigned. I knew him by his calculating brow and restless air. His hands were thrust into his pockets; he was whistling thoughtfully to and fro, a small space having been accorded him by the crowd in deference to his temporary importance . . . I particularly noticed one young woman of humble dress, but interesting demeanour. She was leaning forward among the crowd. . . . to catch some wished-for countenance. She seemed disappointed and agitated; when I heard a faint voice call her name. It was from some poor sailor who had been ill all the voyage . . . at the sound of his voice her eye darted on his features—it read at once a whole volume of sorrow—she clasped her hands; uttered a faint shriek and stood wringing them in silent agony. (Irving, 751)

From within the undifferentiated, heterogeneous crowd Crayon is able to discern two archetypal characters from their outward displays of theatrical self-expression: the proud merchant and the distraught, poor young woman.

Just as many New Yorkers (Federalist and Democrat) had sought to display the validity of their power by means of outward expressions of civic engagement—a circumscribed politics of ritual participation—so Irving elects to focus on the external characteristics of people so as to resist the dangers inherent in romantic or philosophical introspection. In so doing he elevates the intersubjective relations engendered by gestural performance above romantic claims to absolute authority and truth found within the subjective, internalized responses of the individual. The dramatic expressions of pain by the young woman affect Crayon profoundly, forcing him to recognize his isolation and detachment from those around him, but only temporarily, and only within the frame of a single short sketch. "I alone was solitary and idle," he writes. "I had no friend to meet, no cheering to receive . . . I stepped upon the land of my forefathers—but felt that I was a stranger in the land" (751). Rather than a desirable position, as it had been in the case of Addison and Steele's *Spectator* essays, the "solitary" and the "idle" are presented as negative characteristics that ultimately endanger Crayon's sense of self-worth. Despite the young woman's obvious pain, by choosing to have Crayon admit his feelings of isolation immediately after seeing her crying, Irving suggests that his narrator has become envious of her ability to emit a genuine emotional response that adequately communicates her needs and desires to those around her. It is this renewed interest in the theatricalized exchanges between subjects that leads into the concerns of the next chapter of *The Sketch-Book*, the often-overlooked "Roscoe."

In several ways "Roscoe" represents Crayon's reworking of his own aesthetic project in "The Author's Account of Himself" in light of changing circumstances. In the sketch Crayon encounters the English historian, abolitionist, and patron of the arts William Roscoe, whose charity, generosity, and talent serve as a model for him. Reflecting on Liverpool, the narrator remarks that Roscoe was "born in a place apparently ungenial to the growth of literary talent" (753). This statement mirrors Crayon's earlier assessment in "The Author's Account of Himself" of the limited opportunities available to an American writer who is not "merely a lover of fine scenery" (743). Roscoe is a partial reflection of the narrator, but his relationship to the world around him suggests a level of engagement that Crayon is denied through his reliance upon an aesthetic approach to the world based on a detached and passive "sauntering gaze" (745). Roscoe, unlike Crayon, "has turned the whole force of his talents and influence to advance and embellish his native town" (753) and "has shut himself up in no garden of thought, nor elysium of fancy; but has gone forth into the highways and thoroughfares of life" (753–54). The aesthetic of "intertextual reflection, comparison, and immersion" (143) that Paul Giles sees as a key function of *The Sketch-Book* operates here in Crayon's treatment of Roscoe as an uncanny other to himself. This mirroring serves Irving in his project of imagining a radical bond between Britain and America that relies upon a logic of commonality and reflection rather than one of separateness and distinction.

Whereas Crayon screens his own corporeality behind the rich fabric of his language, Roscoe is manifestly present in the world, performing his republican duties and "exhibit[ing] no lofty and almost useless, because inimitiable [sic] example of excellence; but . . . a picture of active yet simple and imitable virtues" (Irving, 754). Following his experiences in "The Voyage" Crayon turns to the body as an instrument of an expressivity that counters and rejects the internalized subjectivity of the mind and text.

> He was advanced in life, tall, and of a form that might once have been commanding, but it was a little bowed by time—perhaps by care. He had a noble Roman style of countenance; a head that would have pleased a painter; and though some slight furrows on his brow shewed that wasting thought had been busy there, yet his eye still beamed with the fire of a poetic soul. There was something in his whole appearance that indicated a being of a different order from the bustling race around him. (752)

In the same way as Federalists sought to create the nation as bound by rites and festivities in the public sphere that marked one's participation in a common historical culture, Crayon imagines Roscoe to be at once a "type" that can be read by the public and serve as a model of civic virtue.

Roscoe is a synecdoche for the wider aesthetic concerns of *The Sketch-Book*. What distinguishes Roscoe from other English writers is his refusal to "steal away from the bustle and commonplace of busy existence; to indulge in the selfishness of lettered ease, and to revel in scenes of mental but exclusive enjoyment" (753). By focusing on his outward appearance Crayon gestures towards a realization that the Englishman and himself share a common bond of fraternity, a condition of being effectively doubles that undermines the nationalism inculcated through romanticism's egocentric subjectivism. As Laura Doyle notes, "To be an embodied subject is to be already double, to belong already to the world of others as well as self, and to arrive at one's own visibility and audibility together with others" (6). By witnessing Roscoe's relationship to the world around him as if through a mirror Crayon *should* come to an awareness of his own flaws, which are also those of America more generally, but oddly fails to. This is because his romanticism is presented as inextricable from his identity as an American and draws him, as Giles notes, "toward the alluring, Lethean rivers of narcissistic timelessness" (158). In Crayon, Irving consciously created a now long-standing stereotype of the American traveller as an individual lacking in sufficient self-awareness to learn much from their experiences of the Old World—a collector of images that he consumes at some distance from reality: a taker of snapshots, or a buyer of print-shop images. In doing this Irving criticizes the picturesque sensibilities that Crayon partially embodies for their naïve inattention to the persistent realities of lived historical experience.

In "Roscoe" Irving invites readers to reflect back on Crayon's description of his own aesthetic in "The Author's Account of Himself." In the sketch, Irving suggests that the exercise of international travel should produce a consciousness in which the claims of the sketch writer to critical distance and authorial control are consistently challenged or undermined. Through the experience of viewing, Irving implies, the sketcher should be forced to reflect upon his own condition and to recognize how his identity is constructed through social entanglements rather than in the exclusive mental space of romantic detachment or sublime providence. In "Roscoe," the formal constraints of the literary sketch (brevity, aesthetic detachment, objectivity) abridge Crayon's engagement with the social world that Roscoe inhabits. Roscoe's genuine historical achievements in the fields of British abolition, dissenting Unitarianism, and the legal profession are reduced to an anodyne meditation on the ahistorical character of his "noble mind" and "classic dignity" (757). He becomes, in effect, a creation of language, not a historical actor. This does little justice to Roscoe and to the actual power he has to inspire a meaningful engagement with the world. What characterizes Crayon's narration here is his inability to achieve the self-reflexivity that Adam Smith had envisioned in *The Theory of Moral Sentiments* (1759) as the logical end point of a sympathetic exchange between viewer and viewed subject, the "invisible hand" that transforms an "impartial spectator" into an involved party by forcing the recognition of commonality.

In this way it is possible to see the schism between Irving's own aesthetic objectives and those of his performed narrator. Crayon always reasserts his neutrality and detachment from the scenes he views, while Irving conceived of the function of literature as establishing a ritual in which the viewer and the viewed subject were connected by a common culture. "Roscoe" operates by demonstrating the construction of identity within a social space of interaction. An engagement with the power of sympathy in "Roscoe" is picked up in the next sketch, "The Wife," where Irving turns his attention to the myth of sentimental womanhood as providing an ideal space of comfort apart from history.

In numerous ways "The Wife" corresponds to the conventions of nineteenth-century sentimental narrative, which, as Elizabeth Barnes defines it, highlights the importance of the familial bond over other forms of association and "works out socio-political questions and conflicts through a gendered body—the woman's" (*States of Sympathy*, 8). Crayon's sketch describes a conversation between himself and a man called Leslie who, like the Irving brothers at the time of the work's composition, had been subjected to "a succession of sudden disasters . . . [and finds] himself reduced almost to penury" (Irving, 760). Unwilling to explain his financial mistakes to his new wife, who is a "beautiful and accomplished girl, who had been brought up in the midst of fashionable life" (76), for fear that it will "strike her very soul to the earth, by telling her that her husband is a beggar" (761), Leslie becomes increasingly depressed and desperate. Eventually he exclaims:

> "To tell her that I have dragged her down from the sphere in which she might have continued to move in constant brightness—the light of every eye—the admiration of every heart—How can she bear poverty!—she has been brought up in all the refinements of opulence—How can she bear neglect!—she has been the idol of society—oh it will break her heart!—it will break her heart!" (762)

Following Crayon's advice, Leslie finally tells his wife about their downturn in fortune and finds to his surprise that she "has been nothing but sweetness and good humour. Indeed she seems in better spirits than I have ever known her—she has been to me all love and tenderness and comfort" (764). In the end, his wife's love has provided him a way of overcoming the pressures constructed in Leslie's own imagination. Indeed, we may assume that his notion that he must protect his wife from dangerous knowledge was actually always a fool's errand and that she may be more relieved that he confesses to her what she already seems to know than she is upset by the knowledge itself. Leslie, in effect, denies his wife agency in seeking to keep the truth from her.

The issue of female agency and the suggestion that gender roles may be performed and are not essential is a recurring trope in the rest of *The Sketch-Book*, which includes a number of significant and self-aware female characters, among them Katrina Van Tassel and Dame Van Winkle. E. D. E. N. Southworth picked up this theme in 1853, when she used "The Wife" as a basis for a short story in her collection *Old Neighborhoods and New Settlements*. In Southworth's version, "The Wife's Victory," Irving's sketch is cleverly reworked from the perspective of the female characters to highlight their agency and the effects of their performances of feminine "virtue" on others. The story extends the frame of Irving's initial sketch to include the events that precede and succeed his version. The story begins with a dialogue between Mrs. Mary Lindal (who on the death of her first husband marries Mr. Leslie and becomes the "Mary Leslie" of Irving's story) and her sister Kate Gleason on the subject of female submission in marriage. Kate chastises Mary for falling in love with Mr. Leslie, who she argues is financially irresponsible in a way that eventually might make him cruel, in "temper a Bluebeard" (31).

Like Irving's story, Leslie's financial speculation leaves him insolvent, a fact that he hides initially from his wife. In Southworth's story the initial investment made by Leslie was taken from an inheritance bequeathed to Mary Leslie's daughter, Sylvia, by her first husband. The plot of Irving's sketch is thereby extended to include the damage patriarchy exerts on multiple generations of women. Additionally, the issue of the will transforms the story from being one about women's duty to one of women's property rights. Mary chooses to bear these trials with the same decorum that does Irving's "Mrs. Leslie," and this initially leads to her being labelled cold and indifferent to her plight, including the loss of her child to a wealthy guardian. Yet her performance of piety and submissiveness ultimately leads Mr. Leslie not only to recognize the value of his wife as *his* supporter but to his own sense of duty to recognize *her* individual property claims. The reversal of the Leslie family's fortunes comes when Mary Leslie stages a scene of private prayer. The narrative is ambiguous about whether she expects to be overseen by her husband and her wealthy relative who has been named Sylvia's guardian. Southworth writes:

> He had seen, and had heard—and never before had the pure and holy heart of his wife been so unveiled as in that prayer; and while it yet ascended . . . he quietly withdrew from the room murmuring "The angel, the angel, how blind I have been! I must save her from this trial; there is but one way, for I must save her without sacrificing Sylvia." (53)

This theatricalized scene of piety leads Mr. Leslie to finally admit his need to confess his insolvency to others who can help him—a thing he regards as essentially demeaning to his "masculine" sense of autonomy. In effect, Mary Leslie's theatre of submissiveness forces Leslie into reliance on a network of social relations, thereby challenging the ideology of inviolate masculine selfhood.

The extension of the frame of Irving's sketch by Southworth serves to critique the patriarchal logic that motivates the sketch form itself—the sense implicit in the genre that events can be abridged around the central figure of the male author and highlight *his* vision and *his* experience alone. Instead, to capture female experience Southworth extends the range of vision beyond the male gaze, bringing in multiple characters and networks of interrelation, as well as considering the significance of motherhood and the performance of domesticity within the purview of the narrative. Such a reworking of the form of the sketch is present in Irving's own initial version, albeit in an embryonic form. When taken out of the context of the narrative of *The Sketch-Book* as a whole, "The Wife" is a tedious and conventional story. However, Crayon's language in the opening paragraph of the sketch sounds alarm bells and casts aspersions on the authenticity of the ensuing narrative. Crayon states:

> I have often had occasion to remark the fortitude with which women sustain the most overwhelming reverses of fortune. Those disasters which break down the spirits of a man, and prostrate him in the dust, seem to call forth all the energies of the softer sex, and give such intrepidity and elevation to their character, that at times it approaches to sublimity. (759)

In the first three pieces of *The Sketch-Book* Irving alludes to the dangerous consequences of a kind of romantic thinking that establishes a utopian space free from the pressures of historical context—a space that Crayon frequently refers to as "sublime." In "The Wife," Irving presents us with a competing utopian space in the shape of the middle-class home. In so doing (and only when *The Sketch-Book* is read sequentially), Irving ironically conflates the two modes of expression: romantic and sentimental. Just as Jefferson sought to present himself both as visionary and as "father" of a mythic "people" in his characterization of America's national providence, so too does Irving's narrative exemplify the parities between sentimental domesticity and romantic intellect through a comparative use of the term "sublime." Michael Warner has argued that Irving's writing in *The Sketch-Book*, with its discomfort with reproductive sexuality (an idea I will explore later in relation to "Rip Van Winkle") and its ideals of fraternal companionship render the text "queer," yet still "misogynistic" in tone. I would not dispute the claim that Irving's language seems uncomfortably essentialist in its treatment of women at times in *The Sketch-Book*, yet it is also worth noting that this language is: first, Crayon's (a narrator Irving does much to undermine); second, always already filtered through an ontology that is both performative and nonessentialist; and third, comic, ironic, even satiric. As I will show a little later in relation to Katrina Van Tassel of "The Legend of Sleepy Hollow," this republican, performative ontology is applied as fully to women as it is to men in Irving's work, even if his vision of fraternity and masculinity is its primary shaping influence, even when applied to women. Irving knew the theatre too well (including early American dramas such as *The Contrast*) to regard identity (even female identity) as wholly essentialist. The fact of everyone always playing parts was always at the forefront of Irving's politics and aesthetics, gesturing towards a feminism that he never openly espoused. Where his feminism falls short, on the issue of voting rights, is not peculiar to women because, after all, Irving's version of democracy was one that cared ultimately very little about practicalities of democratic participation such as the ballot box.

It is following these four sketches and their challenges to the authority of aesthetic detachment and the ideal of a neutral space free from history that Irving presents the reader with "Rip Van Winkle." Although Irving did much to show how the sketch form could operate as a much-needed prompt to historical consciousness, he was also attuned to its limitations. It was with the creation of the short story proper that he was best able to explore how gesture and ritual embedded modern American culture within an older "circum-Atlantic interculture" (Roach) rooted in European ritual, myth, and folklore. Through the short story, Irving was able to highlight how theatricalized forms of exchange and nonlinguistic expressivities might be used to disrupt the ideologically inflected teleology of romantic nationalism and its self-aggrandizing language of newness.

Performing Memory in "Rip Van Winkle" and "The Legend of Sleepy Hollow"

"Rip Van Winkle," as well as being among the first short stories in American literature, is perhaps the most famous. It is the tale of a man in the late eighteenth century who, to escape the haranguing of his bullying wife, goes off into the woods to shoot squirrels near the Hudson River. There he encounters the ghosts of some old Dutch settlers, drinks from a flagon of beer, and falls asleep for twenty years. Upon waking he discovers that the Revolution has taken place and he is the citizen of a new government, the United States of America. As Andrew Burstein has recently noted, "Rip Van Winkle" is essentially a rewriting of an older German folktale, which has its own origins (like many folktales) in pre-Christian myth. Burstein writes, "As for the German antecedents of his tale, the similarities to 'Peter Klaus' are unmistakable; they make 'America's first short story' as connected to Europe as America's first white inhabitants were" (129). Indeed, the capacity of ritual and folklore to provide a model of community and continuity that ties nations together across space and time is one of Irving's primary aims in "Rip Van Winkle."

It is possible to trace Irving's first interest in ritual and folklore to his life in New York City, where as a young man he would have encountered German folktales performed nightly on the stage at his beloved Park Theatre. Bruce A. McConachie has recorded the repertoires of key theatres in New York, noting that "Fairy-tale melodramas, so-called because they share many formal characteristics with folk or fairy stories, were especially popular with upper-class males" (29). In particular, Irving would have seen William Dunlap's translations of the folk melodramas of August von Kotzebue and René-Charles Guilbert de Pixérécourt as well as adaptations of "stories out of the Brothers Grimm or Perrault collections" (36), many of which had not yet had an English major translation in book form. The transmission history of folktales in America highlights the complex exchange dynamic between performance and print that helped to shape the short story tradition. Although the dates of Irving's work on *The Sketch-Book* line up almost exactly with the Grimm brothers' own work in German philology and the study of folklore (and Irving himself read German sufficiently well to interpret much of this popular material for himself), the first impactful English print translations of Grimm and other folklorists did not come until later in the nineteenth century in the widely read 1823 works of Edgar Taylor. Indeed, Anglophone Americans' experience of folktales in the early republic was as likely to come via traditional methods of oral transmission or through stage adaptations as it was from printed sources. Folktales in America did not all start their life as short stories captured in printed form and consumed by an individual bourgeois reader. Indeed, the divide between stage and page was not so fully established in the early nineteenth-century United States for this to be the case. Folktales were often subjected to a process of mediation through performance that rendered the texts as a public property experienced collectively, either as part of the parlor culture of working- and middle-class homes or in public theatres. This leads to the suggestion that the heavily gestural and expressive qualities of works such as "Rip Van Winkle" as well as the story's self-conscious engagement with the power of oral storytelling in the suggestion that Diedrich Knickerbocker's "historical researches, did not lie so much among books, as among men" (Irving, 767), owe much to the fact that European folklore in America was yet to undergo the significant process of ethnographic or philological textualization that would transform them from living texts into less dynamic, printed documents. These processes would effectively historicize folk stories and render them as premodern texts that confirmed the Enlightenment teleology of progress from myth and magic to religion and, finally, science. The history of folk stories in America is one as much of performance as of print, an argument attested to by the fact that Irving's work was so easily adapted for the stage and had a rich afterlife in the work of such successful playwrights and actors as Dion Boucicault and Joseph Jefferson.

As I established earlier, Geoffrey Crayon's interventions in *The Sketch-Book* ultimately enact his own removal from history through his decision to approach life by means of the "sauntering gaze" of the sketch form, which seeks to fashion an ideal disembodied space of objective vision. By contrast, "Rip Van Winkle" begins by establishing its relation to history and myth through the presentation of the story's increasingly baffling series of prior narrators. Irving frames the narrative as "A Posthumous Writing of Diedrich Knickerbocker," which the Dutch-American has collected, in turn, from the wives of "old burghers . . . rich in that legendary lore so invaluable to true history" (767). Furthermore, Knickerbocker begins his manuscript with an epigraph from the seventeenth-century English dramatist William Cartwright that reads: "By Woden, God of Saxons/ From whence comes Wensday, that is Wodensday/ Truth is a thing that ever will I keep/ Unto thylke day in which I creep into/ My sepulchre" (769). Even before beginning the story proper, by referring in the epigraph to the origin of Wednesday in the name of the Viking god Woden, Irving presents the reader with an example of persistence of history in modern language's reliance on mythic or pagan sources. By appealing to Woden, the poem's narrator implies that the "truth" that "ever will I keep" (769) is found in the relation of all consciousness to history and myth. Irving alerts the reader to how history is important in the making of contemporary identities and how what constitutes "truth" is a subject of the effects of social conditioning across large swathes of ethnological time. In this way he attacks the Lockean idealism of the new American republic, which as R. W. B. Lewis remarked in a key text of mid-twentieth-century American myth-and-symbol criticism, *The American Adam*, saw itself as "embodied in a figure of heroic innocence and vast potentialities, poised at the start of a new history" (1). For Knickerbocker (as for Irving himself) the concept of "a new history" is a philosophical fallacy rendered moot by the persistence of expressive culture across Revolutionary temporal and spatial divides. Additionally, the Cartwright epigraph implies a narrative of concealed and revealed knowledge that reflects a distinctly ritualized pattern of behavior in which an initiate that performs certain prescribed gestures receives the secret knowledge of the past from the dead. While living, Cartwright implies, his "truth" is withheld until his death: "thylke day in which I creep/ into my sepulchre" (769).

Just as the myth-and-symbol school attempted to read American narrative as an expression of timeless values, modern theories of the short story that have emphasized the relation of the genre to myth have tended to do so in a somewhat abstracted, dehistoricized way. Claims to the mythic origins of Irving's short stories are common, but few have attempted to show how his early work in the form emerged within the specific historical framework of early nineteenth-century transatlantic republicanism. Mary Rohrberger argues that "the short story proper . . . derives from a Romantic tradition, having its beginning in myths and legends wherein the reader is asked to put the extensional world out of mind and deal in and with a kind of underworld . . . a mystical world of paradox and ambiguity" (*The Art of Brevity*, 6). In referring to the "Romantic tradition" Rohrberger is not necessarily speaking of romanticism in its early nineteenth-century sense of egocentric subjectivism so much as the medieval romance of questing knights and heavily symbolic action. Indeed, folklore invariably blurs the line between text and performance that has been traditionally central to Enlightenment taxonomies. Since such early works of anthropology as Jessie L. Weston's groundbreaking *From Ritual to Romance* (1920) and J. G. Frazer's *The Golden Bough* (1890), mythic narrative has frequently been treated as having its origins in Christian and pre-Christian ritual performances. As Catherine Bell states in *Ritual: Perspectives and Dimensions* (1997), "The study of ritual began with a prolonged and influential debate on the origins of religion" (3). When reading the short story proper it is important to be alert to the fact that the divide between orality and textuality was not yet established when most of the *ur*-forms of contemporary fictional narrative first began to take shape. It is this complex relationship between text and performance, derived from the rituals of an Old World culture, that makes the nineteenth-century American short story especially invested in the actions of the body. By virtue of its "highly patterned structure, its lack of character development, and its thematic limitations" (May in Lohafer, ed., *Short Story Theory at a Crossroads*, 62) the short story proper retains an aura of the sacred that is not reflected in its competitors: the modern realist novel or the lyric poem.

The most frequently occurring ritual pattern that Frazer, Weston, and others saw as the key archetype of Western folklore and myth was "the ritually dying and reviving god" (5) that returns from another world to pass on secret knowledge and so redeem society's ills. In Knickerbocker's tale, Rip's sleep and his subsequent awakening into a new world corresponds with the patterns highlighted by these early works of anthropology, but the world that Irving wishes Rip to redeem is the emergent American nation, a place he saw as rapidly galvanizing around a dangerously ahistorical vision of the power of the individual to shape their own reality—a vision tied to the privileging of textual over bodily sources in Enlightenment discourse. When read sequentially, "Rip Van Winkle" performs an elaborate coup de theatre of its own in *The Sketch-Book* by dynamically transferring narrative focus from the individual to the collective, from Crayon's "modern" spectatorship to Knickerbocker's mythic storytelling. In so doing, Irving fashions the short story proper as a genre that visibly operates according to a different narrative logic than the sketch, an intersubjective matrix closer to the collective processes of ritual or theatre than to the modern spectatorial essay's pattern of aesthetic detachment. It is in this manner that Irving's republican mind resists appropriation by the Jeffersonian liberal, symbolic order, which sought to fuse nationalism and individualism together in its vision of American identity. It is in the short story, with its folkloric and ritualistic origins, that Irving's cosmopolitan consciousness finds its strongest voice in dissent against an ahistorical, culturally amnesiac, liberal, romantic imagination that was increasingly coming to shape popular conceptions of national providence.

The plot of the story enacts this republican logic by raising the question of the relationship between ritualized civic participation and cultural memory. Like the conflation of nullity and sublimity that attend Crayon's vision of the sea in "The Voyage," the "awe and apprehension" (Irving, 776) that Rip feels as he gazes on the mysteriously silent ghosts of the Catskill Mountains results in his withdrawal from conventional temporality: "his senses were overpowered, his eyes swam in his head . . . and he fell into a deep sleep" (776). Indeed, Rip's famous sleep in the woods above his village causes him to pass, however briefly, out of history. It is important to note that Rip's temporary removal from history is made possible through his temporary removal from community. Rip's flight into the woods is presented as a retreat into the internal space of individual, liberal consciousness, rendered by Irving as Rip's entry into what amounts to a wandering fugue state—a psychologically complex condition characterized by total amnesia and a detachment from conventional social relations. As Robert Rudnicki defines fugues, they are "always characterized by a flight from usual surroundings, the mind becoming a virtual *tabula rasa*" (*Percyscapes*, 8). The blankness associated with Crayon's mind in the earlier sketch "The Voyage" (and with Jefferson's treatment of post-Revolutionary American life as a blank page) is transferred onto Rip at this point. In a further turn, Irving uses Rip's fugue to comment further on the limits placed upon memory by the formal brevity of the sketch form. The author's description of Rip's motion at this point in the story resembles the descriptions he had previously used in relation to Crayon. "In a long ramble . . . on a fine autumnal day," Knickerbocker states, "Rip had unconsciously scrambled to one of the highest parts of the Kaatskill mountains" (773). The "rambling propensity" that is so much part of Geoffrey Crayon's character in "The Author's Account of Himself" is recalled by Rip Van Winkle's own movements in the later story. As he "rambles" alone in the woods Rip becomes "unconscious" of his surroundings. Rip's experience of isolation and forgetfulness is the logical inverse of the tale's framing narrative, which implies that cultural memory ("true history") is the province of community and not of the individual.

It is in this state that he encounters the ghosts with whom he cannot interact in any meaningful way in a space that is shown to closely resemble the architectural spaces designated for the performance of Greek mythic drama: "a hollow like a small amphitheatre, surrounded by perpendicular precipices" (775). The scene is worth quoting at length:

> On entering the amphitheatre new objects of wonder presented themselves. On a level spot in the centre was a company of odd-looking personages playing at ninepins . . . Their visages too were peculiar . . . The whole group reminded Rip of figures in an old Flemish painting, in the parlour of Dominie Van Schaick the village parson, and which had been brought over from Holland at the time of the settlement.
>
> What seemed particularly odd to Rip was that though these folks were evidently amusing themselves, yet they maintained the gravest faces, the most mysterious silence, and were, withal, the most melancholy party of pleasure he had ever witnessed. (775–76)

In a moment of lonely reverie Rip is transformed from a figure embodying the spirit of community into a passive observer closer to the kind that Irving had satirized earlier in *The Sketch-Book* in Geoffrey Crayon's narration. Indeed, Crayon's own idiosyncratic lexis is even used to describe Rip's response to the ghosts. Irving has Knickerbocker describe them as "figures in an old Flemish painting," directly referencing Crayon's earlier description of life as a "picturesque stroll from the window of one print shop to another" (745). Furthermore, the "amphitheatre" in which the event takes place is Irving's representation of the nightmarish theatre of the sketcher's literary imagination, a place for viewing images with which one does not interact meaningfully. Rip becomes a passive viewer who receives "new objects of wonder" (775) but yet remains largely invisible to, and unacknowledged by, the subjects he views. The ghosts seem to call for Rip to wait a moment, after which they will communicate with him directly, but they never do. All Rip is able to do is drink and watch them play a game, the coded meaning of which is frustratingly withheld. As Philip Young has noted, this moment in the story seems to call for a symbolic interpretation that is not readily forthcoming: "The action is fairly pulsing with overtones: the men are speaking in signs; their motions cry out for translation as vigorously as if this were, as it seems, some strangely solemn charade" (11). It is only momentarily after this that Rip falls into his long sleep. What Irving seems to be suggesting therefore is that mere spectatorship of history and the failure to participate in the rites and rituals of a community is insufficient to help one avoid the allure of amnesia. Giles's claim that "Rip Van Winkle's twenty-year sleep can be seen . . . as synecdochic of *The Sketch-Book* itself, which attempts to arrest time by expelling historical processes from its frozen tableaux" (157) is only partially true in this sense. Although it is accurate to present Rip's sleep as operating in a similar way as Crayon's sketches—freezing historical time as static tableaux—Irving is self-reflexive about the effects of such a process, which he presents as inseparable from the nationalist consciousness that his cosmopolitan, republican mind rejects. Rip's sleep is the terrifying corollary of the sketcher's romantic vision, a utopian annihilation of history and community through the disembodiment of the viewing subject.

In the story, Rip Van Winkle's decision to escape into the woods of the Catskill Mountains is the result of a depression caused by his "termagant wife's" forceful insistence that his labor be for the family alone. "Poor Rip," Irving writes, "was at last reduced almost to despair . . . his only alternative to escape from the labour of the farm and the clamour of his wife" (773). While Rip "would never refuse to assist a neighbour even in the roughest toil, and was a foremost man at all country frolicks for husking corn," he is unwilling to do "family duty, and keep . . . his farm in order" (771). Irving fashions Rip as the functional opposite of Jefferson's ideal yeoman farmer in *Notes on the State of Virginia* (1787), a man who feels that his duty is to a wider community and not to the individual or the family. In fact, he is a poor patriarch, a condition of political power that is also implied in Jefferson's vision of idealized yeomanry. In spite of his many virtues, Rip lacks the self-interest and willingness to adhere to a sentimental vision of domesticity required for citizenship in Jefferson's future American republic. Through Rip's wife Irving shows how a focus on an ideal domestic sphere and Jefferson's supreme model of individual labor have an uncanny parity: an austere self-interest that is contrary to the festive, collective culture of the Federalist imagination. Furthermore, Irving's treatment of Dame Van Winkle immediately follows his presentation of an "ideal" womanhood in "The Wife." If read sequentially, "Rip Van Winkle" ironically disturbs the previous sketch's vision of a sanctified domestic sphere, presenting it as inseparable from a form of individualism that was rapidly gaining footing in the early republic. It is Dame Van Winkle, not Rip, who through her actions most embodies the self-interest required by the Jeffersonian nationalist imaginary.

It is against the twinned forces of romantic subjectivism and domestic self-interest that Irving depicts theatricalized exchange as a radical force of cosmopolitan antinationalism. Irving's political vision is embodied in the new relationship that Rip has with his son upon his return to the village, which, through the image of their identical physicality, transforms a familial, hierarchical, and patriarchal power relationship into a more egalitarian version of fraternity.

> Rip looked and beheld a precise counterpart of himself, as he went up the mountain: apparently as lazy and certainly as ragged. The poor fellow was now completely confounded. He doubted his own identity, and whether he was himself or another man. (781)

While his first impression is one of confusion and terror at seeing his doppelgänger, upon learning his name is also Rip Van Winkle, he comes to serve as an ameliorating force within the narrative, an identical other that provides a connection between Rip Sr. and the new American nation. An initial revulsion is replaced with a sense of the radical potential within the bodies of the two Rips to rearticulate continuity between the Old World (Rip Sr.) and the New (Rip Jr.) in the wake of the Revolutionary breach. In speaking of the "Revolutionary breach" here I am borrowing from Victor Turner's work *From Ritual to Theatre* (1982), which explores the potential found in theatre to serve as a means of repairing the psychic and affective gulf that frequently develops between nations divided by revolution or political disturbance. In this work, Turner suggests that the pattern of almost all performed "social dramas" corresponds with common forms of fictional narrative, which "can aptly be studied as having four phases . . . breach, crisis, redress, and either reintegration or recognition of schism" (69). The narrative of "Rip Van Winkle" follows this processual formulation almost exactly, since it is structured around four key, ritualized, expressive moments: Rip's alienation from his wife and family, which leads to his panicked encounter with the Dutch ghosts and his fall into slumber (breach), his troubled encounter with the new order (crisis), the intervention of his daughter and son (redress), and his reintegration into the symbolic order through the relaying of his story to the younger generation.

This process hinges on the intervention of Rip Jr., whose mimicry of Rip Sr. turns him into a performative symbol of connection that Joseph Roach has described as "the surrogate." In *Cities of the Dead: Circum-Atlantic Performance* (1996) Roach depicts Atlantic theatrical culture as "a genealogy of linked surrogations" (133)—that is, performances that seek to overcome the radical breach of death or the alienating effects of revolution by means of an ongoing process of embodying the characteristics of one's historical ancestors. Like Irving's own resistance to the egocentric subjectivism of the romantic mode, this "historical model of intercultural communication . . . based on performance," writes Roach, "[is] more resistant to the polarizing reductions of manifest destiny and less susceptible to the temptations of amnesia" (189). In this way, the folkloric origins of the story of "Rip Van Winkle" in the Western mythology of a dead and reviving king are presented as a means of overcoming the emergent nationalism of Irving's own early republican moment. The dangerous neutral space of objectivity that Geoffrey Crayon sought in the disembodied aesthetic of the sketch genre is critiqued through Irving's presentation of the radical potential for transatlantic fraternity that lies within a ritualized treatment of the body. While the sketch form produces a strange cultural amnesia as each event is treated as discrete from every other, the embodied, theatricalized content of ritual and the mnemonic reserves of gestural praxis serve Irving in his attempt to establish a literature of social memory. This challenge though does not take the form of outright rejection of modern American culture. It is rather that Irving couches the potential for a new, more meaningful symbolic order of brotherhood and peaceful coexistence between father and son in terms that recall the old order: Rip Sr. and Rip Jr. are members of different political systems and temporalities but perform the same gestures and behaviors in the social world.

Typically, however Irving's treatment of the radical potential of the body to serve as a lynchpin of communal feeling rests upon a desexualized masculinity. Indeed, in "Rip Van Winkle" (and *The Sketch-Book* more generally) Irving is unable to account for sexual reproduction in his model of historical memory. This is because, unlike historical patterns of performed and learned gestures, sexual reproduction embodies a potential for radically new life that is fundamentally at odds with Irving's aesthetic project. The freedom Rip obtains from the "one species of despotism under which he had long groaned . . . petticoat government" (783) comes with a corresponding "liberation" from any conjugal role that may have attended his marriage—his "familial responsibility." Instead, it is "Rip's daughter that took him home to live with her" (783), and in so doing she provides a "snug well furnished house" (783) in which he can happily "be idle, with impunity" (783), much as she does for the "chubby child in her arms" (781), who worryingly foreshadows Rip Sr.'s own ultimate fate as a symbol of infantile dependence. Irving writes:

> Rip now resumed his old walks and habits; he soon found many of his former cronies, though all the worse for the wear and tear of time; and preferred making friends among the rising generation, with whom he soon grew into great favour. (783)

Even as he brings the Old World and the New into communion and reconciliation through the performing body, that body is one freed from any mature sexual impulse and oddly incapable of strong friendships with adults. This observation leads us to once again reconsider within a transatlantic context the argument Leslie Fiedler first made for American national literary culture in *Love and Death in the American Novel* (1960) that "the whole odd shape of American fiction arises simply . . . because there is no real sexuality in American life and therefore there cannot very well be any in American art" (30). While Fiedler's conclusions are troublingly universalist, Anglocentric, and potentially misleading, it is true that Irving's model of ritualized rebirth is one free of sexuality and desire. To historicize this claim it is worth once again considering Irving's political associations with the elite, and assuredly masculinist, culture of American Federalism. As Waldstreicher asserts, "reportage of . . . nationalist rituals . . . highlights the participation of elites . . . formulaically stresses the unity they displayed and shared with the populace . . . and the equation of elite virtue and public order" (68). For Irving, the redemption of the populace (captured in the tale through Rip's eventual pacifying effect on the village) relies upon the appearance of the respectable body within public civic ritual—a fact that sexual desire always potentially disturbs or challenges. In denying any preexistent sexual role though, Rip effectively denies the patriarchal position often ascribed to the European "Old World" in nineteenth-century America and undergoes a strange process of disinheritance in which he becomes the son to his own daughter. This perverse disassembling of familial power relations registers a challenge both to sentimental fiction's ideal model of domestic nationalism (just as the shift from "The Wife" to "Rip Van Winkle" had done at a larger structural level) and to a hierarchical rendering of transatlantic power relations that marked the United States as the rebel son of the domineering, authoritarian Old World. Instead, Europe and America are rendered as symbolic brothers, united through their performance of the same gestures, manners, and wider patterns of behavior.

Irving though is not deaf to the fact that such fraternalism also occasions the effective removal of women from the public sphere—rendering the new nationalism dependent upon the condition of masculinity. While before the war, Rip had lived under "petticoat government," forced to perform the types of domestic labor he loathed by the cajoling of his ever-present wife, following the conflict his daughter becomes an almost invisible presence whose focused attention to the domestic sphere leaves him with "nothing to do at home" (783). However misogynistically rendered, Irving ascribed to Dame Van Winkle a presence that was equal to the potency of government. Indeed, her "lectures" were part of the very rituals of Rip's public life, described by the narrator as "grown into a habit," ritualized to the point of biological conditioning. In the post-Revolutionary world, though, his daughter is merely a housewife and mother, stripped of her public presence and, for the most part, her voice. Just as Rip's patriarchal authority is undermined by his deposition from the status of father to that of son, so too is female power in the public sphere seemingly undermined by the transformation to a post-Revolutionary, ostensibly more democratic, state. Such erasure of women from public life reflects the realities of the early American republic, where the women who had served such a public role before and during the war were expected to submit increasingly to an emerging national logic of "separate spheres" in peacetime. As Mary Chapman demonstrates in her excellent timeline of the women's suffrage campaign at the beginning of *Making Noise, Making News: Suffrage Print Culture and US Modernism* (2014), immediately following the Declaration of Independence was the first *de jure* restriction on women's voting rights in New York, followed by Massachusetts and New Hampshire, before the rest of the states followed suit over the next thirty years. The Revolution, then, can be seen as the origin point for an erosion of women's political voices.

Returning briefly to theatre history helps to explain Irving's conception of the changing relationship between performance and gender that he explores in his tales. Faye Dudden has suggested that the move towards more expressive and visual spectacles on the American stage was potentially detrimental to female actors, whose presence in the theatre in the colonial era depended upon a cultural preference for the beauties of speech and voice over and above the spectacles of the body. This move towards embodiment in theatre after the Revolution effectively muted women's speech on the stage as performances became increasingly organized around fraternity, masculine daring, and the sexual objectification of women on the stage for the pleasure of primarily male audiences. Consequently, in highlighting the rise of fraternalism as a force in the new democracy, Irving also shows how this version of theatricalized manhood depended upon the wholesale domination of the public sphere by men—whether in the formal sense of political enfranchisement or the cultural sense of participation as audience members in a theatre that was becoming increasingly male.[2] The rise of masculinity as a condition for the construction of a version of democratic participation can be seen in the changes in the theatre from the 1820s through the antebellum era. With the rise of the "star system" and the increasing dominance of melodrama on the stage, playgoers were increasingly forced to conceptualize democracy as dependent less on the spoken word that had driven drama in the colonial era than on the heroic forms of masculine daring performed by figures such as Edwin Forrest. As Amy Hughes and Bruce McConachie have both shown, by the middle of the century the powerful, muscular male body had become a key image of US democratic authority. In this way, Irving sounds a cautious, preemptive note as to the limits of his own fraternal imaginary, and its reliance upon certain conditions of gender identity, that looks forward to antebellum developments.

The centrality of ritual and performance to the meaning of "Rip Van Winkle" is also manifested in the setting Irving selects for Rip's return from the mountains after twenty years. Rip's ritualized "rebirth" conveniently coincides with a time of great festivity, the day of an election. As I showed earlier in relation to Irving's treatment of the New York Seventh Ward hustings, the author here too presents the primary rite of democratic culture as a piece of community or street theatre that provides a counterpoint to the cold "amphitheatre" in which Rip encounters the ghosts of the old patriarchs. While the ghosts "maintained the gravest faces, the most mysterious silence"

(Irving, 776), the American election is "a busy, disputatious" (779) event in which the entire community is involved. However, in "Rip Van Winkle" the festival of election day more closely resembles the conflict-ridden and anarchic culture of European Jacobinism than the respectable events of the American Federalist imagination. Indeed, Rip is nearly lynched as "A tory! A tory! A spy! A Refugee" (780) for his misplaced political affiliations. It is into this environment that Irving reinstalls the body of Rip Van Winkle as a means to provide a continuity denied by the entropic political culture of the early republic.

In "Rip Van Winkle," Irving imagines his eponymous protagonist to be a ritually symbolic force of embodied memory that provides the villagers with a sense of historical continuity that has been disrupted by the vagaries of modern, post-Revolutionary identity politics. As Rip enters the village he sees that the sign above the tavern has changed from the "ruby face of King George under which he had smoked so many a peaceful pipe" into an image of "GENERAL WASHINGTON" (779). In presenting the Revolution as a transfer of signs rather than as evidence of a radically new spirit, Irving questions the essence of the democratic process as a force of the modern. In the story, the election is mapped onto the Christian or pre-Christian rite of purification symbolized by Rip's own "rebirth" into a new community.

Ritual and performance are also important in "The Legend of Sleepy Hollow," in which Irving presents the competition between the romantic and performative modes in his own work as a theatricalized battle between two men, the loathsome Connecticut Yankee Ichabod Crane and the Dutch-American Brom Bones. Whereas "Rip Van Winkle" sought to imagine the possibility of a ritualized union of Old and New World without sexuality, "Sleepy Hollow" concerns the two men's battle for marriage rights over "a blooming lass of fresh eighteen" (Irving, 1065), Katrina Van Tassel. If "Rip Van Winkle" dramatized the limits of fraternalism in the erosion of Judith Gardenier's voice, then "Sleepy Hollow" explores women's roles in the shaping of ritual community—albeit within the perverted Gothic terms of witchcraft and female manipulation.

To highlight the significance of ritual to his vision of community in "Sleepy Hollow," Irving sets the tale around the time of a harvest festival, a "calendrical rite" that marks an "attempt to influence or control nature" through "a communal feast with abundant food, music, dance, and some degree of social license" (Bell, 103). In the story Katrina Van Tassel's own rite of passage into adulthood—the "vast expectations" (Irving, 1065) that attend her future marriage—is mapped onto this festival of rebirth or renewal.

Irving expresses this literally through Knickerbocker's equation of the fertile landscape around the Hudson River with Katrina's own special fecundity. Knickerbocker opens his tale by describing the "bosom of one of those spacious coves which indent the eastern shore of the Hudson" (1058), prefiguring his description of Katrina in a manner that alludes to her own "bosom." Knickerbocker states that she is:

> plump as a partridge; ripe and melting and rosy cheeked as one of her fathers' peaches, and universally famed, not merely for her beauty, but her vast expectations. She was withal a little of a coquette, as might be perceived in her dress, which was a mixture of ancient and modern fashions, as most suited to set off her charms . . . and withal a provokingly short petticoat, to display the prettiest foot and ankle in the country round. (1065)

Irving establishes a connection between agrarian New York and Katrina that resembles Jefferson's claims that American citizens had a natural right to the ownership of a "virgin land." Ichabod Crane, who "is not only a Yankee of Franklin's stamp; he also possesses many of the qualities of his earlier Puritan ancestors" (Roth, 163), equates Katrina in his mind with the "sumptuous promise of luxurious winter fare" (Irving, 1067) that will litter the table at the forthcoming harvest festival. Irving presents his desire for Katrina as qualified by an even greater desire for her father's "fat meadow lands, the rich fields of wheat, of rye, of buckwheat, and Indian corn" and "how they might be readily turned into cash, and the money invested in immense tracts of wild land, and shingle palaces in the wilderness" (1067). In "The Legend of Sleepy Hollow" Crane's sexual impulse is intimately correlated with the politics of land expansion and, through the peripheral presence of "the negroes . . . of all shapes and sizes, from the farm and the neighbourhood" (1077) who gather to watch his courtship of Katrina through Van Tassel's window, the abuses of the slave system. Indeed, Irving creates explicit links between Crane and slave masters in his descriptions of his pedagogical practices. Crane sets "stakes against the window shutters" (1061) to ensure none escape and he is sadistic in his treatment of his pupils: "in the tone of menace or command, or peradventure, by the appalling sound of the birch . . . he urged some tardy loiterer along the flowery path of knowledge" (1061).

In a manner similar to Geoffrey Crayon, who arrogantly believes that the world can be reduced to a series of decontextualized images for his ready consumption, Crane envisions Katrina as a consumable object that, like the parade of doughnuts, apple pies, hams, and smoked beef joints at her father's feast, it is his right to possess and devour. As Richard McLamore notes in "The Dutchman in the Attic," Crane is essentially imperial in his desire for the acquisition of the land and women. For McLamore, Crane is "an American man of letters . . . [and] a parody of imperially ambitious American writers" (48). In fact, Irving makes the link directly between Crayon and Crane in the final sketch of *The Sketch-Book*, which immediately follows "Sleepy Hollow," "L'Envoy."[3] Recalling Crane's position as "a huge feeder . . . [with] the dilating powers of an Anaconda" (Irving, 1062), Crayon describes his sketches in similarly culinary terms. "Few guests," writes Crayon, "sit down to an varied table with an equal appetite for each dish . . . one has an elegant horror of a roasted pig; another holds a curry or a devil in utter abomination" (1090).

Through the intertextual comparison of Crayon and Crane, Irving once again reflects on the limits of the sketch form and its relationship with the emergent American nationalist consciousness. By presenting the Yankee Crane as a functional equivalent of the sketcher Crayon—that is, one who looks to an authentic rural culture for object to either visually or digestively "consume"—Irving once again asks us to reflect upon the ethics of the literary project Crayon first outlines in "The Author's Account of Himself." However, in the short story, with its playful relationship with performance and ritual, Irving resists complicity in Crane's equation of Katrina with the natural bounty of the landscape. By making Katrina "a little of a coquette" (1065) Irving suggests that nature and society are conjoined in her, as she recognizes her role and performs it in the social world. Katrina is hardly the naïve virgin that is there for the taking by a verbose Yankee Crane. Crane's American romantic intellect forces him to imagine her as a product of a genuine, pure, and essential rural culture, when her identity is, in fact, an elaborate, willful, and powerful cultural performance. Her mixture of tradition and modernity exerts an impressive cultural power over the men of the village—both the Yankee Crane and his more traditional antagonist Brom—suggesting that she has agency in controlling the behaviors of the men around her, a fact that she exploits.

If any one of Irving's characters represents the aesthetic intentions of *The Sketch-Book*, it is Katrina, whose body serves to fuse of the "ancient and modern fashions" (1065)—the balance desired by the work as a whole. In aligning himself with Katrina, Irving is engaging not only in an act of transvestitism but also a celebration of threshold states such as the author himself possessed in relation to national culture and the transformations of the traveller he evoked in "The Author's Account of Himself." The name "Katrina" is derived from the Greek name "Hekaterine," which was related to the goddess of liminality and crossroads, Hecate. This goddess of transition was deplored by Athenian, Roman, and early Christian societies, who tarred her and her mainly female worshippers with accusations of witchcraft. Additionally, Katrina's surname "Tassel" connotes the ornamentation on clothing or fabric etymologically derived from the Latin "tassau," meaning clasp or join. Irving's celebration of threshold states is preempted by the narrative, which makes specific reference to Cotton Mather and his famous works on witchcraft and the history of New England, which Crane is shown to read avidly. Again we see Irving confronting the modernity of the American Revolution as a predominantly male tradition, with inevitable implications for the role of women in the new republic. As Laura Plummer and Michael Nelson have suggested, Crane's intrusion into Sleepy Hollow is described in markedly gendered terms. The Dutch, pre-Revolutionary world of Tarrytown is controlled by feminine forces and is assuredly "[f]emale-centred." Control is maintained in Sleepy Hollow "by means of tales revolving around the emasculated, headless 'dominant spirit' of the region, [which] figuratively neuters threatening masculine interlopers like Ichabod to ensure the continuance of the old Dutch domesticity, the Dutch wives hearths, and their old wives tales" (175). Pre-Revolutionary ritual processes like the harvest festival, Irving implies, had a role for women that post-Enlightenment culture has reduced, obfuscated, or else violently repressed.

As I suggested earlier, in the early republic female power and influence became a site of renewed conflict as the increasing attention to the body in performance occasioned a new state of uncertainty as to women's roles in the public sphere—a site of opportunity, but also of objectification. Katrina might be said to organize the rituals in "Sleepy Hollow," but her very body (the "*provokingly* short petticoat") also makes her a subject of suspicion to Irving's modern, post-Revolutionary readers. Indeed, the adjective "provokingly" speaks to a largely male audience in assuming that such personal style would provoke sexual desire on behalf of the viewer.

Irving's attempt to demonstrate the points of connection between "modern," "rational" activities like the democratic election and an agonistic, pre-Christian ritual process in "Rip Van Winkle" is continued in "The Legend of Sleepy Hollow." Like Katrina, the "ghost of a Hessian trooper, whose head had been carried away by a cannon ball" (1059) is at once a product of a modern conflict (the Revolutionary War) and an older folk consciousness. The ghostly trooper is described as "the dominant spirit" of the town, semantically connecting the folktale of a "ghost" with modern, revolutionary Hegelian concepts of "zeitgeist." Furthermore, Irving chooses to make the soldier a "Hessian," suggesting both the historical German mercenaries used by the British Army and, literally, the hessian sacking that would have been used to carry agricultural goods. In this way Irving makes parallels between the ghost and the harvest festival that provide a backdrop to the events of the story. In most European autumn festivals a sacrifice is offered, usually a scarecrow or effigy, to ensure a good harvest and a mild winter by expelling a spirit of famine, death, and destruction. Irving suggests that the ghost is a "Hessian" effigy—that is, little more than a piece of sacking used in a rural ritual of sacrificial substitution.

In selecting the Tarrytown area of upstate New York as his setting for the tale, however, Irving deliberately undercuts the narrator's (Knickerbocker's) own claims in the opening paragraphs to the historical tranquillity of the region. Indeed, the harvest festival that provides the backdrop to the tale has a potentially less generic, more specific historical meaning. Robert Hughes argues in "Sleepy Hollow: Fearful Pleasures and the Nightmare of History" that the town is a society marked not by restfulness but by an especially violent history of trauma and uncertainty. Hughes notes that Tarrytown was on the unsettled border between the British and Continental forces in the American Revolution and that raids by both armies into local towns were common.[4] Indeed, the Dutch of Westchester County were especially harassed by the war as they were remarkably divided in their political loyalties, switching pragmatically between the patriots and British dependent upon the immediate necessities and local concerns. Furthermore, the residents of the village of Sleepy Hollow were known for a history of performing a variety of roles during the war. One especially horrific example was the case of one "Polly Buckhout, shot dead by a Hessian, who mistook her for a man because she was wearing a man's hat" (10). In addition to this, there is the more official history of Major John André's arrest and execution for his involvement in the treason of Benedict Arnold near the town, which rested on being caught behind enemy lines wearing the wrong uniform. Sleepy Hollow, then, was known as a famous site of national and gender play, but was also a location with an especially traumatic history. As René Girard and Joseph Roach have both argued, locations of trauma (either historical or mythic) are often also sites of ritual and performance as rites are repeatedly performed so as to psychically expiate the violence of history, while also retaining it as an embedded cultural memory. Hughes has suggested that in reading "The Legend of Sleepy Hollow," "[w]e can now see that the crucial question of Ichabod's disappearance concerns itself not just with the banalities of love and the pleasures of the imaginative tale, but also with the urgent question of historical trauma and survival . . ." (Hughes, 11). Furthermore, Sleepy Hollow's special history of violence is one of the abuse of women (and "queer" men like André[5]) by the patriarchal forces of nationalistic conflict. The rituals of the town are, like Katrina herself, both old and modern simultaneously. They are located in the history of modern conflict, yet speak to the older magical sensibility of pre-Christian religions.

To prefigure the later events of the story, in which he is either expelled from the village or murdered by an entity that is either a real ghost or Brom Bones in costume, Crane is described as resembling the Hessian trooper in several key ways. Knickerbocker remarks:

> The cognomen of Crane was not inapplicable to his person. He was tall, but exceedingly lank, with narrow shoulders, long arms and legs, hands that dangled a mile out of his sleeves, feet that might have served for shovels, and his whole frame most loosely hung together . . . To see him striding along the profile of a hill on a windy day . . . one might have mistaken him for the genius of famine descending upon the earth, or some scarecrow eloped from a cornfield. (1061)

The ghost is possibly made of hessian, and Irving's comedic technique means that Ichabod Crane resembles a scarecrow—a puppet devoid of spirit whose identity is reduced to a series of symbolic gestures. The brevity of the short story and its legacy in character sketches and spectatorial essays imbues Irving's form with an attention to physicality and gesture as the primary communicative medium. There is a darkly comic undercurrent to an otherwise light story in the fact that Crane may tragically and inadvertently resemble the chosen sacrificial effigy for the village harvest festival. In ritual terms, Crane resembles all that is destructive to the village's (and indeed Irving's) model of community and so is a likely candidate for a scapegoat in a ritual of rebirth and purification. But there is also a further point to make here. As Plummer and Nelson have shown, "Irving's tale is one of perseveration . . . of maintenance of the feminine, and the landscape is predominantly female" (176). Given the known history of raids in the village, the frequent violations of the domestic sphere by the "masculine" forces of war, and the murder of Polly Buckhout, the character of the particular ritual sacrifice that the town chooses (or rather the women choose, as Irving makes a point of noting the centrality of women to decision making) is masculine. In fact, the stories that the "housewives" tell of the Hessian trooper are stories of emasculation: his head serving the Lacanian function of the phallus. The tale is heavily invested in the correlation between "heads" and masculinity, to the extent that Crane's own intellect, and his loyalty to the written word, is set against the bodies of the villagers. Hughes writes, "to be carried away by a word, as Ichabod is by the Mather he so loves, to lose one's head, so to speak . . . is plainly to give oneself over to a fearful death . . ." (17). As in the preceding tales in *The Sketch-Book*, which configured the written word as the passage to a form of devastating historical amnesia or misremembering, Crane's fault is his reliance upon imagination and intellect, synonymous with the written word he valorizes and teaches and the "modernity" he seeks to bring to "Sleepy Hollow." If Irving can be said to be misogynistic, as Plummer, Nelson, and Fetterley have all argued, then this takes the form of his equation of the logic of the body with femininity and the mind with men. Yet, even in this misogyny Irving identifies with the *feminine* body-consciousness as a means to access a history that is obfuscated by male-centered modernity.

Crane fits the mold of a scapegoat according to the understanding of psychoanalytic anthropologist René Girard, who argued that almost all ritual activity could be explained as a culture's attempt to sublimate the fact of their origin in mythic, protean violence by means of the execution of a surrogate victim. In most cases the sacrificial victim is someone (or something) that exists in liminal relation to a community but whose value to that community—in Crane's case as a teacher and man of learning—serves to render them sacred in their eyes. In most cases, the violent desire that Girard describes is transferred onto a substitute, a masked or performing subject that is theatrically, if not in reality, expelled from the community so as to maintain that culture's sense of psychic coherence. This theme of sacrificial threat within the context of transatlantic culture is further established by the haunting presence of "Major André's tree" (1081), the focal point of a Revolutionary-era crisis of sympathy. As I mentioned earlier, the relationship between André and Irving came by way of William Dunlap, whose play on the theme was one of the first major works of postwar American theatre and well known to playgoers of the time.

In *The Scapegoat* (1987) and *Violence and the Sacred* (1977) Girard argues that in order for the sacrifice to be worthy of the gods the value of the victim must be increased, since only visible signs of excess expenditure that demonstrate little or no utilitarian, economic, or practical logic can confer upon a subject the necessary sense of sacredness. For this reason scapegoats often undergo a period of prestige treatment during which considerable expense is lavished upon the victim so as to make them sacred to the community for whom they will serve as a sacrifice. Crane's deluded image of himself as a "man of some importance in the female circle . . . being considered a kind of idle gentleman-like personage, of vastly superior taste and accomplishments to the rough country swains" (1063) is therefore darkly ironic given his eventual fate. Imagining that Sleepy Hollow is an innocuous rural culture incapable of deception or the will to cause him any harm, Crane retreats into a romantic reverie of the kind that had endangered Crayon earlier in "The Voyage" chapter of *The Sketch-Book*. Indeed, Crane is an utterly narcissistic fantasist that Knickerbocker suggests imagines himself to be the king of Sleepy Hollow. In a scene that precedes the final crisis of Crane's failed suit to Katrina, Irving, as Knickerbocker, writes:

> On one fine autumnal afternoon, Ichabod, in a pensive mood, sat enthroned on the lofty stool from whence he usually watched all the little concerns of his little literary realm. In his hand he swayed a ferule, that sceptre of despotic power; the birch of justice reposed on three nails, behind the throne, a constant terror to evildoers; while on the desk before him might be seen sundry contraband articles and prohibited weapons. (1072)

In a satiric inversion of Crane's Yankee modernity, Irving fashions him as a mock king and substitutionary victim in a folk ritual, the very thing that a recent revolution fought in the name of Enlightenment values of rationality was established to eliminate. In addition, Irving's use of the term "little literary realm" returns the mind to Crayon's attempt to establish the world as a series of literary sketches and the attendant position of distance and detachment that such an aesthetic requires. Like Irving's critique of the imaginative, speculative Crayon, Crane's excessive attendance to writing forces him into the path of danger through his belief in the possible annihilation, or inevitable usurpation, of history by a mythologized modernity.

A further irony lies in Irving's decision to cast Crane as a "pedagogue." Even as he proclaims knowledge enough to educate the young he is incapable of the self-awareness and attention to the politics of the body required for him to understand that the community means him harm. In the final moments of "The Legend of Sleepy Hollow" the Headless Horseman symbolically "dethrones" Crane from his saddle by lobbing an enormous pumpkin at him, a symbol that at once refers to the rural Sleepy Hollow economy and, since it is a substitute for a head or brain, the dominance of the performing body over intellect. In the story's ritual drama, the pumpkin head represents the final force of history that encroaches upon Crane's romantic mind, expelling him from Sleepy Hollow as Crayon is finally expelled from *The Sketch-Book*.

Upon finishing *The Sketch-Book*, the reader is left with a final image of the eventual embeddedness of history within modernity, coded as the domination of the folk body over the Yankee intellect. In offering this image, Irving was strangely prescient about the future direction of the short story tradition in America, especially in the context of the new ebullient, carnivalesque magazines and periodicals that were beginning to shape the early nineteenth-century literary marketplace. Ultimately, what would come to be the dominant feature of the short story in America was not its claims to romantic insight so much as the abundance and publicity of the form in print culture. Irving's sense that performance, gesture, and ritual, rather than romantic imagination, internality, and speculation, would come to be the defining characteristics of the American short story tradition was carried forward by figures such as Edgar Allan Poe and George Lippard. These writers' gothic and sensational fictions took Irving's skepticism of the romantic mind, his conception of writing as a style of performance, and his interest in the semisacred, redemptive power of social ritual in new and radical directions. The changes Irving witnessed in the American theatre in the post-Revolutionary era he brought to the short story, particularly concerns around the rise of the body in performance, questions of gender in the new age of spectacle, and the problems of nationalism. These features would become a tradition in the form as print culture began to develop a national and international readership in the antebellum period. Both "Rip Van Winkle" and "The Legend of Sleepy Hollow" would become common source texts for writers in the antebellum era, the former as a major stage show by Dion Boucicault that ran throughout the nineteenth century and the latter as a source for regional humorists such as George Washington Harris and Mark Twain.[6] The *nationalism* of Irving's stories, then, was not his own, but developed vicariously through repeated performance and adaptation: a surrogacy that repeatedly reshaped the original text. After Irving, the short story tradition in America became invested in the concept of cultural memory; a memory maintained and transferred through rituals or theatricalized acts of performance. In using Rip Van Winkle's long sleep or the patterns of culture suggested by the regional and gendered conflicts in "Sleepy Hollow" as a mnemonic or shorthand for certain ideas and concepts, writers such as Poe, Hawthorne, and Melville (all of whom used Irving's work extensively) wrote themselves into a tradition in short narrative—indeed, helped to create it. In effect, they "performed" the short story legacy, reworking it through "surrogations," inherited gestures and phrases.

In the following chapter I show how Poe and Lippard, writing twenty years after Irving, attempted to channel the communal "affect" that Irving associated with femininity in "The Legend of Sleepy Hollow" into forms of male associational bonding that existed at the core of antebellum social relations. For Poe, who often wrote for female-centered publications, there is a certain "queerness" that one encounters in Irving's affiliations with Katrina in "Sleepy Hollow," the peculiar familial relations of "Rip Van Winkle," and an attention to the body as an alternative site of meaning to the written word, which is brought into his discussions of US history in tales such as "The Cask of Amontillado" and "The Pit and the Pendulum." In a certain sense, "The Cask of Amontillado," with its themes of masculine conflict, status, and the violence of history, replays the themes of "The Legend of Sleepy Hollow," whereas "The Pit and the Pendulum" is deeply engaged with the themes of romantic "vacancy" and memory Irving introduced in "Rip Van Winkle." Additionally, Poe and Lippard retained from Irving a sense of the crucial importance of ritual and performance in the creation of republican civic culture, which was sharpened in response to the rise of the "spectacular" marketplace and the entropic individualism of the Jacksonian era. A key element of this argument is that it was through the short story, a form that Poe was well aware was under threat of being sidelined by the rise of the novel in the antebellum era, that Poe and Lippard were able to offer their most cogent critiques of emerging US nationalism—carrying forward the cosmopolitanism that had motivated Irving in the early republic. At times the connections between Irving's writing and the new generation of short story practitioners would take the form of direct references, but more frequently it is observable in a shared desire to negotiate a "middle," nonpartisan position in national and international disputes that Irving began first among his family and friends in the Park Theatre as a teenager. This "middle space" was generated through careful attention to the performing body that Poe, in his famous statements on the "tale," would place centrally in his aesthetic vision by means of his focus on "spectacle," the "dramatic incident," and the circumscription of physical space.

CHAPTER 2

The Rites of Pure Brotherhood
Fraternalism and Performance in Poe and Lippard

> I broke and reached him a flagon of De Grâve . . . He laughed and threw the bottle upward with a gesticulation I did not understand. I looked at him in surprise. He repeated the movement—a grotesque one. "You do not comprehend?" he said. "Not I," I replied. "Then you are not of the brotherhood . . . You are not of the masons."
> —Edgar Allan Poe, "The Cask of Amontillado" (1846)

> The Brotherhood of the Union works by Combination of true hearts— and that Combination is aided by means of rites, ceremonies, and symbols which, in some form or other have been celebrated by the friends of Humanity for untold years. Yet the Brotherhood does not boast of this antiquity of its rites for mere antiquity's sake—nor for the purpose of exacting a superstitious veneration—but in order to show that the Principles for whose fulfilment we are now struggling, have had their believers in every age, and that the smile of God has blessed them . . .
> —George Lippard, "H.F Constitution of Circle of the Brotherhood of the Union" (1851)

On January 31, 1844, over a year before the publication of "The Raven" made him a household name and established his position as one of the foremost American poets of his generation, Edgar Allan Poe delivered a lecture on the state of American poetry to a fee-paying audience at the Odd Fellows Hall in Baltimore.[1] The lecture took place at seven o'clock in the Egyptian Saloon and admission was a relatively sizable twenty-five cents per ticket. Increasingly, lectures had begun to offer Poe a significant and lucrative forum for galvanizing interest in his work, as well as providing a space to discuss the condition of American literature more generally. What is also notable about this lecture in particular though is that it demonstrates the central role occupied by fraternal orders within antebellum cultures of popular literature and performance. Odai Johnson has shown that fraternities like the Odd Fellows and the Freemasons had a long history of supporting the arts in America, especially theatre, which belies the traditions of antitheatricalism frequently attributed to US culture. Johnson notes that looking at lodge records often reveals actors on the books as members of local and international fraternities, suggesting a degree of support for a profession that was often seen to lack esteem among elites. Additionally, fraternities often crossed party-political lines, the very lines that literary history has marked out as divided between pro- and antitheatrical tendencies. Indeed, performers "upon entering a new colony [or city] . . . would need four things in very short order: permission to play, a place to play, a subscription base, and a printer through whom to find his base" (Johnson, 105). In the antebellum era American writers like Poe were a key part of the very same performance landscape as actors and singers and, as such, often sought the support of fraternities in their artistic endeavors.

Given the supposed secrecy of fraternal groups such as the Odd Fellows and their sensitivity to the invasion of sacred, religious space by the noninitiated, the public nature of this lecture, which had received considerable prior notice in Baltimore newspapers, at first seems surprising. What must to be taken into account is the astonishing size and scope of fraternal order membership among men in antebellum America, as well as the role they played in supporting the literary arts. By 1843, the Odd Fellows alone had thirty thousand members, astonishing given that the order had only established its first official American lodge in 1830. Dana Nelson has suggested that this phenomenon is related to the psychic pressures on the antebellum middle- and lower-middle classes, especially in relation to the United States' transformation from an agrarian to a market economy, which frequently threatened to obliterate both Revolutionary-era ties of national sympathy and the economic livelihoods of the young men from whom fraternities drew their largest numbers of new initiates. In the early to mid-nineteenth century fraternities began to fill the emotional vacuum left by the market revolution's gradual obliteration of the traditional apprenticeship system, an organization of labor that had sought to cultivate its own bonds of intergenerational sympathy and support. Nelson writes that:

> Throughout the nineteenth century, fraternal space proliferated in the working and middle classes. From labor unions, political parties

and fraternal lodges, to Christian and reform groups, to professional organizations and sports clubs, men extended the sphere of male sociality well beyond their day at work. These social spaces offered themselves as a corrective to the abrasions of that workday, a haven where a man could be truly recognized apart from his competitive working role, could be rightfully known in his individual particularity. (178)

As well as providing a site free from the pressures of the "competitive working role" though, antebellum fraternities were also synecdochal of larger national tensions between an emergent, liberal, free-market economy and older conceptions of status and power with roots in transatlantic republican tradition. Republicanism required an understanding that the right to political influence was rooted in the performance of the civic rites and rituals that bonded individuals together through collective forms of affect. In this regard, the elaborate initiation and participation rites that began to be a central element of fraternal praxis at this time constituted a form of republican theatre against the backdrop of a marketplace that *could* confer a desirable upward social mobility but was also dangerously entropic, always threatening to place individuals from similar backgrounds into overt competition with one another. Through fraternities, middle-class and artisan American men sought to reconcile their desire for sympathetic community with the emergent liberal-nationalist dream of individual self-determination. Fraternities preached brotherhood and promoted social mobility, while their "sacred" rituals showed how being a successful individual required the social acceptance of a wider group.

The widespread membership of these kinds of organizations is made more intriguing when one considers the changing nature of their ritual practices, most of which initially developed as adaptations of the expressive styles of European Freemasonry. Mark Carnes has observed that although organizations such as the Odd Fellows and the Freemasons proclaimed for themselves the prestige of being global orders of genuine antiquity, constancy of ritual practice, and a traceable line of descent from Egyptian or early Judeo-Christian religious sects, in most cases they were wholly invented traditions. Instead of being the product of ancient Memphis or Jerusalem, the first Grand Lodge of Freemasonry was founded in London in 1717 and the order had continued to undergo a process of invention, adaptation, and accommodation of ceremonial practices throughout the centuries to accommodate the differing needs of subsequent generations and national cultures.

Poe's lecture to the assembled masses at the Odd Fellows Hall occurred at a moment of increasing theatricality in antebellum American fraternal rituals. Throughout the 1840s sacred dress became more ornate, the ceremonies longer, the initiations of new brothers more staged and spectacular, and the names and numbers of possible "degrees"[2] more plentiful, esoteric, and bizarre. Henry Dana Ward's popular 1828 work on American Freemasonry, *Its Pretensions Exposed*, quoted one Professor Robison on a common fear that through the influence of "projectors" dedicated to various causes of their own, the rituals of Masonry had lost their original meanings and were becoming divertingly long, complicated, and dramatic, more like sensational, melodramatic theatre than sincere religious liturgy:

> projectors had contrived to tag their peculiar nostrums to the mummery of Masonry, and were even allowed to twist the Masonic emblems and ceremonies to their purpose; so that, in their hands Free Masonry became a thing totally unlike, and almost in direct opposition to the system (if it may get such a name) imported from England; and some lodges had become schools of irreligion and licentiousness. (Robison in Ward, 317)

Ward drew on a common fear that the American Revolution had disrupted the transnational, imperial logic of Freemasonry and opened it up to the threat of contamination by new ideas and influences. "From 1840–1860 American . . . [fraternalism] was entirely transformed," writes Mark Carnes, ". . . revision [left] only the 'mere shell' of the original rituals" (28). Fraternal orders operated by dramatizing their claims to being both global in their reach and consistent in their vision across vast swathes of historical time but did so through a fairly relentless process of creativity and invention that drew the ire of traditionalists. In a departure from earlier styles of fraternalism that had only a small role for ritual theatre in their overall work, by the early nineteenth century the performance culture of most fraternal orders had become "important in and of itself" (6). Fraternities continued to be formed for a variety of pragmatic reasons, such as insurance and charity, to cultivate reformist or revolutionary activities (as in the case of the American, French, and Haitian Revolutions) or to provide financial support for workers, but by the 1840s most had begun to devote increasing amounts of time to the construction and performance of ritual activities. A lavish and theatrical pomp not unlike that which might have been found on the nineteenth-century stage had begun to inform the very fundamentals of American fraternalism, as drama and ritual became more central to the orders' work. In essence, the affective labor of these orders as a source of associational male bonding became as significant as their charitable and public works.

The Odd Fellows' decision to engage Poe to speak on literary subjects also points to another crucial aspect of fraternalism's work in antebellum society. Fraternities attempted to counteract the insidious effects of what was perceived as a dwindling spirit of community and the rise of a blandly utilitarian market society through the performance of rites and rituals that bonded brothers together by means of what Elaine Hadley has referred to as a "dramaturgy of familiarity, an inclusive form of sympathetic exchange that strengthened . . . ties" (*Melodramatic Tactics*, 31). Crucially though, they also bridged a divide between text and performance by means of their active and visible participation in the era's rich and sensational print culture. In fact, as I will show later in relation to George Lippard's work for the Brotherhood of the Union, the performance and print cultures of fraternal orders frequently reinforced one another. Most fraternities had their own periodicals, many of which had large subscriptions across large geographical areas. In addition to the usual news pages and letters devoted specifically to internal fraternity business, these periodicals behaved much like more mainstream contemporary magazines such as the *Knickerbocker*, *Putnam's Monthly*, and *Harper's*, which were designed for general, predominantly middle-class family consumption and from which they frequently reprinted articles and other content. Publications like the *Masonic Review* and *American Freemason*, and the *Ark*, the *Symbol*, and the *Casket* for the Odd Fellows, had "Family Departments," carried "Literary Notices," and printed essays, illustrations, poetry, short stories, and serialized novels that helped to foster a collective identity between brothers and national and international chapters. A brief list of titles from volume IV of the *American Freemason: A Monthly Masonic Magazine* indicates that many of these works drew on the secret symbols and images of the order: "Brotherly Love: A Poem," "Masonry," "On the Path." As I will show later in my reading of Lippard's *Adonai: The Pilgrim of Eternity*, these works would even serve as sources for the sensational and dramatic theatricalized scenes or dramatic readings that comprised that fraternity's ritual practices. Additionally, the fact that these magazines were traded on the open market allowed different orders to also draw inspiration from each other's publications for rituals of their own. Tied to the growth of fraternal membership, therefore, was a distinct and growing association between literary activity and religious or pseudoreligious ritualism, which were not considered to be isolated, or transcendent, categories but served an equal position in the brothers' social, imaginative, and creative lives.

The writing of antebellum secret societies can be usefully considered as an example of the interactions between performance and print that Ngugi wa Thiong'o called "orature." At once transnational (since fraternities usually borrowed their expressive culture from circum-Atlantic European, Native American, and African sources) and incapable of being considered as solely dramatic or textual phenomena, the work of groups like the Odd Fellows provides a valuable lens on the workings of the wider antebellum public sphere. The attempts of various orders to perform their claims to historical, transatlantic lineage and memory, what Lippard referred to as the desire to "boast of the antiquity of its rites for mere antiquity's sake," inevitably made fraternities subject to criticism from the more patriotic wings of nineteenth-century American society. However, their expressed desire for historical legitimacy meant that even the most avowedly nationalistic orders were in some sense transnational in conception. Indeed, Poe's lecture in Baltimore coincided with the 1844 foundation of the first fraternal order that openly professed nativist political aims, the Junior Order of United American Mechanics, which ironically based its rites and ceremonies on those of international Freemasonry.

This increasing popular interest in ritualism also had a flip side that reflected the hostile class tensions and sectarianism of the antebellum American public sphere. The growing abundance of secret societies in the 1830s and 1840s designed to cater to the middle classes drove a parallel rise in printed works that sought to expose the orders' purportedly suspicious, and often even overtly "traitorous," inner logic by infiltrating the groups and decoding the secret meanings of their ritual practices. In an unregulated marketplace for print that was protected by constitutional First Amendment rights, books, pamphlets, and broadsides aimed at literate, lower-middle-class mechanics and artisans and with sensational and paranoiac titles like *Odd Fellowship Exposed* and *Freemasonry: Its Pretensions Exposed*, contributed to a growing number of popular exposés of sects, political organizations, and religions. Carl Ostrowski has suggested that the realization by popular book publishers "that the exposé pose was adaptable to a variety of subjects in which authors claimed to penetrate a veil of misleading appearances ("Inside the Temple of Ravoni," 3) led to a slew of books such as *Mormonism Exposed*, *The Romish Confessional*, *Awful Disclosures . . . of the Hotel Dieu Nunnery of Montreal*, and *The Blasphemy of Abolition* flooding newsstands in the antebellum era, providing an unofficial mechanic and artisan-republican counterpublic to the official, usually fairly tame, fraternity magazines and books of copyrighted rites and rituals. What motivated these texts though was a sense that in an age of widespread sectarian conflict and religious revivalism things were not as they appeared. Any claim made by a fraternity or religious order to universal brotherhood, sympathy, or a new revelation was met with a violent counterclaim. The narrator of *Mormonism Exposed* (New York; 1842) (writing under the disturbing pseudonym of "The New York Watchman") expressed this pervasive paranoia neatly, appealing to his readers' multivalent bigotry and violent sense of patriotic vigilance: "If the Methodists, or Baptists, or Presbyterians, or Episcopalians, should be *convicted* of forming '*secret societies*,' and binding their members, under the awful penalty of death, to subvert the institutions of this country, would you not do all in your power to make such iniquitous proceedings known?" (iii). The New York Watchman's comments highlight the complex dynamic between a broadly liberal, Jacksonian working-class culture of self-reliance and a more avowedly republican logic of bonding. He refers to the "binding" of members as a curtailment of their liberties and a threat to their very lives, even if in most cases such bonds served to engender a network of support and mutuality. Indeed, while genuine violence related to membership of fraternal orders was actually extraordinarily rare, such events as the disappearance of anti-Masonic campaigner William Morgan in 1826 contributed to a popular perception that these groups had a hidden agenda of deceit or traitorous aggression. Fuelled by this popular paranoia, the exposés of fraternal orders often had the effect of driving retributive action and, ironically, also led to the foundation of secret societies like the Order of the Star Spangled Banner, which formed the basis of the nativist Know-Nothing movement. Such texts as the New York Watchman's *Mormonism Exposed* would eventually lead to the lynching of Joseph Smith (the founder of Mormonism, who borrowed many symbols from Masonry) by an angry mob in Carthage, Illinois, in June 1844. Exposés embodied the complex emotional states of the antebellum lower classes, at once suggesting that it was this group who held the best interests of the nation at heart and displaying a paranoiac class fear of exclusion or the suppression of voice.

These battles over ritual theatre and print were therefore a microcosm of larger conflicts in antebellum society over class identity and the uses of transatlantic memory. Overwhelmingly, middle-class fraternities were drawn to the kinds of Old World ritual and ceremony that Eric Hobsbawm and Terence Ranger have interpreted as gestural markers of a conferred and imagined prestige, while the laboring- and lower-middle classes often saw these things as suspicious signs of a conspiratorial elite derailing the United States from its originally professed aims of individual freedom and liberty. The paradox is that the Odd Fellows, the Freemasons, and others were professing global brotherhood while altering their ritual practices to adapt to the perceived needs of an "indigenous" American democracy as a revived form of nativist nationalism took hold of the imaginations of many Americans. Such tensions produced a competitive feedback loop as fraternities became more theatrical and borrowed more from other orders in the effort to develop a single "ritual . . . [that] is the most beautiful, the most affecting, the most truthful, known to any order on the face of the globe" (Lippard, *White Banner*, 142) to combat "the war of sect and party . . . [and] the strife of hollow and vindictive antagonism" (141). In this way, the workings of fraternal societies closely corresponded to a wider pattern in the performances of sincerity that structured Anglo-American social conduct in the long nineteenth century.[3] In *Declaring Independence* (1993) Jay Fliegelman describes a process in which the increasing need to develop interpretive frameworks to negotiate conduct between men for the purposes of maintaining a national collective identity drove a correspondingly "intensified scrutiny of the body as an instrument of expression . . . [and] led paradoxically to . . . a new social dramaturgy and a performative understanding of selfhood" (2).

In this chapter I propose that in order to comment upon the contradictory pressures of nationalism, global brotherhood, and capitalist citizenship affecting middle- and working-class men, which frequently took on embodied form in the ritual practices of fraternal orders, Edgar Allan Poe and George Lippard developed dramatic styles of short fiction structured around symbolic, gestural, and theatricalized performances of identity. In doing this, Poe and Lippard both drew upon and contributed to the "sensational designs" (Tompkins) of antebellum popular fiction and its attention to the activities of the body, while also highlighting the interactions between print and the performance cultures within antebellum fraternalism. I start by offering a reading of Poe's two Masonic tales, "The Pit and the Pendulum" (which I read partly as a comment on popular sensationalism and fraternal initiation practices) and "The Cask of Amontillado," a dark Masonic revenge drama that appeared, perhaps somewhat incongruously, in the pages of the moralizing, middle-class *Godey's Lady's Book*. As I have suggested though, the Masonic context of this tale would have been widely understood by the readers of *Godey's*, especially since the editor of the periodical, Sarah Josepha Hale, was once married to an important New England Freemason and benefitted from their support in the publication of her early work.[4]

"The Cask of Amontillado" (1846)

In the key expressive moment of "The Cask of Amontillado" Poe explores the notion that ritual and gesture—the rites of a performing body—had become increasingly important to the operation of sympathy between men in the nineteenth-century transatlantic world. Poe does so, however, not by replicating the kind of sentimental plot commonly found in the pages of *Godey's* in which a lasting bond is formed when truths are revealed, but through a hideous inversion that indicates how status relationships interrupt the development of meaningful frameworks of cross-class interpretation and exchange. It is tempting to read such inversion in light of G. R. Thompson's classic study *Poe's Fiction* (1973) as an example of romantic irony, a technique through which the author sought to distance himself from the absurd enthusiasms of his era. However, Poe's treatment of Masonry in "The Cask of Amontillado" is actually remarkably in keeping with the tone, if not the retributive intentions, of popular secret society exposés. Rather than remaining aloof from these other "lower," "inferior" literary works, Poe's story is very much embedded in the class- and status-conscious culture that produced them.

In the story Fortunato effectively excludes Montressor from brotherhood, and by association from his trust, because of his failure to interpret a coded behavior peculiar to a certain sect of the Freemasons. Fortunato states that Montressor is "not of the brotherhood" (Poe, 277) because of his failure to respond to a highly ritualized gestural exchange: "he laughed and threw the bottle upward with a gesticulation I did not understand" (276). In this act we see the great crisis of antebellum American masculinity articulated through the medium of gesture, which carries within it the notion that ritual, properly interpreted, might serve to facilitate an equal grounding in power relations. Poe's story is attentive to the fact that gesture and performance have a long history in the United States and exist as an alternative, parallel, intellectual tradition in antebellum America. Montressor's name ironically recalls the last fortress containing British forces in the United States that was held until well after the Revolution, Montressor's Island in New York. Named after a British military engineer and mapmaker, the name implies the persistence of a "stronghold" of Britishness (something with which Masonry was often associated by radical republicans) within the new US national culture. Additionally, John Montressor himself was one of the organizers, along with the famous English spy John André, of the Philadelphia *Mischianza* of May 18, 1778, a famously elaborate festival and performance given by the British forces during the Revolution in honor of the retiring commander of the army, General Sir William Howe, which was interpreted by American forces as a slight against the recent Continental Congress ban on theatrical entertainments.[5]

For Montressor, Fortunato's gesture becomes a hypertrophy of all the fears of exclusion and inferiority that found their expression in the rise of the exposé form in antebellum print culture. Poe's narrator is not drawn from the lower-middle classes, yet he embodies many of their anxieties, especially since the gesture also situates the tale within the joint contexts of antebellum fraternalism and circum-Atlantic culture. As I have suggested above, the interaction of national concerns with the claims of secret societies to a global reach generated some surprising disjunctions between orders proclaiming allegiance to the same Masonic stem. While one ritualized gesture may have meant one thing to one lodge, to another it may have been meaningless or carried a vastly different implication. In the context of an antebellum print culture that frequently dramatized the changing rites of fraternities, the exploration of the collapse of gestural exchange in "The Cask of Amontillado" participates in a wider cultural critique of the tensional disjunctions between global Masonic ritualism and the emergent forces of antebellum nativism and capitalism. A Masonic gesture is a transatlantic symbol, a sign of participation in a global Enlightenment culture. The "insult" that inspires Montressor to revenge upon his former friend therefore conceivably originates in an exclusion that is not only personal but also indicative of his failure to be allowed to participate in a new international culture of trade and exchange. Indeed, Poe characterizes Montressor as a man bound to the land and culture of his old family line and unable to perform the rites necessary to the new transnational republicanism. The revenge plot of the story, its retrospective narrative, and its pervasive symbols of death and decay indicate the author's interest in the relationship between memory and modernity within a transatlantic setting.

The narrative operates through the implication that the old "great and numerous family" (276) of the Montressors have effectively been supplanted in status by a new transnational middle class, represented through the connections of Fortunato with a fraternal order that were playing a significant role in the gradual middle-class usurpation of aristocratic power in Europe at the moment in which Poe was writing. The incomprehensibility of Fortunato's Masonic gesture highlights for Montressor that his former social position has been lost and that he has been excluded from the primary collective logic that characterized the liberal American middle-class culture of Poe's antebellum readers: the promise of social mobility. Montressor says, importantly, of Fortunato that he is both sincere and "rich, respected, admired, beloved . . . as once I was . . . a man to be missed" (Poe, 276). Montressor believes himself to be less of a man, a fact that disrupts the democracy of brotherhood.

Montressor's failure to interpret the Masonic gesture indicates his exclusion from the relations of trust that maintained this new middle-class power base. The narrative effectively dramatizes these relations of trust in the goading promise of "the Amontillado" by which Montressor leads his quarry through the vault to his eventual end. The story progresses through a series of requests and direct commands that challenge Fortunato to greater and greater states of reliance upon his friend. Montressor can be very direct in his demands that Fortunato press "farther on" and "proceed" to his desired goals, but at various moments he also appears to dissuade his "friend," calling attention to his ill health in a manner that challenges Fortunato's masculinity and his sense of entitlement. In this way, Poe inverts a common trope of Masonic initiations to serve sinister ends. Plays of trust were central elements of most of the popular exposé accounts of fraternal ritual practices upon which Poe drew for his tale. In the usual exposé an initiate would be led by a senior brother through a series of trials or obstacles and be offered at each stage the opportunity to withdraw, further testing their mettle and qualifications for membership and access to new knowledge. Mark Carnes has outlined this common structure thus:

> In every major order at least one ritual developed each of the following themes: (1) an initiate at the outset of his task was portrayed as immature or unmasculine, (2) he overcame obstacles as he embarked on a difficult journey through the stages of childhood and adolescence, (3) this journey or ordeal climaxed when he was killed (or nearly killed) by angry father figures, (4) he was reborn as a man into a new family of approving brethren and patriarchs. In this way the emotional orientations instilled by maternal nurture would give way to the sterner lessons of ancient patriarchs, venerable kings, or savage chieftains." (125–26)

In "The Cask of Amontillado" Poe subverts this form by having an uninitiated brother of lower social status lead his superior through a series of trials that culminate in his eventual death. At each moment Fortunato is offered a chance to turn back, but greed and masculine pride force him to push on.

The theme of disrupted brotherhood is further emphasized by Fortunato's dubious connoisseurship of wine, which disrupts the normalizing influence of brotherhood by introducing a sense of capitalistic competition. Instead of fraternity operating as a release from the divisive pressures of capitalist exchange, an egalitarian site free from the competitive impulse, the presence of the amontillado drives a wedge between Montressor and Fortunato. The protagonist lures his quarry to his doom by direct appeal to the middle-class, capitalistic laws of competition that are shown to be in direct tension with the more benevolent, affective relations promised by brotherhood. The distinction between amontillado and regular sherry is made expressly apparent when Fortunato states of their friend Luchresi that "he cannot distinguish Sherry from Amontillado" (275). Poe implies that amontillado is especially desired and so juxtaposes the desire for egalitarian fraternity with the allure of prestige. For Poe, the kinds of class and status conflicts depicted in his tale owe much to democracy and the divisive effects of capitalist modernity. The author implies that in the translation of Old World aristocratic hierarchies into American middle-class identities, some vital system of exchange has been interrupted.

Unable to find a fraternal space that relieves the dangerous pressures placed upon him by the market society, Montressor is a man alone, and violence is his answer to his isolation. This sense of isolation is further emphasized by the first-person narration of the story. By framing the narrative as a confessional account without a clear or identifiable respondent, Poe suggests that in his loss of brotherhood Montressor has lost the sense of affective connection required for the creation of an inviolate and stable identity. When experienced as text this monologue has the even more perverse and dangerous effect of implanting the expressions of an insane individual directly, and without mediation, into the minds of the reader. Montressor's confession has the double effect of at once describing an event that involved a forceful imposition of the narrator's will upon another and interpolating or possessing the reader by means of written language. In effect, the tale exposes a tension between the internality of romantic subjectivism experienced as text and republican conceptions of the performative roots of power and influence. As Jay Fliegelman has shown, popular oratorical manuals, such as the bestselling *Columbian Orator*, frequently depicted the ideal republican model of conversation as involving two parties understood to operate on an equal footing. An important pedagogical tool in its time, *The Columbian Orator* comprised a series of short, individual monologues (such as Cicero's speech on the Catiline conspiracy) with scenes from important dramas (such as Addison's *Cato*) and Socratic dialogues between two characters on such subjects as "Loquacity," "Civilization," and "Physiognomy." For the author, Caleb Bingham, such dialogue was important for the development of successful "character," a distinct form of republican social performance that locates power and influence in actions and behaviors as much as in intellect. In "The Cask of Amontillado" though, this dialogical element is crucially elided. As readers we cannot be sure to whom the tale is being addressed. Are we overhearing a confession? Are we ourselves the intended respondent, or is there another? This lack of response to Montressor's account—its monomaniacal sense of introspection—is used by Poe as further evidence of the collapse of egalitarian interpretive frameworks necessary for meaningful brotherhood. Poe effectively suggests that with fraternity functioning correctly Montressor would not be prone to violent jealousy. The collapse of the gestural and emotive conduct required for the creation of brotherhood creates a character whose absence of positive guidelines for conduct precipitates his violence. Like Irving's critique of romantic amnesia, Poe's narrator is a hideous extrapolation of Lockean empiricism and psychology—a character shaped singularly by his own subjective experience, whose identity is dangerously internalized. In this way, Poe does not deviate too far from the dominant logic of antebellum fraternalism, even as he stretches its claims and burlesques its typology. He suggests that recourse to narratives of brotherhood that rely upon a transparent visual language and make inner feelings correspond with external expression may provide a way of avoiding the problems of deceit.

To illustrate this Poe turns to heraldry, the dominant visual code of Old World aristocracy, which expresses without confusion the nature, class, and status of the family that displays it. Here Poe shows deference to "European" forms of hierarchical symbolism within the context of democratic America, as a form of visual culture based in familial narratives of the Old World is shown to be a counter to the problem of deceit and the dangers of romantic internality. Montressor states that his coat of arms depicts "a huge human foot d'or, in a field azure; the foot crushes a serpent rampant whose fangs are imbedded in the heel" (276). Within this image are many implications of arrest of social ascendancy and the stagnation of class identity, problems that, while explored by Poe through an aristocratic European framework, express distinct nineteenth-century American concerns. In heraldic tradition the azure tincture is the sky and represents uninhibited social ascendance, while the foot represents movement, which Poe seems to suggest is evidence of social climbing.[6] This process is impeded, however, by the biting serpent, which Poe seems to imply refers to how the Devil, in the form of Montressor's violence, will arrest his social ascendancy. Since the heel carries inferences of the Achilles' heel, this image is suggestive of fundamental weakness.

As evidenced by the misunderstanding of gestures, this collapse of brotherhood precipitates a further collapse of a necessary interpretative framework to negotiate interaction between these two men that emphasizes the failure of Montressor to ascend to the position of influence and class that has been offered to Fortunato. In Poe's text, Jay Fliegelman's "performative [and bodily] understanding of selfhood" is best expressed through Fortunato, whose dress, and, indeed, whose overall countenance, is expressly tied to the drama through the carnival setting in which Poe places him. When Montressor first encounters Fortunato, the narrator takes a peculiarly pathological concern in expounding the nature of his dress and the overt theatricality of his greeting. The narrator states, "He accosted me with great warmth, for he had been drinking much. The man wore motley. He had on a tight-fitting parti-striped dress, and his head was surmounted by the conical cap and bells. I was so pleased to see him that I thought I should never have done wringing his hand" (274).

Fortunato's dress recalls the British, pantomimic, performance tradition of the harlequinade, which is structurally predicated upon the murderous, and often sexualized, pursuit of the silent and hapless Harlequin by the violent and jealous Pantaloon. Like the ritualized behavior of fraternities, pantomime was also characterized by an expressive set of standardized movements and forms. The pantomime genre, which underwent a resurgence in the British theatres of the late eighteenth and early nineteenth centuries, was not only democratic in its cross-class appeal to the many stratified sectors of modern Britain but provided an adaptive mode for critique of complex power relations. As Elaine Hadley reads this theatrical form, "pantomime easily represented both the farce of state power and its physical oppression of the silent underdog" (54). As a genre of performance the harlequinade owed its lineage to the ritualized patterns of the Italian Renaissance *commedia dell'arte*, a genre whose very name is synonymous with the professionalization of acting in the late sixteenth and early seventeenth centuries.

Poe's references to the commedia and pantomime align transatlantic performance traditions with the internal national pressures of American culture. Fortunato's conduct is primarily gestural, while his voice is largely silenced by the alcohol he has consumed, the degenerative effects of the "nitre"[7] in the cellar, and eventually by his being bricked into a wall. Harlequin, whom in the context of transatlantic performance traditions Fortunato most closely represents, is also largely silent, and in this way his body becomes more directly engaged in his performance and is placed under greater public scrutiny. Fortunato effectively accepts the theatricalized and largely silent nature of his role, a role that is similar to Harlequin's "silent underdog." Once he is no longer visible, the possibility of his "speaking" in visual terms is nullified. As a metaphor for the collapse of brotherhood precipitated on the public interpretation and response to gesture, this silence and invisibility are acute. Fortunato cannot be seen, so cannot "speak," because in a culture that increasingly prizes the visual and external and is reliant on the coded, expressive language of gesture, his invisibility silences him.

At the end of the story the narrator waits for Fortunato to speak, but is offered "only a jingling of the bells" (Poe, 279). In the fraternal initiation rituals of the Freemasons, which provide much of Poe's reference material for "The Cask of Amontillado" and "The Pit and the Pendulum," much is made of the manner by which the ascension of degrees is reliant upon receiving a secret code, usually a new gesture, from another brother, a metaphor for receiving the word of God. Carnes writes, "Having descended into the vault and discovered His word, they [the initiates] could set about the work of rebuilding His temple . . . the descent into the vault symbolized man's appropriation of divine power" (48). "Word" here becomes synonymous with the visual language of gestural exchange. In Poe's story the knowledge that might be conferred is withheld and, as such, Montressor's class identity is left stagnant. He does not ascend in class terms as a result of his descent into the vault because his purpose was the disruption rather than the maintenance of brotherhood. Poe suggests that men should not be tricked or deceived into passing knowledge on to one another, as fraternity and reason need an acknowledgment of the democratic power of equality to function. By overlaying theatricalized ritual onto the pantomime, Poe follows a dominant line in the short story tradition in his suggestion that viewing the spectacle of the body can confer democratic knowledge, whereas obscuring it behind the walls of status and class only serves to disrupt the all-important visual codes of republican culture.

Poe's message in "The Cask of Amontillado" concerning the importance of social performance and visibility is indicative of a wider change in American society in the antebellum period: the transition from a Revolutionary-era ideal of oratorical simplicity as the medium of choice for the generation of sympathy, into a more visual, sensational, and avowedly melodramatic style of public performance. Poe would explore this theme in an essay on

"The American Drama" that appeared in the August 1845 edition of *American Whig Review*. Looking at American dramatic production, Poe (himself a failed playwright who was known for the power of his lyceum performances and poetic readings) concluded that the "spirituality" of the drama has remained essentially constant even though the physical means of representation ("the mechanisms" in Poe's terminology) have undergone improvement during the centuries. In this manner Poe defends the American theatre against detractors by suggesting that the "spiritual" work of drama is actually improved upon by the new mechanical capacities for spectacular visual expression. Unlike the central Neo-Platonic hypothesis of the romantic mode, which characterized the visual world as a disturbing illusion that detracted one from meditation on reality, Poe echoed the peculiar sensationalism of antebellum literary culture in his hope for a possible fusion between aesthetic, haptic, and "spiritual" truths.

> Coming to Drama, we shall see that in its mechanisms we have made progress, while in its spirituality we have done little or nothing for centuries certainly . . . and this is because what we term the spirituality of the drama is precisely its imitative position- is exactly that position which distinguishes it as one of the principal of the imitative arts . . . In dramatic writing, no principle is more clear than that nothing should be said or done which has not a tendency to develop the catastrophe, or the characters. (Poe, *Essays*, 358)

Poe's essay on "The American Drama" is usefully considered alongside his more famous comments on the short story or tale. In an essay on Nathaniel Hawthorne's work that appeared in the May 1842 edition of *Graham's Magazine*, the author outlined his theory that "if wise," a successful short story writer "[would] not fashion his thoughts to accommodate his incidents; but having conceived, with deliberate care, a certain unique or single *effect* to be wrought out, he then . . . combines such events as may best aid him in establishing this preconceived effect" (572). For Poe, the short story, like the drama, is an imitative art and should not aspire to utter originality of mental conception, as such pieces tend to become "excessively diffuse, extravagant, and indicative of an imperfect sentiment of Art" (573). Instead, the necessary element for success in short prose fiction, as on the stage, is careful attention to the roles played by form and "mechanism" in creating "the immense force derivable from totality" (572). Unlike the category of romantic or "spiritual" originality favored by such groups as the New

England transcendentalists, which ultimately located meaning and value in the internal motivations of a singular author, Poe's dramatic "effects" are outwardly expressive and avowedly social in conception, being, as they are, directed towards the pleasures of the audience or reader. By bringing the effects of the stage into the arena of prose writing by means of his attention to the importance of collective affect and symbolic action, Poe developed a theory of short fiction that was less representative of the individual subjectivism of the romantic movement than it was of the totalities that symbolic anthropologists like Victor Turner and Clifford Geertz have attributed to ritual. As such, Poe's understanding of short prose narrative and drama as an attempt at a synthesis of "mechanism" and "spirit" foreshadows a tradition of modern ethnography that would come to define what Edward Sapir called a "genuine culture" by its ability to develop forms of expression that navigated between order and irrationalism—what Victor Turner described as "structure" and "anti-structure." However, Poe also reflected a greater theatricalization of social behavior and conduct in his own era, which, as Karen Halttunen has shown, was perfectly in keeping with the character of publications like *Godey's Lady's Book*.[8] Indeed, his theory of the importance of dramatic events and "effects" to nineteenth-century artistic culture and society drew upon popular discussions that attended the late eighteenth-century rise of melodrama as a dramatic form on the transatlantic stage. In his 1832 essay on "Melodrama" in France, popular playwright René-Charles Guilbert de Pixérécourt suggested that the expressivity of melodramatic style was indicative of both the rise of democratic publics and a new grandeur in social behavior. In a typically high-flown manner, Pixérécourt outlined a progressive narrative of development in which the aesthetically low quality of most melodramatic performances was merely a stage of development in what was, at its core, the perfect modern art form. Pixérécourt's suggestion that the melodrama's combination of music, speech, mime, and other genres allowed it to achieve the status of a total art was similar to Poe's claims for the power of short prose fiction. Pixérécourt writes, "Melodrama is spoken, it is sung, it is danced, it is mimed; it has replaced everything else, turned everything upside down . . . There is only one genre . . . the same thing will happen with melodrama as has happened with everything else in this world; out of chaos order is born."

This greater theatricalization of public life led to a crisis in fraternity membership in the transatlantic nineteenth century. In a world that was visibly becoming more performative, secret societies increasingly needed to be publicly acknowledged in order to fulfil their mandate to the needs of republican brotherhood and national political concerns, while also responding to commonplace anxieties concerning the possibility of deceit. In effect, brotherhood had to be performed in order to allow the generation of a republican body politic. Just as the initiation rituals of fraternal organizations invariably include an element whereby the body of the initiate is exposed to the assembly, either actually naked or as a result of the focus of the gaze, Fortunato's body takes center stage in Montressor's tale. Poe's first-person narrative effectively excludes Montressor's body from his own account of events, turning the readers' gaze upon the gestural conduct of Fortunato in a similar manner to how the staged harlequinade focused viewers upon Harlequin. The theatrical and gestural, embodied in Fortunato's exchanges, *should* mean that he is saved from Montressor's violence, because in the intellectual terms of nineteenth-century fraternalism gestural conduct allows for republican brotherhood. However, the setting of the tale disrupts the possibilities of fraternal brotherhood, since carnival, a legitimated site of class conflict, works to reverse the model of deferential exchanges that bound brother to brother. Poe chooses "the supreme madness of the carnival season" (274) as the setting of his story, because it elevates the underlying class tensions beneath the supposed egalitarianism of fraternal brotherhood. By reversal of positions, suggested by the murder of the rich and respected Fortunato by the less-accepted figure of Montressor, the differences in their identities are brought to the fore.

In *Carnival: A People's Uprising at Romans 1579–1580*, Emmanuel Le Roy Ladurie explores how the festivities of the Catholic carnival were used by elites and subalterns respectively to voice inherent concerns about the structure of the society in which they lived. Carnival, a festival that originated in pagan spring rites of purification, is a politically and socially legitimated site of class conflict. Unlike at other times of the year when the full force of medieval repression was frequently deployed to maintain elite order, during carnival artisans could mock their patrician masters, patricians lampoon their "primitive" rural servants, and the rustic underclass challenge the hierarchical order of Old World Catholicism by resurrecting the traditions of pre-Christian animists. Le Roy Ladurie says this in relation to the Romans carnival of 1580:

> Carnival . . . dealt with social sins or ills, on which the community unfortunately could reach no consensus. In other words, the elimination of social ills implied class struggle, with greedy notables on one side and rebellious peasants on the other. Each group entered in

to Carnival, confronting the other with theatrical and ritual gestures leading up to the final massacre. (xx)

The primary political technique of carnival was "the supreme and truly Carnival rite of inversion or role reversal" (Ladurie, 189). In the European carnival tradition that Poe evokes, on *lundi gras*, the day before the official beginning of the feasting and celebration, one of the sectors of the society would appoint an official carnival king or "lord of misrule" who would decree that many of the town's official laws be reversed. In this way, the forms of social control peculiar to hierarchical societies, such as traditional impositions on the consumption of certain wines and foodstuffs by certain classes, would be removed. Poe's reference to amontillado, an expensive product that was made by aging sherry in American oak casks, is intriguing in this context. Amontillado sherry was extremely expensive and, as such, one product that in early modern Europe would have been the preserve of the wealthy and legally prohibited to certain classes.[9] At carnival season, however, as long as the carnival king sanctioned it, increased license would be offered to revellers. This role reversal did not always alleviate class tensions and in fact often heightened them. As Ladurie notes, however, "this vision unwittingly substantiated through its hysteria what it was ridiculing" (192), since these reversals could be used to taunt the lower classes, reinforcing essential differences through the exposure to the peasants or artisans that which would ordinarily be denied them.

Poe uses the Catholic tradition of carnival to explore the class tensions that underlie American middle-class identity and fraternal brotherhoods. Through the murder of Fortunato at carnival season, Montressor both expresses his desire for a reversal of their respective positions and reinforces his own essential difference of class and status. The torch that Montressor drops through the "remaining aperture" (Poe, 279) in the wall where Fortunato has been confined is a taunt based on the reversal peculiar to carnival and it explorations of class identity. In Catholic ritual the bearing of a torch at carnival season was typically reserved for the upper classes and suggested the "shining, Christian, purifying, and fertile flame" as an antidote to the "black, macabre, demoniac masquerades of the poor" (Ladurie, 240). By placing the torch, a symbolic image of purification and of upper-class status, in the darkness where Fortunato has been buried, Poe makes an ironic statement about Montressor's uncomfortable middle-class identity and the reversals peculiar to carnival season.

I will here return to the treatment of the body in "The Cask of Amontillado," since it is not just Fortunato's physicality that carries an important visual coding, but Montressor's. The irony of carnival reversals lies in the fact that although they attempted to ameliorate or placate the tensions that arose from differences of class and status they often inadvertently reinforced them. This irony is replicated in Poe's treatment of Montressor's use of his body, which is remarkably different from his treatment of Fortunato's. By drawing attention to this difference, Poe dramatizes how frequently disparities of class and status can disrupt utopian and egalitarian dreams of a collective, universal, transnational brotherhood. Most understandings of class relations operate around the role of the body in production. Usually those whose labor requires the frequent use of their body are excluded from elite social status, while those whose work is more avowedly intellectual occupy higher echelons in the class structure. In "The Cask of Amontillado" Poe's narrative frame effectively excludes Montressor's body from interaction within gestural exchange. However, when Montressor fails to interpret Fortunato's gestural conduct, his response is to mock his former friend with a gesture of his own that sarcastically parodies fraternal ritual practices and hints at his murderous intent. Poe writes that Montressor "produce[d] a trowel from beneath the folds of [his] *roquelaire*" (277). This trowel, a common symbol within Masonic art that appeared on nearly all the regalia, amulets, and bodily adornments of the higher degrees, will eventually be the tool that seals Fortunato's doom but is interpreted by him as a joke about "masonry." By making reference to the trowel, Poe not only implies Montressor's failure to understand the required gestural exchange, and therefore be included within the new culture of middle-class cosmopolitanism, but also evokes the origins of contemporary Freemasonry in craft and building. Montressor reveals an actual trowel, a workingman's tool, as opposed to the excessively decorative and purely symbolic trowels used in Masonic rituals.

    By Poe's time many of the associations with artisanal pursuits that had been such a feature of earlier forms of Freemasonry had begun to be excluded from fraternal ritual practices. This exclusion of the artisanal element from ritual owes much to the increasing membership of middle-class men within fraternities. Since middle-class men's bodies seldom labored as a result of the changing economic practices and mechanization, the rituals were altered to accommodate new truths in antebellum society. Ironically, Montressor's body becomes central to the tale at the point at which he labors, which further signifies his failure to be included within the socially mobile new middle classes. Despite his claims to historical familial lineage, what ultimately identifies Montressor is labor and work, which features increasingly at odds with prevailing middle-class conceptions of self. When he is building the wall, the narrator minutely describes the processes required to brick his friend into the masonry. Poe writes of Montressor:

> It was now midnight, and my task was drawing to a close. I had completed the eighth, the ninth, the tenth tier. I had finished a portion of the last and the eleventh: there remained but a single stone to be fitted and plastered in. I struggled with its weight; I placed it partially in its destined position. (278)

The author places great attention upon the labor of Montressor's body. He "struggles" with stones and lifts great weight. When positioned contextually within the codes of nineteenth-century American class relations, the perceived necessity of Montressor's labor must lead us to infer his disenfranchisement. The irony of the tale lies in how rather than assuaging his problems with class in the murder of Fortunato, Montressor reinforces them through the act of building a wall, a process associated with the lower-class status of which he is attempting to rid himself.

Poe's tale explores how the collapse of fraternity and interpretative frameworks between classes effectively leads to social decline. Albeit in a perversely inverted way, Poe ultimately supports the central project of fraternal orders: that the continuation of expressive performances of deference and exchange might serve to bind society and lead to cooperation. Through his support for the power of expressive and performative codes, Poe incorporates a fraternal symbolism into his tale so as to comment upon the forms of collective association increasingly being used by men to respond to the divisive effects of modern market society. "The Cask of Amontillado" is predicated upon these expressivities, which place transparency and the performed dynamics of the body in juxtaposition to the invisible and dangerous hidden exchanges of romantic subjectivism, liberal self-reliance, and capitalist culture.

"The Pit and the Pendulum" (1842)

> Impia torturum longas hic turba furores
> Sanguinis innocui, non satiata, aluit.
> Sospite nunc patria, fracto nunc funeris antro,
> Mors ubi dira fuit vita salusque patent.[10] (Poe, 246)

"The Pit and the Pendulum" displays Poe's concern for the role played by Masonic history and ritual in the transatlantic world. As he would do often in his career, Poe uses Old World conflict as a framework to discuss ideas that would have resonated within American popular print culture. Focused upon the torture of the hapless narrator by "the black-robed judges" (Poe, 246), the tale seems initially to concern itself with a history of oppression associated with the Spanish Inquisition and is therefore at a substantial critical distance from American republican national concerns. However, what has been missed in readings of this story is the importance of the Latin epigraph, which places the tale firmly within the context of republican brotherhood and fraternal ritualism by means of an implied association with the history of the French Revolution. Read in conjunction with wider concerns related to republican politics, brotherhood, and class in America, Poe's tale engages in a complex balancing act by which he pastiches both the claims made by fraternal orders of their capacity to embody enlightened liberty, fraternity, and equality in opposition to the violence of the Old World *and* their opposite, the terrors found in lower-middle-class city mysteries and exposés of secret societies. The epigraph mentions the "Jacobin Club House in Paris,"[11] a censured fraternal order connected to the *ancien régime* of the Masons, whose head was Maximilien Robespierre, leader of the French Revolution. The quatrain, supposedly to be found at the gates of a market where the Jacobin Club was formerly housed, concerns themes of fraternity, nationhood, and redemptive rebirth. Poe locates his tale in a specifically European context, but the reference to the Masons also situates the story within a shared transatlantic space organized around historical Enlightenment political connections between America, Spain, and France.[12]

Through careful allusions to "the condemned cells at Toledo" (248) and "General Lassalle," Poe alludes to the Spanish suppression of international Freemasonry by Grand Inquisitor Francisco Xavier de Mier y Campillo in 1815, an event that played a major role in the emergence of modern Spanish and French nationalisms. Importantly, Poe alludes to the fact that the Jacobin Club House will soon become a market. Factually this is inaccurate, a point that Baudelaire, with his encyclopedic, historical knowledge of Paris, was quick to point out in his critique of Poe. However, for the purposes of his discussion of fraternity, revolution, and Western political culture, it is important. When Poe writes that the "quatrain [was] composed for the gates of a market to be erected upon the site of the Jacobin Club House at Paris" (246), the author connects fraternal orders with the birth of capitalism. What seems like a story of redemption from oppression through capitalism though must be understood in the context of popular antebellum print culture and the exposé, which frequently evoked the dangers of market capitalism to the production of sympathy among artisan republicans. As with the role played by the sherry in "The Cask of Amontillado," Poe implies that the ideal model of Enlightenment, universal republican fraternity that brought about the Revolution, one that provided a counterpoint to free-market liberalism, has been sullied or suppressed, literally buried, by the rise of capitalist competition and nationalistic fervor.

Consequently, the tale's outward attention to the Catholic inquisitions of the early nineteenth century is framed by an epigraph that evokes threats to liberty within the context of an emergent market culture. In the tale, Poe evokes a universal, Protestant brotherhood that is rendered as an alternative both to the divisive social effects of modern capital and the dangers of Catholic ritualism, which lies buried beneath the ground: a memory awaiting an embodied revival. The author connects Catholicism with capitalism by means of the shared trope of covering or masking, which serves to damage the forms of sympathetic exchange based upon the visibility of the individual body, which was often seen as a necessary base for a progressive political body. Just as the market covers over the Jacobin Club House and its history of revolutionary fraternalism, so the Spanish inquisitors are "black-robed" and masked, their bodies hidden from view.

This resistance to covering and masking reflects a popular republican narrative in which Enlightenment, Protestant openness and transparent social conduct were presented as an alternative to the dangerous, hidden, and suspicious activities of mercantile elites and Catholic clerics. As the fraternities of the early nineteenth century increasingly set themselves up as sites in which brothers could be free from the entropic effects of competitive capitalist exchange, the masks that had hidden the faces of the brothers in the eighteenth century began to be removed from the ritual practices of all but the most conservative orders. Carnes writes,

> Without explanation, the use of masks soon disappeared. This suggests that the purpose of the ritual was not to efface personal identity utterly and replace it with a socially induced alternative, but to bring issues of personal identity to the fore, where they could be challenged and examined within differing contexts and environments. (Carnes, 35)

Carnes's account of the changing role of masks in fraternal rituals suggests that the orders were more concerned with the celebration of one's personal identity within a framework of universal brotherhood than its suppression. In the nineteenth century, ritualistic gestures such as unmasking conferred an understanding of the relationship between one's brothers and one's self.

Poe's equation of Catholicism with capitalism is an uneasy one since, as scholars such as Max Weber and Walter Benjamin have shown, "the spirit of capitalism" resides more easily within the discursive economic and social patterns of secular or Protestant societies motivated by the "work ethic." By drawing this parallel though, Poe was drawing on a common trope of nineteenth-century mechanic-class fiction. Popular novels like George Lippard's *The Quaker City* often depicted Catholicism and laissez-faire capitalism as sharing similar roots, intentions, and activities. According to Lippard and others, both Catholic clericalism and an elite form of capitalism that focused power upon bankers and speculators were inimical to the values of self-reliant individualism and honest labor espoused by the urban lower-middle classes. Michael Denning has argued that one need only look to the shared lower-middle-class readership of Catholic exposés and city-mysteries fictions like *The Quaker City* for evidence of how for Protestant American artisans, the dangers of rising capitalist control and Catholic ritualism occupied an equally fraught position in their minds. The fears that drove the emergence of the exposé form in popular print and the rise of nativist parties in the political sphere were galvanized in the 1840s when both Irish Catholic mass immigration to the United States and the burgeoning market revolution were threatening the traditional livelihoods of Protestant tradespeople. In "The Pit and the Pendulum" Poe fuses these two functionally disparate models of society as a means of providing the reader with a monolithic image of tyranny: a hypertrophy of the collected anxieties of the lower-middle classes.

The most expressive moment in the tale is when General Lasalle of the conquering French Army saves the narrator from the brink of death. Lasalle represents the ideal fraternity brother, a man whose position as a general in the French Army is suggestive of physical masculine power, intellect, reason, and, through his connection to the modern military, martial order. Lasalle saves the narrator, who is "fainting, into the abyss" (Poe, 257), from certain death, and in so doing reinstates the sympathetic relationships and male bonds that have been lost to the narrator in the "blackness of darkness" (240) that has supervened. This ending is best read as a resurrection of both the protagonist himself and of a form of fraternity that is able to challenge the violent orders of the Old World. The preponderance of swoons, faints, and collapses in "The Pit and the Pendulum" is testament to Poe's use of an expressive sensational and theatrical melodrama as a response to modern capitalism. The swoon represents both the emasculation of the narrator and his return to brotherhood at the hands of a man who in a moment of gestural exchange (the grip of his hand) becomes his equal. The degraded state of the figure in a liminal condition that Victor Turner sees as an important recurrent feature of "the ritual process" is present in the swooning man. As the narrator faints, Lasalle is said to extend "an outstretched arm [which] caught my own" (257), a gesture that at once implies a reinforcement of the bond of brotherhood and an acceptance of the narrator by a man in a higher degree. In the context of antebellum American society, Poe's melodramatic effects show how brotherhood was seen as a positive response to tyranny.[13] Lasalle effectively pulls the narrator from a solipsistic understanding of self, expressed through his paranoiac first-person narration, into the shared nature of brotherhood. In ritual terms the narrator finds what Turner calls "communitas": a temporary state of collective feeling. The conclusion to the story dramatizes a moment in which the narrator, whose torture has precipitated a long mediation on his loneliness and isolation, is dragged back into collective association. In effect, the narrator is saved from a solipsistic conception of selfhood.

The French link again becomes important here, as Poe overlays fraternity with the kinds of affective excess first found in the French stage melodramas of the late eighteenth century. Later readers of Poe's tale, including William Butler Yeats, have interpreted the savior of the hero by the deus ex machina device of General Lasalle as evidence of the American writer's critical and literary weakness. However, this response is framed by the failure of many critics to read Poe's tales as literary melodramas, and the skepticism of much modern criticism to that significant popular, emotive, and gestural mode in nineteenth-century letters. By evoking melodramatic effects, Poe is engaging in a transatlantic dialogue between his tale and the modern, democratic performance tradition of the French melodrama. This style, as Peter Brooks notes, was designed to serve the needs of a diverse citizenry, "that extended from the lower classes, especially artisans and shopkeepers, through all sectors of the middle classes, and even embraced members of the aristocracy" (xvi). By referring to an important fraternal order at the beginning of the tale and juxtaposing that to the excessive emotional expressivity found in French Revolutionary melodrama, Poe suggests that themes of performance, initiation, and fraternal brotherhood are related to the formation of a functioning republican body politic. By depicting themes of torture in relation to wider concerns for the role of fraternities in the history of republicanism,

Poe shows how trial is implicated in the formation of republican institutions such as the theatre and the fraternal lodge.

This leads to the suggestion that the events of Poe's tale are really a carefully contrived hoax and that the torture enacted upon the anonymous hero is more a form of elaborate theatre, with its own stagecraft, than a genuine imprisonment. Poe uses the historical framework to simulate the kinds of mental and physical trials described in popular exposés of fraternal initiation rituals, as a metaphor both for the difficult passage of Old World culture into modern democracy and the struggles of antebellum American manhood against the competitive pressures of capitalism. Moreover, the physical spaces of "The Pit and the Pendulum" reflect the character of the initiation rituals that proliferated in the early to mid-nineteenth century. With their "grisly scenes . . . gruesome iconography" (Carnes, 56), and oftentimes expensive and elaborate mechanisms, trapdoors, and stage effects, these rituals included the complex excess of simulacra that typified nineteenth-century popular drama. A seemingly incoherent mix of historical reenactment, perverse imagery, and symbols derived from religion and popular culture, fraternity initiations interacted in fascinating ways with aspects of nineteenth-century performance culture. Just as in domestic settings the rise of interest in parlor theatricals drove a market for increasingly spectacular stage effects, the theatrical initiations and hazings that would come to take up more and more time throughout the nineteenth century became correspondingly more spectacular and elaborate.[14] Brothers were known to dress up in strange "historical" or "indigenous" costumes and use magic lanterns to project grotesque images on the walls of their lodges as a means to disorientate and discombobulate initiates. David Reynolds has noted, for example, that the equipment list for the rites of the Brotherhood of the Union, which borrowed heavily from other orders like the Masons (of which the founder George Lippard was a member), included "a large Magic lantern," and "Indian costume," "Collars of Merino, Robes of Cambric," "urns, and torches" (*George Lippard*, 20).

Despite their apparent incoherence to outside observers, a fact that also undoubtedly drove the prurient interest seen in popular exposés, such rituals were also designed to present to the initiate the complex typology of Masonic thought and culture, and were, in turn, designed to assist him in coping imaginatively with new social and political realities of nineteenth-century life. The rituals of fraternal brotherhoods elevated the importance of performing the gestures and behaviors of one's forebears as a means of generating continuity with the past in a time of unprecedented social change and instability:

The powerful symbolism could confer upon the lives of the Masons a spiritual significance of events in the Old Testament. An arch in a railway bridge station might bring to mind the temple of Solomon, an onerous business contract might gain meaning as a form of Babylonian captivity. (Carnes, 48)

Initiation rituals sought to remind the young initiate of his bodily weakness, and therefore his weakness under God, through physical challenges and vicious theatricalized assaults upon his person. In a typical ritual, the initiate would face two dramatized obstacles that presented him with the choice of yielding to the will of God (embodied in the sacred congregation of his brothers) or facing the consequences of certain death—namely, a forced exclusion from the security and affective bonds of that brotherhood. In both instances initiated brothers would save the young man just as the trial reached its horrific climax. In his tale, Poe represents these choices by means of an elaborate stagecraft, which includes features reminiscent of the new melodramatic dramaturgy.

In "The Pit and the Pendulum" each of the visual effects and mechanical contraptions seek to represent a certain spiritual knowledge required for the development of the young hero's character. The first, "a circular pit" with "a sudden plunge into water" (250), represents certain death. Just as in "The Cask of Amontillado," which would follow nearly six years later, this suggests that invisibility, in a time of increased concern for the visual, is tantamount to a form of social obsolescence. The second, a vast sharpened pendulum depicting "the painted figure of Time" (252), is a common symbol in Masonic art. The fact that the narrator notes that "the crescent was designed to cross the region of my heart" (253) suggests that Poe is making reference to the Masonic initiation practice described in works like Henry Dana Ward's *Masonry: Its Pretentions Exposed* of drawing a sword across the chest of the new brother, a symbol of yielding to the will of God as well as opening the heart, an emblem of sympathy, to the congregation. Much of the typography of Masonic initiation is present in Poe's tale, depicted through a staged and contrived physical environment. In addition, the "hideous and repulsive devices . . . the figures of fiends in aspects of menace, with skeletal forms [that] overspread and disfigured the walls" (251), recall the devices that began to adorn fraternal lodges from the early nineteenth century onwards.

What characterizes the physical spaces in the story is their relation to the notion of the perceived need for visibility. From the start of the tale what strikes the narrator is a profound sense of being watched, to the point that he questions whether or not the whole diorama is an elaborately staged piece of theatre with events planned out in advance. As he prepares to escape from the pendulum, the narrator muses: "the result of the slightest struggle, how deadly! Was it likely, moreover, that the minions of the torturer had not foreseen and provided for this possibility? Was it probable that the bandage crossed my bosom in the track of the pendulum?" (254). Upon escaping, the narrator states that "the hellish machine ceased, and I beheld it drawn up," before claiming that "my every motion was undoubtedly watched" (256). The network of interactions between popular print culture, transatlantic history, and the rites of fraternal orders that shape the narrative of "The Pit and the Pendulum" ultimately coalesce around the act of observing the behaviors of an expressing body.

Poe's Masonic tales use a transatlantic framework to present a dark inversion of masculine sympathy. Poe thus participates in a debate that was conducted in popular print about the role of international fraternities and their rituals within antebellum society. In each case the transatlantic setting of the tale allowed Poe to explore the confusion of simulacra that occurred when the Enlightenment and Christian claims to universal brotherhood clashed with emerging national cultures and stratified regimes of class and status. The author's use of Masonic symbols did not therefore diverge from the broad skepticism about all nationalistic and utopian schemes that characterized much of his fiction, whether his satires on transcendentalism and literary coteries ("The Fall of the House of Usher," "Hop Frog") or burlesques of popular pseudoscience ("Mesmeric Revelation," "The Facts in the Case of M. Valdemar"). For Poe America was too scarred by history to serve as a site for utopian schemes, but for his friend and fellow writer George Lippard US national culture would serve as an organizing principle for the rituals of his socialistic labor organization, the Brotherhood of the Union. In his rituals of the order, and in its short-lived, financially disastrous paper, the *White Banner*, Lippard would attempt to build a model of fraternal sympathy that responded to popular fears about the dangerous, "traitorous" work of secret societies, while also drawing on their activities as a collective reserve of memory that could form the basis of a revised, racially pluralistic, politically nonpartisan, and religiously ecumenical version of American patriotism.

Labor, Nationalism, and Sentiment: Lippard's *The White Banner*

The Brotherhood of the Union was George Lippard's most ambitious utopian project and the most fully developed example of his interest in the importance of the body as a site of meaning and medium for cross-cultural and intergenerational communication. Between 1849 and his death in 1854 the popular author and radical reformer began to direct the majority of his time and considerable energy to work for the union. Most critics have seen this as evidence that by 1851 Lippard's best work was behind him. His productions for the Brotherhood have even been interpreted as a sign of his attempt to cope with an emotional breakdown after the death of his wife and son (Reynolds). Such perspectives ultimately confirm a critical problem with the traditional purview of American literary studies and its perennial fetishization of text (and in particular the novel) as a subject of interest. Unlike those authors whose primary work was in the field of the novel (a prose form usually considered to be the work of a single author and directed to a unified purpose), writers like Lippard who dedicated themselves to other, more unstable genres of expression have seldom fared well in the process of building a nineteenth-century American canon. This inevitably leads to a view that the novel, or occasionally short stories considered in a decontextualized way as autonomous pieces of prose, triumphed in the antebellum period as the dominant form of literary expression. In particular, dramatic or magazine and editorial work has fared particularly poorly in an American studies context. Jared Gardner has noted of the early nineteenth-century magazine work of George Lippard's favorite author and fellow Philadelphian Charles Brockden Brown, "part of the problem for our contemporary readings of early magazines lies in the fact that almost all of these early works were financial failures, and therefore the work . . . smacks of dilettantism, a hobby taken up after more 'serious' work as novelists was largely behind them . . ." (*The Rise and Fall of Early American Magazine Culture*, 141). The Brotherhood of the Union, especially the construction of its rituals and mythology, has usually been seen similarly as an odd hobby or evidence of Lippard's extraordinary confidence and ego, certainly not as a major moment in the history of nineteenth-century American literary culture or the history of the left. However, the union was Lippard's attempt to develop a patriotic fraternal organization that amalgamated the powerful emotionality of antebellum temperance and religious revivals with symbols drawn from antebellum popular culture and the ritualized bonds of association cultivated by groups like the Odd Fellows and the Masons. Ultimately, this combined ritual and spiritual power would be directed towards the socialist goal of transforming the United States into an anticapitalist "Palestine of Redeemed Labor" (*TWB*, 142). The Brotherhood of the Union went further than almost all of the preexisting fraternities with which it claimed heritage by actually turning US political history into a source for its sacred rites. Degrees within the Brotherhood were named after "the founding fathers" of the US state. Lippard himself was named "The Supreme Washington" of the order, while other executives went by the titles Supreme Jefferson, Franklin, Wayne, Fulton, or Girard.

A surviving fragment of the secret "Constitution and By-Laws of Progress Circle, No. 9 of the Brotherhood of the Union" from 1850 describes the work of the society as a dramatic attempt to reclaim the "H.F"[15] once embodied in the work of "a Great order of Brotherhood" that was lost "in far distant ages, when man was enslaved by the Oppressor" (v). The anonymous author (presumably Lippard) makes a grand claim that "La Fayette and Washington" (who definitely were Masons) "firmly believed" in the "mysteries of the H.F" and created "our own Revolution" in order to fulfil a global prophecy "written alike in the pyramids of Egypt, and in the monuments of Mexico" (v).

The imaginative world of Lippard's Brotherhood resembled in most key ways the kinds of imagined traditions and surrogations that structured the rites of almost all nineteenth-century fraternities, whether American or foreign. However, in writing the myths of his order and drafting their rituals Lippard also adapted the distinctly nationalistic rhetoric of popular, apocalyptic, religious revival movements to argue that the American Revolution was an exceptional moment in a divinely scripted historical drama and the founding of the Brotherhood of the Union would accelerate a teleological process that would end with the Second Coming of Christ. Lippard writes,

> We have done more. We have shrouded the honorable and venerable degrees of the Order, under names, titles, rites, and ceremonies, altogether peculiar to this Continent, and thoroughly American. We have invested our mysteries with a two-fold glory—one shines in the far-distant past, and reveals the ancient grandeur of the H.F—the other glows upon the deeds, the men of the Revolution, and perpetuates them by impressive rites, forever. We have added to the original vow of the H.F,—that tender and awful invocation of Brotherhood—another vow, which obliges every brother to maintain, at all hazards, the sanctity of American Union. (vi)

In his work for the Brotherhood of the Union Lippard attempted to develop a form of ritual practice that could balance competing visions of American identity rooted in antebellum sectarianism and class conflict, which frequently pitted the suspicious patriotic sensationalism of lower-middle-class print culture against the internationalism and Christian moral revivals of the middle classes. By "surrogating" the deeds of "the men of the Revolution" through the "impressive rites" of the Brotherhood, Lippard sought to ameliorate conflict across two temporalities. Embodying the spirit of the Revolution would have the immediate effect of dispelling the fierce disputes over patriotism that commonly flared up around fraternities in the laboring-class press. Additionally, it would also serve to shore up modern American national identity by rooting it within a framework of tradition, conceived as a previously suppressed or obfuscated history of radical thought and action.

The grandeur of Lippard's vision for the union lay in how it was conceived as a bridge between the imaginative, visionary power that romantic poets and authors had shown was possible within printed text and the embodied theatricality of ritual performances. Like most fraternal orders of the period, Lippard's Brotherhood had its own publication, the *White Banner*, a magazine that was designed to serve simultaneously as the mouthpiece of the group, a prompt to its ritual activities, a record of its philanthropic works, and a vehicle for the publication of George Lippard's fiction.[16] The *White Banner* is a complex material artifact that contains elements reminiscent of many of the dominant forms of reading matter that were available in the nineteenth-century American literary marketplace. Weighing in at 152 pages (over 200 if one includes the appended "Articles," rule book, and "H.F Constitution" of the order included at the back), the *White Banner* was considerably longer than the cheap story papers usually sold to the laboring and lower-middle classes and eschewed the reliance on illustrations that would come to characterize that form, especially after the 1852 founding of *Frank Leslie's Illustrated Newspaper*. Stylistically the journal was more reminiscent of elite publications like the *Knickerbocker*, even more since it carried literary notices of recent works by established European novelists such as Dickens, Thackeray, Sue, and Bulwer-Lytton. Additionally, by virtue of its epistolic structure, heavy reliance on mythology and symbolism, and guides to worship and successful living, it recalled certain "sacred" written works like the Bible, Torah, or Qu'ran.

Unlike a novel collected in book form, which as Shelley Streeby has claimed is "isolate[d] . . . from other printed contexts, offers the narrative as a whole, in its entirety, and thereby furnishes a rigidly bounded, self-enclosed narrative space for readers" ("Opening Up the Story Paper," 185–86), the magazine reflects an alternative logic of the collective that was more suited to the aims of the Brotherhood of the Union. Instead of aiming for unified coherence or a "plot" constructed by a single author, the *White Ban-*

ner operates by means of repeating motifs, mnemonics, and synecdochal phrases across a variety of different forms of short prose narrative. In reacting to the text, readers are required to patch together ideas, contributing to a sense of smaller entities shaping a wider political or social imaginary. In effect, the text operated through cultural memory with phrases and images serving as what Richard Dawkins called a *meme*: a fragment designed to be reappropriated and reused by a variety of individuals to permit the easy transmission of important cultural information. Through the use of short stories and sketches Lippard also attempted to cultivate a kaleidoscopic sense of pluralism that reflected the diverse needs of the different trades and crafts that comprised the Brotherhood. Formally, at the level of the material artifact, the *White Banner* reached beyond the partisanship and regimes of class and status cultivated and perpetuated in much antebellum print culture. The physical object of the text embodied the values that Lippard sought to inculcate in members of the union: a sense of religiosity, collective responsibility for reform, and a certain cosmopolitan interest in world history and culture.

Much like its predecessor, the *Quaker City Weekly*, the magazine was composed of a variety of different genres and styles of short prose, including essays, written accounts of lectures delivered at group meetings, a short story/novella (*Adonai: The Pilgrim of Eternity*), and a collection of brief, visionary sketches described by Lippard as "Legends of the Everyday." Taken collectively, the magazine's underlying logic was that literature could be made to serve genuine political ends. Men and women should not just reflect upon the importance of American history or Christ's sacrifice at the intellectual, internalized level suggested by the Calvinist tradition in theology but embody these things in the practices of their everyday life. Indeed, Lippard's editorial pose in the text is that of a reluctant romantic prophet whose visions of a Christian socialist republic drew upon popular preexisting nationalist tropes and narratives to ground his call to arms. For example, in "Legend IV" (a sketch billed as the "sequel" to his popular bestseller "The Legends of Mexico") Lippard describes "a most singular dream" that he self-deprecatingly claims he is "altogether afraid to make . . . public (107), in which Zachary Taylor's American "Army of Occupation" in Mexico dramatically lay down their rifles, pick up "ploughs and spades and all that kind of thing" (109), and charge forward across the continent felling trees and ploughing fields until "his soldiers had transferred the Desert of Pennsylvania into a very garden, adorned with the homes of one hundred thousand poor men" (109). The tone of this piece, which is constructed like all of his "legends" as a series of short paragraphs or aphorisms, resembles at once a millennial vision of the Second Coming and a piece of militaristic, national propaganda. However, the sketch also reveals Lippard's commitment to the importance of collective work and the actions of the laboring body. As Washington Irving had done before him in *The Sketch-Book of Geoffrey Crayon, Gent.*, Lippard's sketches (or "legends," sometimes "visions" or "dreams") in the *White Banner* operate around a central paradox or ambiguity: the use of a seemingly detached style of intensely visual narration to argue against any form of political or social detachment that reeked of elitist complacency.

For this reason, David Reynolds has suggested that Lippard's primary theological target across his career was rather different from the traditional targets of popular print culture. In his writings and speeches Lippard opposed neither the religious fanaticism of evangelizing groups like the Mormons and the Millerites nor the aesthetic beauty and ritualism of Catholics (who, unlike the Masons, Odd Fellows, and the nativist fraternities, the Brotherhood welcomed warmly), but rather "the coldly logical, grimly deterministic Protestantism of John Calvin . . . [whose] distinction between the elect and the damned found secular enactment in contemporary class conflicts between the rich and poor . . ." (*George Lippard*, 75). As Lippard writes in an essay contained within the *White Banner* entitled "The Three Types of Protestantism":

> Let this idea of a predestined family of Elect, and a predestined family of castaways, be carried into political action, and you have at once, the explanation or the theory of the growth of our Modern Civilization, which treats the largest portion of the Race, as beings born to utter misery, and the Few as the chosen people of God. You have the Modern Oligarchy of the Money power. . . . Reduce Calvin's theology to political economy and you have this result—The poor, the laboring, the unfortunate, are the castaways, damned in this world, beneath the hoof of oppression and destined to damnation in the next, beneath the frown of God . . . (134)

For Lippard and his Brotherhood the Calvinist notion of election that was in the process of being reworked by elite coteries like the New England transcendentalists into a distinctive "American" tradition of thought was inimical to the active principles of Christian socialism he favored. Throughout the *White Banner* Lippard rails against any form of religion that promotes mere speculation, passive indoctrination, or preaches predestination as intellectual justifications of preexisting class and status hierarchies. The greatest force of his anger is reserved for "the coldly intellectual form of Protestantism . . . that *reasons* but cannot *feel*—Protestantism without a heart,—Protestantism that protests not only against the evils of the Catholic Church, but against all that is tender and affectionate in the hearts of homes of men" (133). Such austerity and intellectualism Lippard traced back to Calvin and the New England traditions of thought he had helped to inspire. As a Philadelphian, rather than adopting a form of romanticism with its roots in the egocentric subjectivism of New England Calvinism, Lippard sought to bring to bear his city's Quaker heritage—with its focus on discussion, ecumenical tolerance, and feeling—on social and political questions. In fact, so concerned was he that the Brotherhood of the Union would become doctrinal and dogmatic that in the *White Banner* Lippard even warns against perceiving his own written "visions"—which he deliberately underplays by his description of them as "absurd dreams" (109)—as prompts to such passive reflection or internality. As the author states in "Legend IX," "Religion is not found in elegant churches, or prettily bound books—much less is it heard from the lips of Smooth-speech, the polite preacher, or Sodom-speech the wrath-preacher" (120). Powerful oratory, medievalist Gothic architecture, and the intellectualism of "highbrow" printed biblical texts, the author implies, might actually be hazardous to the spiritual life of working men, ultimately promoting the sectarian divides and class antagonisms that only "Pure Brotherhood" can overcome.

To do justice to Lippard's vision for the *White Banner*, it is important not to adopt a critical position that fetishizes the text and isolates it from the rituals that were "produced alongside or within [its] mediated literacies" (Roach, 11). Such a New Critical or formalist approach to Lippard's work would only reinforce the antiliturgical, Calvinistic logic of inwardness that Lippard abhorred. The *White Banner* preached a message of embodied Christianity in its texts but also existed in parallel with a secret society that inscribed that message onto the very bodies of its members through performed gestures and rites. The Brotherhood of the Union was laboring-class sentimentalism written on the living flesh. An example of how Lippard's sensationalist fiction and his ritual work interacted can be seen through a comparison of a chapter entitled "The Gospel of the Manacle" from the novella (or series of sketches) *Adonai: The Pilgrim of Eternity*, which was included in the *White Banner*, with an extant fragment of the Brotherhood of the Union's ritual book, *The BGCI Of the Circles of the Order* (Philadelphia, 1850), currently housed at the Library Company of Philadelphia. Before doing so, it is useful to briefly outline the plot of *Adonai*.

Adonai: The Pilgrim of Eternity displays Lippard's virtuosic command of the dominant evangelical, melodramatic, sentimental, allegorical, and sensationalist styles of antebellum popular fiction. It details the life (and afterlives) of a young patrician man in the service of Emperor Nero called "LORD LUCIUS." Towards the beginning of the story, Lucius is asked to sit in a beautifully adorned room and "act as sentinel" before an "IRON DOOR," behind which a multiracial group of one hundred Christians are to be "starved . . . until the fairest of them all, the Maiden whom Nero desires for his bed, shall deny her Madness, and solicit the mercy of the Emperor" (15). These events are frequently punctuated by asides from the author during which he muses on how "the great world itself [is] but a luxurious chamber, and a charnel-vault, only separated from each other, by an Iron Door, sometimes called Custom, Law, and often in a lively way, Religion!" (16). After three days (a passage of time heavily redolent of the Easter story of the death and resurrection of Christ), Lucius opens the iron door expecting to find that the Christians have devoured each other in an effort to survive. Instead, the protagonist finds that they have all died quietly in attitudes of prayer save an "Aged Slave" (20) who then proceeds to convert Lucius to Christianity. For his treasonous faith Lucius is then sentenced to death. As he is about to be beheaded the executioner challenges him to testify that Christianity will last for "sixteen centuries" (22), which he does with a considerable excess of oratorical flare. Lucius then sinks "back, like one in a dream" (22) and falls into a trance-like state reminiscent of Irving's Rip Van Winkle. The rest of the story is a series of sketches of important moments in history, during which Lucius (renamed Adonai, a Hebrew name for God) is repeatedly reborn and searches the globe for evidence of "a word, spoken from the lips of the oppressed and poor [that] shall give peace to the world . . . Brotherhood" (93). When the narrative reaches the nineteenth century, Adonai visits Mount Vernon and resurrects George Washington in the body of a young dying laborer who then accompanies him on his travels as the "Arisen Washington." Eventually an illustrious parade of men including Adonai, Washington, Franklin, Hancock, Sherman, Paine, Plato, Socrates, Swedenborg, Sir Thomas More, and Charles Fourier join together in a union that banishes Satan from America.

The story's themes of embodied Christian virtue, ritual rebirth, and brotherhood can be seen as textual analogues of the ritual performances the author wrote for the Brotherhood of the Union. By reenacting "the deeds [of] the men of the Revolution, and perpetuat[ing] them by impressive rites, forever" ("Constitution," vi), Lippard sought to confer dramatic grandeur to the lives of laborers whose increasing participation in mechanistic means of production had alienated them from traditional outlets of artisanal prestige and esteem. At a key moment in *Adonai*, the protagonist and the Arisen Washington visit Boston. There they encounter a man who is conducting a ritual in honor of the founder of the Jesuit brotherhood, Ignatius Loyola. Lippard writes:

> And standing beneath the column of Bunker Hill, Adonai recounted to the Arisen Washington the deeds of the Three Lords.
> "And it was for *this* that you fought the Revolution."
> To this the Arisen Washington made no answer, for his heart was full. After a pause, he said, "Let us go into the City. There is a man there of whom we have heard much. He is said to preach the true Gospel. Let us go."
> They entered the city, and inquired of every one concerning this man, and at length were conducted up a narrow stairway, at the head of which was a door, covered with black cloth. Here their conductors left them.
> They opened the door and entered a spacious room, whose windows were hermetically sealed, so that the light of the sun might not shine, even through a single crevice.
> The walls, the carpet and the ceiling of this room, were alike of scarlet red. In the centre, on an altar covered with scarlet, a red light was burning in a skull. Beside the light stood a goblet filled with human blood. (*TWB*, 72)

Crucially, certain elements from this written narrative are picked up in *The BGCI Of the Circles of the Order*.

A section on the correct protocols for the presentation of the sacred "Circle of the Union" includes the following passage on how to prepare the tabernacle for an initiation:

> 4. The Tabernacle is erected [for the Initiatory Degree] at the point designated in the plan. It is composed of four black curtains, supported by posts, or attached to the ceiling by cords and rings. These curtains form four sides or walls in the shape of a square. Within

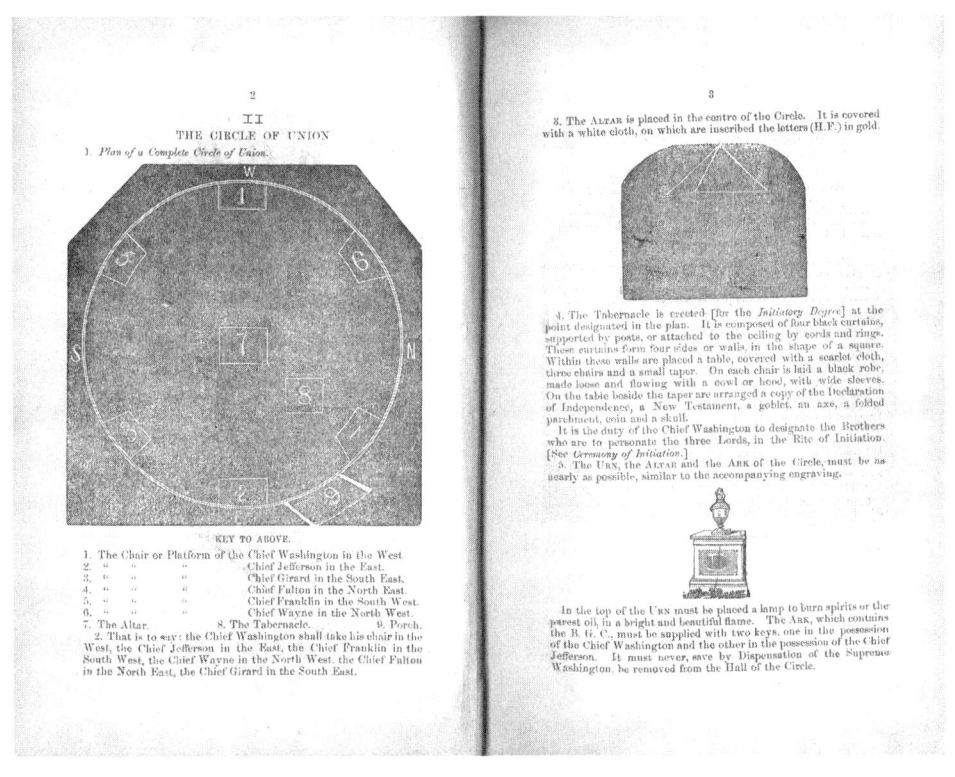

Fig. 1. From *BGCI* "Of the Circles of the Order," George Lippard. Reproduced courtesy of the Library Company of Philadelphia.

these walls are placed a table, covered with a scarlet cloth, three chairs and a small taper. On each chair is laid a black robe, made loose and flowing with a cowl or hood, with wide sleeves. On the table beside the taper are arranged a copy of the Declaration of Independence, a New Testament, a goblet, an axe, a folded parchment, coin and a skull.

It is the duty of the Chief Washington to designate the Brothers who are to personate the three Lords in the Rite of Initiation.

5. The Urn, the Altar and the Ark of the circle must as nearly as possible, similar to the accompanying engraving. (3)

The references to a blacked-out room, "an altar covered with scarlet cloth," a "skull," "a goblet," "an axe," a "coin," and a "folded parchment" made in both of these texts suggest that the performance and George Lippard's novella were designed to function as intertexts. Indeed, the suggestion that there were present three brothers who "personate the three Lords" (3) would have forced the initiate to reflect back upon the adventures of Adonai and the Arisen Washington, who are followed throughout their travels by three figures symbolizing the corrupt elites: "the Lord of the Land, who was busily engaged in buying up land . . . the Lord of Labor, who governs men by transforming Labor into *Coin* and strips of paper . . . the Lord of Law, a portentous personage, known by his dress of *old parchments*, by the *axe* he carries in one hand while the other brandishes the rope of a gibbet [all italics my emphasis]" (72). When undergoing an initiation, a new brother would have been expected to recall the meaning of these symbols in the context in which they appeared in the *White Banner*. The text therefore serves to imbue significant objects for the order with a sense of sacredness. In *Adonai* "The Gospel of the Manacle" is revealed to be a false rite, the purpose of which is to galvanize the Catholic "soldiers of Loyola . . . [who] "drink to the subjugation of the American Continent" (74) into acts of treason against the American Constitution. As with Masonic initiations, such enactments of false rites and rituals often served to dramatize the potential fragility of the order's sentimental brotherhood and its susceptibility to infiltration and subversion. Like the different initiatory stages dramatized in Poe's "The Pit and the Pendulum," the enactment of "The Gospel of the Manacle" from *The Pilgrim of Eternity* would likely have been one act in a longer initiation process. These most likely would have dramatized other significant moments from any of the short fictional narratives and "legends" contained within the *White Banner*. For example, another "vision" of Adonai's is entitled "The Gospel of the Rifle" and includes a moment where copies of the Declaration of Independence and the New Testament (props also listed in the Brotherhood's inventory of objects) are handed around and read aloud. Yet another ("The Holy Sepulcre") is a description in striking italics and block capitals of a moment when "THE SWORD OF WASHINGTON [is] *grasped by the hands of* THE LABORERS OF A WHOLE WORLD" (89). Despite the loss of much of the *BGCI* ritual book, such melodramatic moments strike the reader as cues for another rite of the brotherhood.

Traditional Americanist literary scholarship has had little room for Lippard's style, either relegating it to the second tier of US antebellum writing or dismissing it as too excessive, too incoherent, or too anti-intellectual to justify significant attention. This perspective, however, belies the fact that by combining print and performance Lippard deployed short prose fiction in remarkably inventive and effective ways. Failure to consider the various activities of his career holistically has rendered much scholarship prone to overlook the fact that for nineteenth-century audiences reading fiction was frequently a participatory and active process that involved engaging the body as much as stimulating the mind.

In the following chapter, I turn to the influence of the English Benthamite Edward Bulwer-Lytton, and British imperial state culture more generally, in shaping the character of Herman Melville's short, transatlantic diptychs from the mid-1850s, "The Two Temples," "The Paradise of Bachelors and the Tartarus of Maids," and "Poor Man's Pudding and Rich Man's Crumbs." By investigating the intersections between two national literatures at midcentury, I consider how Melville sought to develop forms of short narrative that borrowed from British writing a sense of the affective and institutional connections between art and the public sphere of politics and government. In much the same way as the ritualized culture of fraternities provided a site in which men could develop and renew emotional bonds and allegiances between individuals, I show how Melville drew from Bulwer-Lytton a sense of the importance of emotionality to the successful operations of the state. This search for a means to renew his political faith, I suggest, occurred during a period in which the American author was undergoing disenchantment with both the sectarianism of antebellum culture and the romantic liberalism of the Young America movement. The question Melville would pose to his readers in his fiction of the 1850s is whether transatlantic art could provide a model for society that averted civil strife, and whether republican models of respectability and virtue could ever be a truly progressive social force.

CHAPTER 3

"The Rule of Men Entirely Great"
Richelieu, Ritual, and Republicanism in Melville's Diptychs

> Beneath the rule of men entirely great
> The pen is mightier than the sword. Behold
> The arch-enchanter's wand—itself a nothing—
> But taking sorcery from the master-hand
> To paralyse the Caesars, and to strike
> The loud earth breathless!—Take away the sword—
> States can be saved without it!
> —Edward Bulwer-Lytton, *Richelieu; or, The Conspiracy* (1839)

Since Charles Olson's important study of Melville and Shakespeare, *Call Me Ishmael* (1947), scholars have been interested in exploring how the American author's frequent references to theatre in his fiction help to shape the aesthetic and political character of his work. "The Two Temples," a story that went unpublished in Melville's own lifetime, is built around a key transatlantic, theatrical reference to the English playwright and politician Edward Bulwer-Lytton's 1839 work *Richelieu; or, The Conspiracy* that the narrator sees performed in London by the famous actor William Macready. While it may seem like a passing reference, Melville's use of *Richelieu* has been a subject of some concern for scholars. For critics such as Barbara Foley, Melville's reference to Macready is a blunt and sarcastic jibe at the English actor, whose decision to stage *Macbeth* at the same time as Edwin Forrest led to a night of intense and violent rioting at the Astor Place Opera House in New

York on 10 May 1849: "Nothing daunted, Macready attempted to rehearse *Richelieu* . . . but the Opera House was closed" (Foley, 101). However, if we adopt more a transatlantic and comparativist approach, in which Melville's nationalist sympathies are not so readily assumed, the reference can be understood as less cynical or ironic. Indeed, a critical tradition of reading Melville as a subversive ironist has often obscured many of the important political and contemporary meanings of his life and work. After all, as Foley notes, Melville had initially signed the petition that called on Macready to play at the Astor Place Opera House on the night of the riot, suggesting a level of respect for the English actor that Foley is unable to adequately account for. While this may have been merely an act of courtesy to Macready (who became acquainted with Melville's brother Gansevoort during his time with the American Legation in London and was friendly with Melville's wife's family, the Shaws) and not, as Dennis Berthold has implied, an overtly political act, at the very least it suggests some level of intimacy or polite association. This does not render it insignificant, however, for as critics interested in Anglo-American culture have suggested, subtle gestures of respect, courtesy, and politeness are loaded with social significance in transatlantic terms. Indeed, respectability and courtesy serve a highly significant thematic function in *Richelieu*. By reading the thematics of *Richelieu* into Melville's story, "The Two Temples" transforms from purely a discussion of attitudes to theatrical and religious culture in nineteenth-century America into an engagement with contemporary debates concerning republican political culture that were, in turn, a response to calls for respectability and order in the wake of the bloody Astor Place Riot. According to many contemporary accounts, the feud between Macready and Forrest that led to so much death began with a simple gesture—Macready's excessive flapping of a handkerchief—that offended Forrest's sensibilities, demonstrating how important what seems from the critical distance of time to be minutiae of etiquette could be in international terms.

In this chapter, I show how "The Two Temples" and Melville's other diptychs of the 1850s are intimately connected with Melville's own political turn away from Young America's celebrations of rugged, radical, and working-class liberal democracy in the wake of the Astor Place Riot, towards a decidedly more republican vision of politics structured around symbolic acts of "respectability," deference, and virtue that recalled British imperialism. Additionally, I wish to demonstrate that the short story form served Melville as an especially effective means of considering the role played by ritual and performance in the political operation of states. As Dennis Berthold has shown, the Astor Place Riot was an important turning point in Melville's development as a writer. The violent protest against Macready in New York, which ended with the deaths of twenty-five young men, precipitated Melville's increasing suspicion of the working-class culture, unfettered individualism, and "ruthless democracy" that had informed works like *Typee* and *Omoo*. Dennis Berthold writes:

> Melville's writing after Astor Place reveals a gradually deepening suspicion of democratic literature and drama. Although New York life normally provided him a rich populist literary resource . . . Melville could not confront the bloody ironies of the Astor Place Riot. (441)

Berthold's assertion that Melville was unable to "confront" the Astor Place Riot does not do justice to the complexities of "The Two Temples," where Melville seeks in part to develop a different form of political philosophy based upon civic ritual that can be used to address the sectarian problems that dogged antebellum liberal democracy. Rather than regarding Astor Place as the limit of Melville's democratic imagination, it is more useful to consider Melville's change of direction after the riot as an example of the author's long meditation upon the form that democracy should take in America. Just as Melville lampoons Pierre Glendinning for his reluctance to engage with the public sphere in *Pierre* (1852), so "The Two Temples" expresses a discontent towards the truly individualist, romantic, and mechanic-class attitudes towards democracy that contributed to the civil disorder of the Astor Place Riot. Taking Melville's short work as well as *Moby-Dick* and *Pierre* as archetypal of this change, what is noticeable about this period of Melville's career is the particular influence of a ritualized concept of political power that is decidedly different from the populism of his earlier work. Indeed, Melville's apparent defense of Macready and the popular affective relations he develops around him in the London theatre in "The Two Temples" suggests a newly found political support for a form of democracy that is characterized by cultural leadership and a desire for increasingly respectable civic space.

While the riot was certainly a crucial moment in both transatlantic and American class relations, none have attempted to understand his work after the Astor Place Riot in relation to the politics of *Richelieu* or, indeed, given the play much attention at all. What Berthold, Foley, and others attribute to Melville's ambivalence towards democracy—or perhaps his increasingly urgent desire for cultural prestige—can also be understood in relation to his interest in the "irrational" forms of affiliation that structure Anglo-American culture. In contrast to Berthold's claims that Melville was unable to "confront the bloody ironies of the Astor Place Riot," I argue that by turning to *Richelieu*, Melville responded directly to Astor Place by engaging with theatrical and ritualized expression as a means of generating a positive form of collective political association. Melville's story seeks to draw potency from the "ancient associations with the Court and the central institutions of government" (Stephens, *The Censorship of English Drama, 1824–1901*, 37) that were central to British theatre but had never developed in America, where the dramatic arts had usually taken a largely amateur or market-oriented form with little in the way of official state patronage. It is in British theatrical traditions that Melville locates the potential for a new culture in America: a sort of "stage-managed" version of democracy that called for the new role of professional, engaged authors.

Consequently, this chapter draws upon Elisa Tamarkin's influential study of the relationship between US democratic culture and British imperialism, *Anglophilia: Deference, Devotion, and Antebellum America*. In this study Tamarkin shows how American reverence for British culture is not always either purely conservative or subversively ironic, but can be deployed to "register . . . a critical sense of disaffection with American society, including its politics of slavery and its anti-intellectualism" (xxv). For Tamarkin, "*Anglophilia* describes a condition of our national experience centred not around a revolutionary rejection, or a project of exclusion, but around a common [British] focal point of our endearments—[a] sort of collective feeling" (xxxiv). In this formulation, Melville's critique of American nationalism in "The Two Temples" reconfigures Britishness into a catalyst for the "collective feeling" by using the short story form to evoke a sense of ritual theatre. To begin to unpack the complex relationship between a British play and an American short story, it is worth considering *Richelieu* within its original English context. In particular, the play's first public performance highlights many of the elements that are crucial to Melville's own understanding of its value and significance as a symbol in "The Two Temples."

On March 7, 1839, William Macready took to the stage at the Covent Garden Theatre as the lead in the first performance of Edward Bulwer-Lytton's new play, *Richelieu; or, The Conspiracy*. The play, written specifically for Macready by Bulwer-Lytton, had garnered such attention in the London press in the preceding weeks that the young Queen Victoria had on March 6 sent the "Lord Chamberlain's Deputy to Macready to ask him for a copy of the play" so that she might read it in advance of the performance. The queen's request to the great tragedian stipulated, "in any state she was to have it" (Shattuck,

Bulwer and Macready, 124). Although the occupation of the Lord Chamberlain usually involved the defense of the monarchy against potential sedition from the theatre, Queen Victoria's enthusiasm for Bulwer-Lytton's drama suggests less censorship than a genuine personal excitement at what was, in effect, the must-see performance of the spring season. Judging by Macready and Bulwer-Lytton's journals, one would not have thought that there was any concern on behalf of its author and leading actor as to the play's subject matter for the new British monarch. The queen's attendance takes center stage in their accounts, not with the fearfulness of conspirators—which they certainly were not—but with the knowledge that with the queen's patronage they may in fact have a real success on their hands. Indeed, Macready seems more concerned with whether or not his own performance is ready for a royal audience—that is, subject to his own excessively high standards. As the lead actor and manager of the Covent Garden Theatre, one would expect a certain trepidation over the politics of *Richelieu*, a play whose characters include a reprobate king, a powerful career politician, a nostalgic appeal to Catholicism, and a cast of generally badly behaved aristocrats. However, at this time Macready and Bulwer-Lytton were at the very height of their fame, and it was the public face of Macready, as well as Bulwer-Lytton's respect as a novelist and the playwright of the successful *The Lady of Lyons* (1838), that helped to push through what may have been otherwise seen as a potentially seditious piece of theatre.

Despite Macready and Bulwer-Lytton's relative ease with the censors, staging the play would not have been without its complexities, especially considering the plot, whose themes concerned no less than examinations of a religiously controlled civil service, revolution and conspiracy, and the relative weakness of kings. Stranger still was to make the rather manipulative Cardinal Richelieu the hero of the piece at a time when tensions in Parliament were high due to the accession of the new queen, the emergence of the Chartists, and the growing influence of the professional middle class in British political life. As Richelieu states in the 115-line soliloquy from the 1839 version, "For private life, scripture the guide—for public, Machiavel . . . day or night . . . ambition has no rest" (73). In its dialogue between monastic devotion and Machiavellian strategy, *Richelieu*'s classical republican vision has next to no place for the much-vaunted judicial function of constitutional monarchy. In fact, Richelieu remains one of the most bureaucratic heroes in literature, appearing more like a virtuous civil servant than the ubiquitous melodramatic gallant of the early Victorian stage. This role is filled by the love interest of Richelieu's ward Julie, De Mauprat. Even despite the significance of placing a bureaucrat at the center of the drama, the play still conforms to the romantic norms of Victorian melodrama, whereby the future security of France is eventually secured by the young lovers' marriage. Most of the action happens offstage and is reported to Richelieu through his spy network, making the play an essentially bloodless affair punctuated by monologues attacking the nobility for their vices.

As John Russell Stephens notes in *The Censorship of English Drama, 1824–1901*, the political landscape of the English theatre had, since Sir Robert Walpole's Licensing Bill of 1737, been subject to considerable state censorship and control. In part this was because systems of royal patronage helped to perpetuate the theatre's "ancient associations with the Court and the central institutions of government" (37). This was not so in America, where such a personal and thematic relation to the politics of state was uncommon and where censorship was performed more by audience choice than official regulators. In no figure of early Victorian drama is this more manifestly apparent than Bulwer-Lytton, who as a playwright, novelist, committed disciple of Jeremy Bentham, and Whig member of Parliament was intricately enmeshed in the complex fabric of nineteenth-century political and artistic culture. Indeed, the popularity of Bulwer-Lytton's work and the fact that it was staged in the legitimate patent theatres of Covent Garden and Drury Lane made him even more likely to draw the gaze of the censors before the Theatre Regulation Act of 1843. This act, shepherded through Parliament by Bulwer-Lytton himself and known as "Bulwer's Bill," limited the power of the Lord Chamberlain to censor material for the stage in almost all cases except those related to the preservation of order and public decency. Prior to 1843 the Lord Chamberlain regulated all plays and only the patent theatres (Drury Lane and Covent Garden) were allowed to perform spoken-word drama. Following 1843, responsibility for censorship was transferred to local magistrates and away from the crown, sanctioning a boom in new theatrical entertainments and reducing the stranglehold of the patent theatres over spoken-word performance. Consequently, in works like *Richelieu* Bulwer-Lytton was exploring not only the potential of middle-class respectability to undermine the power of aristocratic privilege in fiction but, crucially, at the level of the law.

Bulwer-Lytton cut extremely close to the bone with his three historical dramas of the 1830s, *Richelieu*, *The Lady of Lyons*, and *The Duchess de la Vallière*, in depicting "the gradual shift of power from despotism to republican democracy" (Stephens, 45). In each of these plays the monarchy is comparatively weak next to the clever courtier, through whose respectability and professionalism the Victorian audience was offered a prehistory of government that foresaw the bureaucratic developments of the modern, liberal state. Bulwer-Lytton's French trilogy was especially piquant in the context of the young and inexperienced Victoria's recent, contested succession to the throne, and his own support for the antiaristocratic Reform Act of 1832. But no official censorship occurred, and while the Tory press had attacked Bulwer-Lytton for the politics of his prior theatrical works, no such attack was levelled against *Richelieu*.

The queen was detained on the night of March 7 and was unable to see the opening night of the play, appearing finally on March 14. However, as William Jerdan, the influential editor of the *Literary Gazette* described it, "The house overflowed in every part . . . and even what are called the slips, were fully tenanted by a respectable audience." Macready's performance caused the crowd to rise "*en masse* and cheer . . . him for some moments" (126). As Melville notes in "The Two Temples," the response of the crowd to Macready, while deafeningly loud and "unmistakably sincere," is peaceful, and the "gladdened crowd, are harmoniously attended to the street" (Melville, 312). Uplifting, enlightening, and composed, the play presents to the author's imagination the very ideal of a well-governed republic. As a ritual it stands in positive relationship to both the solemn, exclusive, and dictatorial Gothic church of the diptych's first section and the chaotic mob violence of the Astor Place Riot. After its success in London it was not long before theatres across the country, and abroad, had begun staging productions of the play. The first American version would appear at Wallack's Old National Theatre in New York on September 4 of the same year with William Macready's future transatlantic rival Edwin Forrest in the title role. Although never staged nowadays, Bulwer-Lytton's play became a staple of British and American theatres for the next sixty years.

It is useful to return to the reception of *Richelieu* in London, since it is here that Melville's narrator sees the play in order to establish its significance. As Jim Davis and Victor Emeljanow state in *Reflecting the Audience*, attempts to show the theatre to be respectable

> reflect the results of a concerted effort on the part of both journalists and theatre managers in this period to paint a picture of theatre's eventual triumph over adversity—religious opposition, urban degradation, "mob rule and working-class domination"—and of the acceptance by the general public of its right to respectability and cultural leadership. (168)

In Victorian Britain, many managers, playwrights, and theatre critics, through their descriptions of theatre culture and the thematic engagements of the plays themselves, sought to generate an image of decency in the theatre as a means of counteracting pervasive, residual prejudices surrounding drama and theatrical culture. Jerdan's reference to a "respectable audience" is telling, as Davis and Emeljanow have shown that "respectable" was often used as a term by journalists that referred more to conduct than to the social composition of theatre audiences, which even in the legitimate theatres of Covent Garden and Drury Lane frequently comprised almost all of London's classes and castes. When speaking of "respectability," journalists most often meant "respectful." This differed greatly from American drama, where theatres remained more highly stratified along class lines until the twentieth century. In London, the working-class presence in the theatre was almost always underplayed through carefully structured journalistic language and subjected to the values that defined middle-class theatregoers. The effect of this was to draw greater numbers of middle-class patrons who would ordinarily have steered clear of the theatre on the grounds of attitudes towards its morality and the presence of the working class in the cheap seats.

The construction of a discernible middle-class sensibility in Britain was therefore as much an artistic and journalistic exercise as something purely economic. While the genuinely increasing presence of the middle class was certainly, and discernibly, affecting the composition of England's public, it was the creation of a middle-class art in the print and theatrical culture of the time that was having the greatest impact in institutionalizing themes of respectability, duty, and virtue. As Davis and Emeljanow state:

> [R]eports about theatregoing tend to focus on the performances, the costuming both on and off the stage, the comfort or discomfort of the theatrical ambience, and the presence of notable patrons and the general aura of respectability. (169)

Spoken-word dramas such as *Richelieu* were designed to appeal to middle-class values as a means of implementing attitudes of "respectability" in the theatre. However, they did so with knowledge that their audiences were drawn from many social strata. Simultaneously antimonarchical and antimob, *Richelieu* expresses this kind of cross-class appeal in a way only theatre really can, through the elevation of grand gesture and oration that could be seen and understood even by those in seats farthest from the stage.

The success of Bulwer-Lytton and Macready's partnership is interesting for a number of reasons in regard to its influence on American literature. *Richelieu*, as a play and phenomenon in early nineteenth-century transatlantic culture, was notable for the way that it emphasized the role of the public, professional statesman as the harbinger of legality and social order over and above traditions of inherited aristocracy or "natural nobility" that were essentially extensions of a familial narrative framework. This was quite different from earlier transatlantic successes such as John Home's *Douglas* or Sheridan Knowles *Virginius*.[1] When transposed onto the American scene, the ornate republicanism of the play, along with its melodramatic conspiracy plot and its calls for respectability and order, engaged with issues that were rapidly becoming of paramount importance in a country that was fragmenting into sectarian disorder, even as it was building new national institutions. In Bruce McConachie's seminal work on the American melodrama, *Melodramatic Formations*, the author accounts for the waning influence of agrarian and Jacksonian conceptions of democracy in the theatre by suggesting that in this period melodramas began to turn their attention increasingly to urban-industrial themes. McConachie writes, "For the most part, the tradition of agrarianism . . . constituted Jacksonian theatre as a residual culture" (xviii).

To modern readers, particularly trained to regard romantic thought as a liberation from the stultifying pressures of modern life and state bureaucracy, the play seems fiercely conservative, but accurately historicized it verges at times on a strangely progressive piece of drama. This is because what is conservative to modern liberal readers informed by Foucault's famous critique of Bentham's panopticon is often, though not exclusively, a system of power that emerged from classical liberalism, such as Bentham and Bulwer-Lytton's model of state control as a curb against tyrannical dictatorship. As an idea this would have historically been associated with the pre-Marxist left, while modern readers would see greater correlations with later fascistic or totalitarian models. This is evidenced in part by John Stuart Mill's essay on Bentham, in which he sets his utilitarian mentor in opposition to the romantic mind of Coleridge, concluding that the former is the more progressive of the two. Mill suggests that Bentham was able to articulate, where transcendental philosophy was unable, that:

> the changes that have been made, and the greater changes which will be made, in our institutions, are not the work of philosophers, but of

the interests and instincts of large portions of society recently grown into strength . . . Bentham gave voice . . . to those who found our institutions unsuited to them. (134)

For Bentham, the rise of the middle class constituted the rise of a potentially progressive force in politics and culture: a group whose aesthetic interests were finding their voice in the complex negotiations of Victorian popular culture.

For Americans seeing *Richelieu*, the play's oratorical and gestural style came close to the performative qualities that had characterized earlier heroic melodramas of the Jacksonian theatre, but with the added value of a republican appeal to the middle-class values more frequently associated with Victorianism than with the nineteenth-century United States. In this way *Richelieu* reflected the dominant expressive mode of oratorical and performance culture that had come to define antebellum lecturing, preaching, and acting. The play's success in America is very telling as it implies a certain level of receptiveness to this formulation of the republican ideal was present in the national populace, which was tied to the waning influence of Jacksonian agrarianism in the American theatre around the time that *Richelieu* was staged in New York.

While many critics have sought to demonstrate Melville's radical democratic strain (most famously C. L. R. James) by showing the influence of Bulwer-Lytton's theatrics on Melville's work, it is possible to see how the American author may be understood as a significantly more republican writer than previously thought. Whereas James elevates the crew of the Pequod in *Mariners, Renegades, and Castaways: The Story of Herman Melville and the World We Live In* as a potential site for communitarian power, historicizing Melville and reading his work through republican conventions suggests that it may be more useful to understand the unity of the crew in terms of fraternal power in opposition to aristocratic tyranny. Melville defends sympathetic exchange and attacks tyrannical personalities but ultimately shows openness to the idea of elites as educators of the people in the ways of democracy.

Indeed, Melville's "The Two Temples" is structured around ideal images of fraternity and knightly virtue that are challenged by the negative aspects of capitalist exchange. "Temple Second" begins by describing how a "lady rich as Cleopatra" enlists the narrator as a "knightly companion" from the "fraternal, loving town of Philadelphia" (Melville, 306) to chaperone her on her European tour, buys his transatlantic passage, and then leaves him penniless in London because of an illness that is never fully defined. It is in this state of disgrace that he discovers the higher life of the theatre and the politics of Bulwer-Lytton and Macready's republican drama.

In the story, the narrator passes through the streets of London on a Saturday night. He expresses discomfort with the street life and its "indescribable crowds which every seventh night pour and roar through each main artery and block the bye-veins of great London, the Leviathan . . . the one unceasing tide" (307). Essentially it is this market and its culture (most likely Covent Garden by the description of its character and geography) that is regarded by the narrator as dangerous and threatening. Composed in the aftermath of Astor Place, this fear of the majority in an area known for its street theatre and shops is particularly acute. The masses of London are depersonalized and equated with the corruptions of unchecked cupidity: "Better perish amid myriad sharks in mid Atlantic, than die a penniless stranger in Babylonian London" (307). The narrator continues by describing "Saturday night . . . and the markets and shops" as a "Norway Maelstrom" (307). Like the symbolic maelstrom, the forces of London market are both centripetal and centrifugal, as likely to drive people apart from one another as they are to force them into an undesired association.

The narrator's difficulty with the masses is only assuaged by the presence of what Barbara Foley identifies as the Royal Lyceum Theatre just off the Strand: a "wide and far less noisy street, a short and shopless one" (307). It is this location, a "blessed oasis of tranquillity" (308), in the mass of noise and people that the narrator finds solace. The theatre, with its "two lofty brilliant lights" (Melville, 307) becomes a visual metaphor for the illuminating and educating power of the public sphere to overcome the corruptions and dangers of the marketplace. Situated almost precisely between the center of London's cultural district around Covent Garden and the formal state institutions of the Inns of Court ("The Paradise of Bachelors" that Melville would explore in another of his diptychs) and the Royal Courts of Justice, the Lyceum suggests an ideal balance between the formal and the informal, between "rational" state power and "irrational" human feeling. It is in the illuminating presence of this institution that the narrator encounters charity from both the "working-man" (309) who offers him the ticket and an English child in the gallery who offers him a drink of ale.

The exchange with the young working-class boy is intriguing given the nationalistic and class hostilities between America and Britain that had come to a head at Astor Place in the years preceding the story's composition.

"Thank you", said I, "I won't take any coffee, I guess."
"Coffee?—I guess?—Aint you a Yankee?"
"Aye, boy; true blue."
"Well dad's gone to Yankee-land, a seekin' of his fortin'; so take a penny mug of ale, do Yankee, for poor dad's sake."
Out from the tilted coffee-pot-looking can, came a coffee-colored stream, and a small mug of humming ale was in my hand. (311)

The charity of the English boy is presented as a critique of belligerent nationalism, class antagonism, and the corrupting influence of the market. The narrator makes specific reference to the fact that it is an "*unpurchased* penny-worth of ale" (311) that the boy offers the "Yankee" narrator, performing a sympathetic and ritualized exchange (that of drinking together) as an antidote to the divisive, centripetal forces of the market. As anthropologist Catherine Bell writes, shared participation in the act of consumption "is a common ritual means for defining and reaffirming the full extent of the human and cosmic community" (*Ritual: Perspectives and Dimensions*, 123). Through this ritual act of gift giving, the "cosmic community" of Anglo-American relations is reestablished, supplanting any possible nationalist antagonism through recourse to the quasi-Christian symbol of the boy's absent father, to whom they toast.

In cultural anthropology, rituals are often understood as operating around a central absence, which serves as an emotional glue between individuals or groups. Victor Turner and Joseph Roach have both shown how in societies divided by revolution this absence serves a political function, since there usually exists within both cultures either a sense of disruption or a desire for reconciliation that stems from access to shared experiences or history. This reconciliation may not be directly juropolitical in nature—that is, reparative at the level of state institutions—but may instead take on a sublimated form through ritual acts between individuals or groups. As Turner notes of these breaches, "there may be an attempt to transcend an order based on rational principles [such as the Enlightenment logic that informed the American Revolution] by appealing to that order which rests on a tradition of co-existence among predecessors of the current community" (91). In this instance, the physical absence of a predecessor (the boy's father) because of migration creates a shared transatlantic history between the American man (who is himself a migrant of sorts) and the English child. In this dynamic space of transatlantic cultural interaction their bond fills the vacuum left by the missing individual or the political entity of British North America.

The child's act of generosity does not follow the "rational principles" of the market, in which the mug of ale has a definable exchange value. Instead, in Turner's terms, it serves the emotional function of a ritual object by transcending that "rationality." In fact, the author's language is marked by frequent allusions to the religious culture of the Old World and a strong sense of the sacred. He is the "knightly companion" (Melville, 306) of the rich lady, the Lyceum Strand is a "transatlantic temple" (311), the beer he receives is made of "blessed hops," and the act of giving is sanctified: "God bless the glorious boy!" (311). The fraternity established between the narrator and the boy is based on a ritualized exchange, conducted within the sacralized space of the theatre. It transcends enforced national differences through a theatricalized act of deference, which makes recourse to a shared heritage that preexists the nationalist divisions of the modern era.

Although the act of receiving charity from an English child might be interpreted as a demeaning or infantilizing threat to the "rugged individualism" of the American narrator, it is best understood as compatible with Melville's broader project in the story of imagining a transatlantic community based upon the radical potential of mutual respect and admiration. In the context of Astor Place and the increasingly hostile transatlantic relations that the riot pointed to, this project was paramount. As Tamarkin has noted, the antebellum vision of a sanctified, transatlantic community rested upon a distinction between "deference" and "power" that was rejected by liberal thinkers but central to republican political culture. While the liberal tradition in this period largely conceived of acts of deference as a symptom of unequal power relations, republican thought did not always see ritual as incompatible with democracy. Instead, as Tamarkin remarks, "while power demands submission . . . deference [is] a desire to submit that is compatible with democratic practice—an effect that says, I am free enough to admit your worth and to take my pleasure in it" (xxix). Consequently, in republican thought the elective nature of certain acts of deference make them affirmations, rather than negations, of the freedom of the two subjects. Melville's generous child seems not to recognize the significance of his act, smiling "merrily" and "offering his coffee-pot in all directions" (311). As such, the effect of his charity is heightened, since to be effective ritual must be unselfconscious and, in the terms of Adam Smith's *Theory of Moral Sentiments*, "disinterested." To be otherwise would transform the act into a mechanical process of means and ends, in which charity expects a return in kind.

Earlier, the narrator had mused on the nature of charity when offered free entrance to the theatre, asking whether receiving gifts was inimical to the construction of inviolate selfhood. He apostrophizes, "Why these unvanquishable scruples? All your life, nought but charity sustains you, and all others in the world. Maternal charity nursed you as a babe; paternal charity fed you as a child; friendly charity got you your profession . . ." (Melville, 309). The meaning of the story rests upon the narrator's comprehension that voluntary acts of deference or offering may serve to affirm a sense of community that is not necessarily contradictory to individual self-determination. The things that have shaped the narrator's character, his mother's nursing or his father's will to provide, are acts that have no especially "rational" meaning. Melville would continue this theme in several shorter works from this period, especially "Poor Man's Pudding and Rich Man's Crumbs," "The Paradise of Bachelors and the Tartarus of Maids" and "Bartleby, the Scrivener." "Bartleby" in particular explores how polite deference—the famous "I would *prefer* not to" of the "pallidly neat, pitiably respectable" clerk—might be misinterpreted as a sign of servility, with disastrous effects. The distinction is crucial, as while the former recognizes social ritual as a spur to equality, the latter recognizes them merely as the action of power.

This transatlantic, republican understanding of ritual and deference, in which emotionality and civil society are mutually interdependent and reinforcing, accounts for the strains of medievalism that run through both Melville's tale and Bulwer-Lytton's play, which initially strike the reader as peculiarly conservative or outmoded. To read it as such is to buy into a critical tradition of Melville studies in which the author is always assumed to be ironic or mocking in his approach to the Old World. Furthermore, it is to miss the complex meanings attached to the medieval in mid-nineteenth-century Anglo-American culture. As Clare Sponsler has persuasively argued, such an inattention to the European-American cult of the medieval reflects "the inclination on the part of many historians to emphasize processes of nation-building, while downplaying the pull of allegiance to a European homeland; the result has been to deflect interest from cultural forms [like ritual] that resist nationalism and assimilation" (*Ritual Imports*, 5). As Sponsler shows, transatlanticist readings of mid-nineteenth-century American culture benefit significantly from serious critical engagement with the complex and surprising meanings attached to the Old World in both Britain and America. In particular, Victorian culture often used the medieval to imagine a version of state power that relied more upon filial devotion than the more mechanical apparatus that Foucault describes as the analogue of modern liberalism. In *Richelieu* the eponymous hero is *both* a symbol of religious power in the Catholic Old World (a power based on submission and devotion) *and* a model of an emerging democratic culture (one based on modern bourgeois individualism and self-determination). Like Bulwer-Lytton himself, whose own life bridged the divide between art and politics, Richelieu is shown as the embodiment of the reconciliation between these two, apparently irreconcilable, forces and highlights the paradoxical nature at the heart of republican thought.

At several key moments in the play, Richelieu professes the simultaneity of his positions as bureaucrat, knight, priest, and sorcerer, while acknowledging that he adopted all of these roles because of his filial devotion to the state. In his self-reflexive monologues, Richelieu emphasizes the significance of desire, as opposed to mere coercion or force, in his decision to serve France. He announces that he possesses "a knightly heart/ that beats beneath these priestly robes" and that "beneath the rule of men entirely great/ The pen is mightier than the sword/ Behold the arch-enchanter's wand . . . / taking sorcery from the master-hand/ To paralyse the Caesars" (31). Richelieu deliberately recalls Ciceronian republicanism as he transfers influence away from the French monarch, a "Caesar" who in the unchecked exertion of his hereditary will is the literal embodiment of the forceful application of feudal state power. Instead, Richelieu places influence in the hands of "men entirely great," whose own power rests upon both an embryonic form of modern bureaucracy and the voluntary devotion suggested by their adoption of monastic or chivalric vows. Oddly though, Richelieu's Catholicism is imagined without the pope. Instead, Bulwer-Lytton's Richelieu is devoted to the state, which is also his lover: "My mistress France—my wedded wife—sweet France/ Who shall proclaim divorce from thee and me" (27). Consequently, Bulwer-Lytton's rendering of the seventeenth-century French nation more closely resembles the ideal political unity between church and state of the nineteenth-century Anglican imagination than the conflicted loyalties between monarchy and papacy peculiar to early modern Catholicism. In the play, secular love trumps ecclesiastical hierarchy. Consequently, in Melville's story he takes on the significant role of connecting the Old World and the New in a symbiotic relationship, structured around elective affinities rather than forced, hierarchical relations of power.

Since the figure of Richelieu operates to generate such a sense of communal purpose and collective affect, my reading in part challenges many of the critiques of Melville's story that have seen his diptych as a sarcastic attack on religion in general. Rather, if Melville's later work (particularly the poetry) is anything to go by, religion and ritual were highly significant to his aesthetics and thought after 1850. By showing the relationship between the story and the republican logic of *Richelieu* it is possible to see that Melville directs less criticism against religion *per se* than against the increasingly hierarchical nature of its rituals in America. Following Tamarkin, the ritual acts of worship in the first half are shown to be acts of "power" that provide a counterpoint to the acts of "deference" in the second section. Consequently, it is useful to turn to Melville's treatment of "Temple First," a thinly veiled sketch of New York's Grace Church.

In the first section, the narrator states that despite the "theatric wonder of the populous spectacle of this sumptuous sanctuary" (Melville, 303), he is unable to hear the minister. The silence highlights the absence of dialogical interaction between the speaker and his audience, for while they offer him "all-approving attention" they do so as a "mass of low-inclined foreheads . . . [in] hushed silence, [and] intense motionlessness . . . as if the congregation were one of buried, not of living men" (303). The congregation appear to have no will of their own and from the narrator's peculiar viewpoint of the bell tower their devotion to the pastor seems an involuntary act. In effect, Grace Church exists not to inspire a democratic involvement or affective connection, so much as reinscribe the tyrannical power of a prior aristocratic culture. For the hapless narrator, the minister is not so much an ideal republican orator, with the power to enliven and inspire social exchange across classes, as a "necromancer" who preaches to the dead within the spectacular spaces of antebellum religious revivalism.

Melville's criticism of religion rests upon the way that the Gothic architectural style seeks only to inspire hierarchical relations in opposition to sympathy and exchange. The irony of this is that the Gothic style of Grace Church was conceived to inspire emotional worship and continue a legacy from the 1830s that had endeavored to erode the distinction between the theatre and the church. Instead, the earlier period of religious revivalism in the 1830s and 1840s, which had sought to borrow from the theatre as means to inspire democratic relations between the congregation and the preacher, was damaged by the ostentatious and expensive architecture, whose grandeur only served to inspire an image of an all-powerful and unknowable God. Although, as Beryl Rowland has shown, it was the similarity to Grace Church that forced *Putnam's* to refuse the sketch for publication, the comparison with the theatre in the second section would have forced contemporary readers to draw parallels with New York's Broadway Tabernacle Church, a space that had been famously converted from a theatre by the abolitionist Lewis Tappan. However, the conversion was widely considered a failure. As Jeanne Halgren Kilde has shown in *When the Church Became Theatre*, concerning the Broadway Tabernacle Church, "This building was designed for liturgical services and hierarchical social relationships, not the affective worship and egalitarianism that had characterized the congregation's revivalist foundations" (56). As in Melville's fictional church, the problem was money and the ostentation that followed it. This resulted in the abandonment of the space by the poorer and more devoted churchgoers and an eventual shift in denomination from Tappan's Calvinistic Presbyterianism to an elite form of Congregationalism.

For the narrator, the dizzying height of the church supports the image of an all-powerful God who inspires silent devotion. Indeed, the author's ironic quip "Here . . . is a fitter place for sincere devotions, where, though I see, I remain unseen . . . I like it, and admire it too, because it is so very high. Height, somehow, hath devotion in it . . . Heaven is high" (Melville, 302) implies an altered relationship to God that is generated by the awesome height of the church. The phrase "though I see, I remain unseen" (302) conflates the untouchable power of aristocratic privilege with a transcendental ideal of disembodied Emersonian consciousness: the "transparent eyeball." Instead of expressing himself in the affective and embodied relations of his worshippers, God becomes (in the physical spaces of the Protestant Gothic church) unable to distinguish individuals within a crowd of his worshippers. Through the image of the stained glass as "a Cuban sun," Melville implies that the God of the earlier religious revival has become an indifferent sun god who bathes his congregation as if they were merely "beds of spangled pebbles" (303). The architecture of the church separates God from the people and their feelings, making the position of the narrator an ironic inversion of his desire to engage in the communal rituals of worship. Forced to look down upon the congregation from the bell tower, the narrator is higher than the people, so is, as he sarcastically remarks, closer to God. Thematically and aesthetically, therefore, Melville's America is shown as a site of increasing division, while Britain is a fantasy in which classes and cultures are united by ritualized and theatrical bonds of affection.

The comedy of his attempt to leave the church, where his endeavor to alert the patrons to his presence results in criminal charges being filed against him, is suggestive of the fact that the narrator has been utterly separated from the public spaces of emotional worship. In fact, in the context of the narrative, the American church literally makes him fear the public, rather than desire to commune with them. As the narrator states, "no one can adequately respond to my summons, except the beadle-faced man; and if he see me, he will recognise me, and perhaps roundly rate me—poor humble worshiper—before the entire public" (304). By attacking the Gothic church, Melville attacks money and its corruptions, because it is money that divides the congregation and interrupts the emotion of worship. This even goes as far as to influence the process of law, which, in its ideal form, should operate as an unbiased force. Melville writes that the narrator:

> Represented as a lawless violator, and a remorseless disturber of the Sunday peace . . . was conducted to the Halls of Justice. Next morning, my rather gentlemanly appearance procured me a private hearing from the judge. But the beadle-faced man must have made a Sunday night call on him. Spite of my coolest explanations, the circumstances of the case were deemed so exceedingly suspicious, that only after paying a round fine . . . was I permitted to go. (306)

Not only is the "beadle-faced man" allowed to influence the judge in the first instance, the "gentlemanly appearance" of the narrator allows for an ironic second manipulation of the law. However, in America no amount of gentlemanly decorum can offer the narrator a fair hearing. When first attempting to gain access to the church at the beginning of the story, the narrator remarks, "had I . . . tickled the fat-paunched, beadle-faced man's palm with a bank note, then . . . I would have had a fine seat in this marble-buttressed, stained-glassed, spic-and-span new temple" (300). There is an irony in the fact that a small, initial bribe would have helped him avoid a legally mandated fine. When viewed comparatively, Melville appears to be reflecting negatively upon the liberal tradition in antebellum America, in which deference and politeness are not valued above the more morally compromised world of capitalist exchange. Melville's America is a place of irony and schism, in which there is a radical separation between the real and ideal that is only compensated for by the sincerity that the narrator finds in British imperial culture. In Melville's treatment of the American Gothic church the scale has tipped dramatically. Power is shown to rest increasingly in the hands not of the just but of the wealthy and influential. The ritual spaces of American worship are shown to be corrupt and hierarchical, aping the unequal powers of an older aristo-theocracy.

In Melville's story the incapacity of the narrator to interpret fully the ritualized gestures of the minister suggests that the power of embodied, theatrical affect has been interrupted. Melville writes:

> At length the lessons being read, the chants chanted, the white-robed priest, a noble-looking man, with a form like the incomparable Tal-

ma's, gave out from the reading-desk the hymn before the sermon, and then through a side door vanished from the scene. In good time I saw the same Talma-like and noble-looking man re-appear through the same side door, his white apparel wholly changed for black. (303)

For the narrator, the minister's gestures have become a perverse and confused version of the pantomime, in which his seemingly phantasmagoric and spectacular transformation from white to black seems like a hollow act whose color shifts imply a form of minstrelsy. Furthermore, the equation of the minister in the mind of the narrator with Talma is telling, as the French actor in some ways represents the very inverse of the democratic and emotional potential of the drama. Talma's art was used as propaganda by Napoleon and as such is intimately connected with tyranny and dictatorship in France as the ideals of the First Republic gave way to the Napoleonic Empire.

Two figures from different stages of French history, Talma and Richelieu, stand on either side of Melville's transatlantic virtualization of London and New York. One shows America's potential for the reestablishment of tyranny and dictatorship (understood as a consequence of the divisive effects of money); the other shows the way of sympathy and duty. In "The Two Temples" Melville configures transatlantic exchange as an actual, symbolic theatre crossing the Atlantic, with European history providing the proscenium arch or framing device. Crucially though, like the absent father that provides a site through which the child and the narrator are brought into ritualized communion, Melville's short diptych form operates around the symbolic function of an elision or absence. The joined sketches are not formally united but ask of the reader that they find a common point of connection, much in the style of ritual, which, as I have shown, often asked communities to generate commonalities around an invisible presence, surrogate, or shared myth. Melville's narrative project in "The Two Temples" is to generate a third stage in the symbolic interaction between the New York church and the London theatre, a larger, symbolic memory of transatlantic bodies in motion, which is formally evoked in the short story by means of that body's deliberate elision. Through the narrator's movement and action (happening largely, as it were, offstage), Britain and America are brought into transatlantic symbiosis with the author functioning as the stage manager or high priest.

The form of Melville's short story though also alludes to the medieval, religious art form of the diptych panel painting, or "travelling icon," that would serve as an *aide-mémoire* to the virtues of the saints while on pilgrimage to the Holy Land (something that Melville would do himself in 1857). These hinged artworks would be used to set up temporary altars in an age before the widespread availability of bibles enabled more private and textual acts of worship. Kneeling before a "travelling icon," the worshipper would be forced to consider their own bodily presence in direct relation to the religious history of two saints, triangulating their spiritual selves. By alluding to the sacred structure of the diptych, Melville collapses the distinction between the New World author and Old World ritual, instilling reading with the performative and devotional aura that Macready's depiction of Richelieu emphasized in Edward Bulwer-Lytton's play, while also asking that a third body—either the reader themselves or the narrator, consider themselves in direct relation to that transatlantic history. Within the context of a work that frequently alludes to the significance of acts of transatlantic devotion and deference, the image of the book as altar suggests that Melville's vision of the author is as a guide for the reader in a quasi-religious communion in which to read is also to share. The diptych form simultaneously points to an older, public culture of worship and to newer, private acts of reading, conferring its own sense of ritualized "theatre" upon an otherwise isolated act. Unlike his romantic nationalist contemporaries, Melville does not see this communion as lying within a transcendental space of pure imagination or intellect, but instead in the embodied and material relations of theatre and ritual that were central to British imperial power. Macready and Bulwer-Lytton's Richelieu is a model for the author, as by suturing public expression to private devotion, he serves as an inspiration to a feeling of common human nature between otherwise divided individuals. Consequently, Bulwer-Lytton's play successfully negotiated the complex territory between the politics of the state and artistic creation that Melville had always struggled to capture in his own work. In his work for the theatre, Bulwer-Lytton displayed a similar kind of reasoning in bringing the pomp and circumstance of government into a line with the personal performances of selfhood. As the American Federalists had in the early republic, Melville too saw theatricality, the performance of one's subjectivity, as a crucial means of ensuring the persistence of both ritualized bonds of national community and personal morality. As such, Melville and Bulwer-Lytton were drawing on a shared, specifically transatlantic, history of republicanism that took the form of constitutional monarchy in Britain and in America emerged as Federalism. Much in the same way as Irving had before him, Melville saw the maintenance of links between Britain and America as a crucial element in the fight against modern sectarianism. By imagining the act of reading as a form of ritual theatre imbued with a strong aura of the sacred, Melville's story ultimately seeks to offer both a personal, spiritually enriching experience and one that is politically important to the project of reasserting a history of transatlantic republicanism in a time of increasing division and hostility organized around performances of Anglophilia and Anglophobia.

Paper, Professionalism, and State Power

If "The Two Temples" is Melville's consideration of how cultural borrowing from British political culture could reinvigorate US democracy, then "The Paradise of Bachelors and the Tartarus of Maids" is a study of the increasing role played by a professional class of men in the operations of modern states. In the story, Melville's treatment of class relations is predicated upon an economic shift from an agrarian (represented in the text by the American, Jeffersonian seedsman-narrator) to urban professional mode of government (represented by the English lawyers). In the first section of the diptych Melville makes the seedsman-narrator the subject of the Englishmen's "fraternal, household comfort" (Melville, 319) and hospitality, suggesting that the American market revolution has generated a fraternal bond of equality between America and Britain as both undergo a process of industrialization and modernization. In the story both British and American power is shown to rest with the middle-class bureaucrats who monitor the law courts and man the new social institutions of democracy.

It is useful to begin this discussion by returning, once again, to *Richelieu* as a dramatization of the changing conditions of transatlantic power. When Bulwer-Lytton has his lead say that "Beneath the rule of men entirely great/ the pen is mightier than the sword" (5), he is implying that the ideal model of a functioning republic (one that is constantly vigilant against the power of aristocratic privilege) relies upon the elevation of the authorship and the rule of small numbers of educated elites—in this case "men entirely great." In Bulwer-Lytton's play, the republican impulse relies upon the fraternal bonds of educated "knights-bachelors" (Melville 315) to defend against both Tocqueville's famed "tyranny of the majority" and dictatorship. The logic followed that since such people upheld the virtues most desired by society, they were best designed to instill those virtues in the populace. Bulwer-Lytton's play implied that these elites should be drawn from the emergent professional classes, whose commitment to duty, honesty, and work made them ideal candidates for power in the context of the development of a Victorian imperial, bureaucratic culture.

A key aspect of the play's plot involves the hyperdramatized transfer of letters and legal documents between parties. In the course of the narrative, paper becomes the primary means of establishing guilt, appealing to the professional aspirations of the Victorian middle class and implicating production and control of documents within the nexus of relations that comprise the epic motif of kingship and nobility. Although documents were a common trope in theatrical plots during the nineteenth century, prior to *Richelieu* these props were usually used to defend the familial narrative, as a proof of legitimacy to an inherited land claim, a bloodline, or to uncover a previously unknown relationship between characters. In *Richelieu* the device is used to deconstruct nobility and attack the structure of aristocratic power (and the significance it attaches to family bloodlines) by appealing to republican virtues of duty, honesty, respectability, and work. The notion that underpins the play is that if Richelieu had not been doing his job properly then evil would have triumphed. As the character of Joseph says to Richelieu at the high point of the play's dramatic tension:

> Tears are not for eyes
> That rather need the lightning, which can pierce
> Through the barred gates and triple walls, to smite
> Crime, where it cowers in secret!—The Despatch!
> Set every spy to work;—the morrow's sun
> Must see that written treason in your hands,
> Or rise upon your ruin. (Bulwer-Lytton, 115)

This speech reflects the panoptic logic that Foucault famously attributed to Benthamism. In it crime is covert, hiding behind the "barred gates and triple walls" of aristocratic privilege and historical lineage, whereas visibility, light, and governmental transparency are positive virtues associated with the heightened expressivity of Bulwer-Lytton's melodramatic rhetorical style. Tied to this is the notion of documents—the all-important "Despatch"—as legal and judicial markers of the will to eliminate the dangerous aspects of inherited privilege. In Bulwer-Lytton's play the middle class drive a wedge into notions of the value of inheritance and nobility through their supposed duty to the rule of law and just government.

After Richelieu shows the king documentary evidence of his brother's involvement in a plot to depose him, no further appeal to bloodlines can be made in Orleans's defense. Effectively, the pen has triumphed over the sword and paper over blood. Working as a member of Parliament in an era of Victorian constitutional monarchy that saw the rise of parliamentary press coverage, official printed government reports (the famed "Blue Books"), and Hansard transcripts, Bulwer-Lytton knew how important the interaction between oratory, performance, and the printed word was to the successful operation of the state.[2] In response to the widespread criticism of George IV's era of aristocratic misrule, by the late 1830s British government had at least outwardly begun to adopt an agenda of transparency that found its fullest force of expression in the growing number of publically accessible official printed materials drafted and printed by governmental and quasi-governmental commissions and bodies. Bulwer-Lytton came to political prominence at a time during which the majority of the political speeches and debates conducted in Parliament were being transcribed in real time by skilled reporters and relayed to the press. Additionally, works by governmental commissions and observers exposing the conditions of labor, domesticity, and other previously privatized endeavors flooded the print marketplace. Indeed, read through the lens of anthropology, these new printed archives of memory commissioned and published by the state corresponded as much with a sacred ritual logic of abundance (the notion that cultural power resides in the performance of excessive, overinflated modes of production and consumption) as they did with the ocular regimes of power Michel Foucault identified with the growth of modern, transparent state apparatus. Instead of power lying purely in the private realms of aristocratic households, it began to be displayed though the state's printed outputs.

The suggestion that forms of ritualism that liberalism would designate as premodern, or primitive, are implicated in the construction of modern state power is explored in both "The Paradise of Bachelors and the Tartarus of Maids" and "Poor Man's Pudding and Rich Man's Crumbs." The latter diptych investigates the relationship between modernity, expressed through the liberal individualism of the American poet Blandmour (a thinly veiled reference to Emerson) and the ritualized culture of monarchist Europe. The story questions whether the modern subject's insistence on his or her own romantic self-sufficiency is actually progressive or improving. Blandmour appears to suffer poverty acutely and, due to his insistence on refusing state or individual charity, dines on a "bitter and mouldy" (292) porridge of rice, milk, and salt, whereas the English poor accept the more morally degrading, but physically more sustaining, charity of the prince regent as they eat the leftovers of one of his lavish and opulent parties. For Melville, this distinction between America's proud but impoverished individualists, who reject the interventions of the state, and the collective masses of the London poor, who rely upon it, raises the question of state power and influence in the context of nineteenth-century political change. Indeed, while the archaic English ritualized "civic, as well as civil" (Melville, 295) solution to poor relief seems regressive, it is also pragmatic, whereas American liberalism is rendered as self-defeating. Both, in effect, are shown to shape transatlantic modernity, even as they seem mutually incompatible forms of government. Blandmour (a writer) has the power of the printed word and the right to individual expression but no food, whereas the London poor have access to food but no selfhood, as they are captured by the state's gaze as a debased, recognizably abused, collective. The British state performs theatrically, whereas the American state has its values and ideas expressed by the individual through print. Taken together, Melville comments upon the changing nature of transatlantic power, which had become as reliant upon performance as the written word, seeking in his diptychs to explore the middle ground, something like a form of democratic, state-sponsored authorship. Like William Dunlap in *A History of the American Theater* several decades before, then, Melville conceptualizes art and writing in the diptychs as a state good that should be supported and overseen by government—as a form of endeavor captured by the exercise of something like a rudimentary, Benthamite welfare state. Dunlap suggested that art would flourish in America when censors, of an idealized, benevolent sort, were given the power to endorse and patronize cultural institutions—rather than leaving the measure of quality up to the *laissez-faire* free market and the audiences alone. In effect, government had to involve itself in theatre, Dunlap argued, to improve the conditions both of that theatre culture (or American art more generally) and of the lives of its citizens, by taking on the mantle of culturally improving them and not leaving the citizenry to form their own liberal, individual versions of selfhood. The state, in the republican tradition of social-sanctioned and -created rights, had to be performative, active, theatrical even, in its expressions of power.

This concern with capturing the performative aspects of power in print was reflected in Bulwer-Lytton's plays, which often limned the borders between text and action to explore the changing character of nineteenth-century state power. When in *Richelieu* the cardinal announces (in a line that is perhaps now Bulwer-Lytton's only remaining contribution to English letters) that "the pen is mightier than the sword" and that it is a "wand . . . to paralyse the Caesars" (55), he connects professionalism, law, government, and performative action together, implying a link between the notions of justice or fairness and the expressive, ritualized histrionics of drama. In Bulwer-Lytton's work (as in Melville's) gestures participate in important ways in the action of modern law and government. This key dramatic moment in *Richelieu*, during which the pen becomes a magic wand, makes the private act of writing subject to public exchange. In effect, the writer and the orator are endowed with the power to educate others in the correct model of just virtue through the public sphere, placing power in the hands of those who performed in civic life the highest ideals of duty and work within the social imaginary, namely commissioned bureaucrats and civil servants. The line "Behold the arch-enchanter's wand" is a cue to flourish the pen in a richly gestural and expressive manner, showing the audience the visuality that underpins Bulwer-Lytton's words and demonstrating how the author of printed words and the actor were equally important in the translation, and therefore meaning, of any performance.

In this way, claims to nobility and the familial narratives of the past are challenged by the emergence of a system of exchange that is based on the copying and transmission of documents through official or semiofficial state channels. Consequently, the role of the middleman is elevated and more directly implicated in the modern system of relations that govern state power. This is as true of Melville as it is of Bulwer-Lytton, as the American author's short work ("Bartleby, the Scrivener" and "The Paradise of Bachelors" especially) engages with how new forms of bonds, fraternal and economic, replace the family bonds of the past, just as Richelieu's concern for the written word disrupts the claims of the nobility to a monopoly of power over national and political culture. As an influence upon Melville's short work in the 1850s, Bulwer-Lytton's great stroke in *Richelieu* was to make bureaucracy exciting enough material for drama. Just as Masonic and fraternity culture in America inscribed a religious typology into the banalities of the workday as a pharmacon that both relied upon and counteracted those banalities, Bulwer-Lytton—himself a Rosicrucian and Freemason—made paper trails, that pervasive mark of the new middle classes, the basis for the foundation of grand notions of nationhood, nobility, and divine power. Bulwer-Lytton draws a picture of society where princes, spies, star-crossed lovers, murderers, and cardinals are all ultimately in the thrall of paperwork.

In "The Paradise of Bachelors," Melville's narrator partakes in a ritual of feasting that symbolizes his partial initiation into the sympathetic economy of a group of "nine gentlemen, all bachelors" (Melville, 316) who claim lineage to the medieval brotherhood of the Knights Templar, an order whose radical form of monasticism historically opposed the rule of kings and the papacy. As a result of the connections he makes in London he is "ceremoniously enrolled as a member of the order" (315). Like the ceremony of drinking together in the second section of "The Two Temples," the feast generates a commonality among a group of upper-middle-class lawyers, whose fraternal relationships reflect the shift of power in the nineteenth-century Anglo-American public sphere from an aristocratic order structured around ties of blood to a corporate, middle-class form of government organized around the professions. Indeed, when Melville refers to the "nine gentlemen" as "a sort of Senate of Bachelors" (316), he makes a link between fraternity and republican power. As the narrator states, "the nine bachelors seemed to have the most tender concern for each other's health" (318). The reference to tenderness is telling as Melville implies that feelings that Victorian culture would normally reserve for the private sphere (love, tenderness, affect) underpin the public culture of law and government. The relationship they have is one of "tender" love mediated by "the general celibacy of the Temple." Through the ritualized elements of the feast, including the excessive consumption of alcohol, the corporeal elements of love are transferred into the process of eating. In other words, their excessive consumption stands in symbolically for a reproduction that is impossible within an all-male space.

The relationship of the lawyers to one another is based upon a ritualized culture that is nonutilitarian and, because it relies upon excessive consumption, wastefulness, and expenditure, also nonrational. However, the process of international market capitalism that first brings the narrator into relational discourse with the London lawyers (the trade of paper) rests upon a form of reproduction that *is* mechanized and rationalized. When the two sections of the story are read in conjunction, the tale becomes a meditation upon the Templars' paradoxical ideal of fraternity and legality. Even as the Templars see their actions as an alternative to the unequal relations of market, national, or aristocratic culture, the diptych's second section reveals how the reliance of their profession on the unfair practices involved in the international trade of paper renders their ideals hypocritical. By fusing images of pseudomedieval ritualized feasting and mechanical reproduction together through the diptych form, Melville shows how nonrational affective and ritualized exchanges between professional men of government are implicated in the development of capitalism and modern mechanized production.

Melville therefore uses the idea of professional culture to comment upon the act of writing itself: a creative, artistic, and critical process that is made possible both by the utilitarian, capitalistic process of mechanized production and, increasingly, by the extension of state and federal power. Since the short story in particular owes its development to magazine culture, Melville's juxtaposition of the images of a nonutilitarian fraternal ritual and a utilitarian factory constitutes a self-reflexive critique of the form itself. In this diptych Melville simultaneously reflects the fraternal ritualized culture of the Anglo-American transatlantic world and comments upon its increasing reliance upon an unfair, even abusive, mode of production.

With Melville's short work, the republican sympathy that characterized the earlier century, which emerged from the largely aristocratic model, is reconfigured into some form of cross-class association through the emergence of the mass production of paper—a process that is shown to involve all classes at some level. By using the diptych form Melville shows how each class is bound together through labor and sympathy. During this period, popular plays began to reflect societal changes and develop new uses for their generic conventions. In effect, the "respectability" that was becoming common in writing about the theatre became apparent within the plays themselves as a byword for structural shifts in the nature of social composition. The familial narrative that had structured early melodramas gave way to the narrative of respectability and fraternal relations characterized by Bulwer-Lytton's work.

In "The Paradise of Bachelors and the Tartarus of Maids" the author reflects the changes in mid-nineteenth-century political culture from aristocratic power to a more republican, civic culture of government demonstrated in *Richelieu* by using the story's second section to present a sketch of working conditions in a New England factory that partly resembles the kinds of bureaucratic "investigations" that were being increasingly conducted by civil servants under the official auspices of the British or US state. Read without sufficient attention to the first section, Melville's tale resembles the traditional sketch, a form that Kristie Hamilton has described as "doubly detached—above a scene . . . and purportedly independent of society's prejudices" (21). However, when read in light of the first section, "The Tartarus of Maids" does not operate in the same detached way as the traditional sketch. Instead, Melville deploys the form to comment upon the unprecedented powers of access wielded by elite middle-class men in Anglo-American society—a power that was performed in public life through the social investigations conducted by the professional classes. But Melville goes further than this in the story by drawing attention to how reliant the observational and regulatory functions of modern, Anglo-American legal and governmental institutions were upon the control and use of paper by this new elite coterie of men. In the opening to "The Paradise of Bachelors" section of Melville's story, the narrator writes that "sick with the din and soiled with the mud of Fleet Street . . . the Benedick tradesmen were running by, with ledger-lines ruled along their brows" (313). With this the author makes a link between the Benedick [ergo bachelor] class, paper, and the current way of organizing society through the "ledger-lines" in account books and documents. These men are shown to be the most prevalent class of this district of London, separated from the rich lawyers of Temple-Bar by class and economics, even as they are tied by the rule of paper and the ideal of professionalized manhood. The idea of these men as single is interesting in regard to the tale's reinterpretation of the relationship between paper and the familial narrative. In the era of the market revolution in America and the development of a male professional class in England, labor imposes limits upon the normative, traditionally heterosocial realm of domestic interaction by reinterpreting the relationship between the individual and time.

This image of hardworking bachelors ruled by paper and professional culture has its equivalent in the young women of the story's second section. In the opening of "The Tartarus of Maids," where the narrator gazes upon the Gothic image of the mill, "frost painted to a sepulchre" (324) among the "Alpine corpses" (323), the mill itself recalls Poe's House of Usher: solitary, desolate, and ruined. Just as "The Fall of the House of Usher" represents the collapse of a family in the face of a new culture, so "The Tartarus of Maids" looks at the deathly girls of the Black Notch as a symbol of the collapse of the familial life occasioned by the new production economy. When the narrator notes that "I seemed to see, glued to the pallid incipience of the pulp, the yet more pallid faces of all the pallid girls I had eyed that heavy day" (Melville, 331), the author offers us an image of how modern print culture cultivates a sameness that is synonymous with a certain kind of spiritual death.

As Wai-Chee Dimock explains in *Empire for Liberty: Melville and the Politics of Individualism*:

> Antebellum America, the age of individualism, was also a period of sharpening tension and polarities. The economic revolution that promoted massive migration westward and southward, and from rural areas to industrial centers, also resulted in the destruction of the self-sufficient farm economy, the collapse of the artisan and apprenticeship system, and the breakdown of traditional familial and communal ties. (11)

Melville explores this "breakdown" of traditional ties by reference to the production of paper, which plays an important role in the creation of an international public sphere of male sociality that challenges the centrality of the family to modern life even as it establishes new bonds of affection. The "seedsman," a kind of imperially and creatively ambitious Johnny Appleseed figure, uses the paper he buys to disseminate his seeds "all through the Eastern and Northern States, and even . . . into the far soil of Missouri and the Carolinas" (Melville, 321), and so dramatizes the ambitions of the short story writer seeking national and international fame within the context of an emergent Anglo-American print culture. The allegory at the heart of Melville's diptych is therefore one of male sociality and its participation in the bureaucratic extension of state power in the antebellum and early Victorian eras.

While the bachelors of the first section are ironically depicted as hermetically removed from the world of labor and injustice, the second section suggests that their very condition of power, since it rests on the trade and use of commodities like paper, cannot escape the realities of new transatlantic industrial conditions. Melville implies that the power wielded by the new professional classes, which in Bulwer-Lytton's Benthamite imagination would have been conceived of as a radical force of reform, has been misdirected into a support for new versions of laissez-faire capitalism. The narrator of "The Tartarus of Maids" is a sympathetic observer of the mill girls' plight, for whom his very condition as a writer dependent on paper renders him complicit in their oppression. It is useful here to turn to the work of an American contemporary of Melville, Orestes Brownson, whose writings exhibit a similar transatlantic model of Christian virtue, adopt similar influences, and also look to fraternal power as a model to overcome the dangers of unrestricted capital.

In his inflammatory tract *The Laboring Classes* (1840), Brownson takes up the mantle of the British writer Thomas Carlyle, whose work *Chartism* (1839) had theorized an end to the laissez-faire capitalism of early nineteenth-century England. By applying Carlyle's anti-laissez-faire model to the American scene and adding a protest of his own against Catholic and Episcopalian church hierarchy, Brownson appeals to his educated middle-class readers by suggesting that the roots of protest against oppression lie in an earlier model of Christian virtue and solidarity. Brownson writes,

> Moreover we are Christians, and it is only by following out the Christian law, and the example of the early Christians, that we can

hope to affect anything. Christianity is the sublimest protest against the priesthood ever uttered, and a protest uttered both by God and man; for he who uttered it was God-Man. (Brownson in Hollinger et al., 303)

In *The Laboring Classes*, Brownson assimilates British and American traditions of reform and includes a Unitarian attack on Catholicism and Episcopalian priesthood. In doing so he demonstrates the attitudes to cultural leadership that characterize Melville's own transatlantic model of Christian virtue, fraternity, and affect. It is interesting to note that in framing this discussion, Brownson, like his intellectual comrades Carlyle and Melville, first looks to the oppression of women under capitalism to incite the sense of injustice necessary to propel his critique of American labor relations. Brownson adopts a melodramatic mode of sublime gestural and emotive language in depicting the life of Lowell factory girls, the same caste who are so important to Melville's "The Tartarus of Maids." Importantly, by making reference to how their morality is damaged by such conditions, Brownson suggests that sexuality in any form is as dangerous a consequence of capitalism for women as the destruction of the physical body. In this way he appeals to the melodramatic tenor of antebellum reformism. Brownson writes of the female laborers thus:

> the great mass wear out their health, spirits, and *morals* [my italics], without becoming one bit better off than when they commenced labor. The bills of mortality in these factory villages are not striking, we admit, for the poor girls when they can toil no longer go home to die . . . The average life, working life we mean, of the girls that come to Lowell . . . from Maine, New Hampshire and Vermont . . . is only about three years. What becomes of them then? Few shall ever marry; fewer still ever return to their native places with reputations unimpaired. "She has worked in a Factory," is almost enough to damn to infamy the most worthy and virtuous girl. (298)

Philip Young's essay "The Machine in Tartarus: Melville's Inferno" theorizes the journey of the narrator into the "Black Notch" through the "Dantean gateway" (Melville, 321) as an updating of Dante's passage into the Inferno accompanied by Virgil. However useful Young's decoding of the classical and Christian allusions in the work is in establishing an influence for the second part of Melville's story though, it does little to consider the second section in relation to the first. Young even goes as far as to say that "The Tartarus of Maids" "might command more attention if it stood alone" (208). In my reading, Melville's narrator is implicated in the formation of the public sphere of ritualized male sociality that is transatlantic in scope. This consequently forces both sections of the tale to be given equal critical weight in analysis, since fraternity as a concept of governmental, economic, and social power is transatlantic. In the story Melville does not attack male power except where it endangers women through association with the vagaries of the market. The mill functions to expose the dangerous, competitive side of fraternal power. Once again money appears to corrupt what Melville, with his transatlantic imagination, sees as the positives of fraternal power by placing women in physical danger even as it generates a space for fraternal culture.

In "The Tartarus of Maids" section of the story Melville explores the hellish conditions of labor through allusion to Dante, whose journey back from disgrace into respectability and Christian virtue is precipitated through initiation into the male sociality of Virgil, a figure of the orator and Roman republican culture. In much the same way as Masonic initiation for Poe required the active participation of the young man in the processes of his indoctrination, so Dante's journey through Purgatory and Hell with Virgil is an active process that facilitates his ascendancy and arrival into knowledge. In *The Divine Comedy* the return of the hero to a model of Christian virtue is enacted by his inclusion into the secret knowledge of previous generations and the fraternity of Virgil and the poets. This, in turn, is figured as a release from the dangers of sexuality and physical love, engendered in the figure of the she-wolf that attacks him in the woods at the opening, and his discovery of a desexualized form of affiliation rooted in male bonding. Like the narrator of "The Two Temples," whose implied relationship with the rich woman ultimately leaves him destitute and alone, sexual desire threatens to corrupt him and turn him away from the one true path. As Dante says to Virgil in the first canto:

> You are my master and my author, you—
> the only one from whom my writing drew
> the noble style for which I have been honored.
> You see the beast that made me turn aside;
> help me, o famous sage, to stand against her,
> for she has made my blood and pulses shudder. (61)

When the narrator first arrives at the "Devil's Dungeon paper-mill" (Melville, 322) he is met by a "dark-complexioned man" (326) who greets him with a peculiar intimacy, and whom he later discovers is the mill's boss "Old Bach, as our whispering girls all call him" (327). Before he is able to conduct his business with the mill owner, the narrator states that the man "without pausing for a word instantly caught up some congealed snow and began rubbing both my cheeks" (326). The "horrible, tearing pain" that the narrator feels is a component of his initiation into the fraternity of bachelors, a theatricalized, embodied exchange like a handshake or bow that provides the context for the following business transaction. However, even as the intimacy of the exchange recalls the tenderness of the bachelors towards one another in the first section of the story, Melville inverts it to be a cause of pain to the body rather than comfort. In doing so, the author shows how capitalist exchange perverts the republican political ideal by introducing a dangerous component of competition into fraternal sympathy. Old Bach becomes a demonic inversion of masculine sympathy in a transatlantic space of sympathetic exchange, expressing the complex oscillations of elite power between tyranny and democracy. Like the images of Talma and Richelieu that frame "The Two Temples," the blackness of Old Bach is a counterpoint to the model of law and positive fraternal power found in the first section.

The introduction of the "dimpled, red-cheeked, spirited-looking" (326) Cupid into the narrative further emphasizes the theme of the oscillation between tyranny and democracy present within ritual through elite power and cultural leadership. Since Cupid in Roman culture both represents love and material greed, Melville's Cupid becomes a motif that at once represents the ideal of boyish fraternal love and the corrupted "cruel-heartedness" (328) that is its inverse. When he is first introduced he is said to be "gliding among the passive-looking girls—like a gold fish through hueless waves—yet doing nothing in particular that I could see" (326). Unable to sympathize with the women under his charge, his capacity for expressing the ideal of fraternal love that Melville sees among the Templars of London is under considerable question. Cupid becomes the narrator's guide and, in the tradition of Dante, he should represent an ideal of fraternal sympathy, justice, and order. Cupid is a childlike god of love found to be incapable of such love and as such initiation into his world is a cruelly inverted ritual of base greed and manipulation. When the narrator marks Cupid's name on a piece of paper and drops it into the "exposed part of the incipient mass" (329), purportedly to test the speed of the machine, it emerges "with my 'Cupid' half faded out of it" (330). Through this image Melville implies that the forces of pressure placed upon the boy by a fraternal power based on competition rather than feeling reduce his identity to a dulled cipher, while the love that his name symbolizes is weakened and thinned. When the narrator then remarks, "my travels were at an end, for here was the end of the machine" (330), he implies that the end is not the narrator's but Cupid's as his innocence is corrupted and his identity all but lost.

The excessive style Melville adopts in "The Paradise of Bachelors and the Tartarus of Maids" has its origins in Dante's support for wisdom, virtue, and fraternity but goes further than the medieval poet by implying that these virtues are dangerously subject to corruption at the hands of the unequal processes of capitalist exchange. The danger to the maids in Melville's diptych signifies the author's growing concern that male power not come at the expense of the "feminine" capacity for love. The mill, with its phallic allusions to functionality and productivity, works to undermine the sympathetic power of the female attendants and their child overseer, stripping them of their emotional affect by making them subject to the process of diffusing tyrannical power—the production of paper. The mill seems to remove them of their blood, both figuratively since the "strange-colored torrent Blood River" (321) seems to carry away the "blood" from the land, and physically in the implied danger to the health and virginity of girls in the "rag-room." When the narrator states that the girls are "their own executioners; themselves whetting the very swords that slay them" (Melville, 328), he expresses the paradox at the heart of his tale. The paradox is that the paper that helps to generate the sphere of male sociality in print too often becomes reliant upon the very processes of capitalist exchange that endanger women and can corrupt young men by introducing violence and competition.

In this regard, Melville's fraternalism finds a strange, intellectual bedfellow in the figure of Margaret Fuller, whose own transatlantic, feminist imaginary echoes Melville's logic by appealing for female exclusion from the dangerous market spaces of masculine mid-nineteenth-century culture. In *Woman in the Nineteenth Century* (1845) Fuller notes that if the impediments put in place by men (namely the unequal processes of transnational capitalist exchange) were removed and women allowed to compete freely on their own "platform," then their conditions would be infinitely improved. Fuller suggests that the supposedly "feminine" capacity for sympathy should be utilized in the creation of a more just society. The concept of a separate platform echoes Melville's fraternalism in seeking to develop a form of association that extends beyond the familial narrative as a means of generating a more just concept of power and cultural leadership—literally a society based on separate but equal spheres of sorority and fraternity. As Fuller states:

> We will not speak of the enthusiasm excited by actresses, improvisatrici, female singers, for here mingles the charm of beauty and grace; but female authors, even learned women, if not insufferably ugly and slovenly, from the Italian professor's daughter, who taught behind a curtain, down to Mrs Carter and Madame Dacier, are sure of an admiring audience, and what is far better, chance to use what they have learned, and to learn more, if they can once get a platform on which to stand . . . If there is a misfortune in woman's lot, it is in obstacles being imposed by men, which do not mark her state; and, if they express her past ignorance, do not her present needs. (Fuller in Hollinger *et al.*, 390)

As with Melville's other diptychs, "The Paradise of Bachelors and the Tartarus of Maids" is structured around a significant elision. In this instance, the fraternalism of his narrator results in a blindness to the reality of working-class female life. The women depicted in the second half of the diptych, like the young men in the first section, are voiceless and rendered as merely spectral presences by the semiofficial eye of the gentleman-narrator. In reality the mills girls of New England were not passive victims of the factory owner's cruelty or the male observer's institutionalized gaze, but were actively involved in the creation of significant counterpublics (printed "platforms") of their own. Such mill-worker-authored publications as the *Lowell Offering*, the *Factory Girls' Garland*, and *Factory Girls' Album* constituted, according to Benita Eisler, "the first writings by and about American blue-collar women" (*Lowell Offering*, 41). These magazines combined political agitation for the ten-hour movement with traditionally "feminine" styles of sentimental prose. Reprinted stories from *Godey's Ladies Book* and genteel mill-girl-authored love stories were nestled alongside more incendiary Fourierist tracts and debates in these magazines. Additionally, the mill girls of Lowell and other industrial towns were responsible for organizing lyceum lectures, trade-union protests, religious services, and other activities that cultivated a sense of collective sympathy and participation. This mixed tone that fused forms of love drawn from the private sphere to the new antifamilial models of association shaped by the realm of public culture perfectly encapsulates the ideal version of performed democracy that Melville himself favored in his diptychs.

Across his diptychs Melville seeks to find an ideal version of transatlantic democratic authorship that can speak simultaneously to different classes in antebellum society and so serve as a means to unite the nation in a time of increasing sectarian and economic tension. In the following chapter I show how Melville's ideal of transatlantic democratic authorship as theatrical and ritualized exchange finds an apt metaphor in the image of the child on the stage, specifically the twelve-year-old Irish actor Master William Betty. The male child for Melville simultaneously represented the possibilities generated by new public forms of discourse and the "feminine" capacity for love and emotionality and so was able to balance the competing class-based registers of modern American society. As such, Betty served for Melville as the ideal symbol of nineteenth-century democratic art. In the American author's little-studied story from 1854, "The Fiddler," Master Betty appears reflected in the figure of Hautboy, an American who offers an antidote to the narrator's romantic malaise through his childlike enthusiasm and expressive performances that perfectly encapsulated the spirit of modern magazine and short story writing.

CHAPTER 4

The "Child of Nature," or the "Wonder of the Age"
Melville's Child Prodigies

> The lovely boy as I beheld him then
> Among the wretched and the falsely gay,
> Like one of those who walked with hair unsinged
> Amid the fiery furnace. He has since
> appeared to me oftentimes as if embalmed
> By nature, through some special privilege
> Stopped at the growth he had—destined to live,
> To be, to have been, come and go, a child
> And nothing more . . .
> —William Wordsworth, *The Prelude* (1805)

By 1852, Melville was facing bankruptcy and personal ruin after the critical and commercial failures of *Moby-Dick* (1851) and *Pierre, or The Ambiguities* (1852). On the advice of Charles Briggs, who became editor of the New York–based *Putnam's Magazine* in 1853, Melville turned to writing short magazine fiction to make ends meet, producing works for *Putnam's* and its main rival, *Harper's*, throughout the 1850s. Even though his literary reputation and contacts permitted him access to two of antebellum society's most prestigious publications, magazine writing was fraught with problems regarding the intersections of class and authorship, issues that he had previously explored in *Pierre*. While journals like *Putnam's* positioned themselves as the vocal piece of an upwardly mobile middle-class audience and featured work by many of the elites of antebellum literature, the cultural authority of short fiction was a subject of some debate. Whereas a small number of editors and readers "considered 'magazinish' writing a reputable and serious literary form" (Post-Lauria, 152) that was in the process of attaining the privileged status of the novel, most considered the new genre a lesser cousin of the book and somewhere closer to the newspaper in status. Owing in part to the editorial decision to publish certain works anonymously, as well as the considerable access that magazine writers seemed to possess to a much-maligned urban world, they were often treated with a degree of suspicion.[1] While *Putnam's* published works anonymously, other journals, like Robert Bonner's *New York Ledger*, openly flaunted their access to celebrity authors like Fanny Fern. Indeed, Bonner proudly announced that Fern was to be paid $1,000 for the rights to serialize *Ruth Hall* in his periodical. *Harper's* adopted a mixed approach to publishing, with some works attributed to named authors and others published anonymously. The increasing need for copy to satisfy the demands of a growing and diverse body of readers often meant that within antebellum journals the work of certified literary and intellectual elites was presented alongside unsolicited contributions from anonymous writers. Indeed, "The Fiddler" appeared in the same issue of *Harper's* as a serialized chapter of *The Newcomes* that is directly attributed to W. M. Thackeray. Consequently, the antebellum magazines posed the problem of attributing fiction to an embodied figure whose status and sincerity could be verified within an increasingly complex and heterogeneous marketplace.

In order to overcome this potential difficulty, magazine writers often combined their work in this field with achievements in other literary endeavors. Indeed, the markets for books and journals were not wholly discrete entities. Many of the most successful literary figures of the day, such as Dickens and Stowe, made their careers out of exploiting the new periodicals while simultaneously publishing in the more established and culturally authoritative field of books. Another approach taken by antebellum authors was to seek success on the lyceum lecture circuit before publishing in the magazines. The most significant figure in this regard must certainly have been Ralph Waldo Emerson. As R. Jackson Wilson has suggested, Emerson's cultural and class status depended on accounts of his lectures that noted his "sincerity" when speaking in the lyceum. Melville would try this route himself in the late 1850s, attaining moderate though short-lived success.

Melville's magazine fiction was not the first time he had sought to match popular appeal with critical esteem. It is, in fact, a recurrent feature of his broader aesthetic. Sheila Post-Lauria has highlighted the manner in which

"Melville's *Pierre* closely resembles French sensationalist fiction" and "stood in stark contrast to literary forms demanded by cultivated readers" (128) even though the novel was published in a form that was too expensive for the lower-class readers of the very type of fiction that the novel mimics. To turn to magazine writing after such a literary disaster as *Pierre* raised a particular set of problems. The failure of that novel to convince readers of the author's value meant that Melville was entering a new marketplace without a preestablished claim to status. Without the class and cultural authority that came from success in the book market to undergird his short fiction, Melville's decision to turn exclusively to writing for the magazines radically destabilized his already-unsure class status.

Unlike novel reading—an exercise primarily seen as contributing to a sentimental economy of domestic and private consumption—the circulation of journals and monthly magazines within the more public spaces of the market tended to contribute to an understanding of the media as the textual analogue of theatre (Lehuu). Like the frequent hostility that was felt by actors towards their craft, magazine writers ran the risk of being seen as deceivers, tricksters, or hacks whose intentions were purely economic and whose professional status was questionable. As John Evelev has noted, new magazines like *Putnam's* were deeply distrusted and often accused of mounting an "attack on traditional professional status" (5). In the antebellum popular imagination, when not fortified by status claims drawn from other areas of life or literary production, the more public and market-oriented work of magazine writers was more often associated with "the festive and somewhat transgressive quality" (Lehuu, 4) of a carnivalesque, working-class, street culture than with the sanctified realms of the upper-middle-class salon.

As I established in the previous chapter, following Charles Olson's *Call Me Ishmael* (1967), critics have noted that Melville's work is filled with references to the stage that structure his critiques of American society and artistic practice. However, it is not just at the level of reference that Melville's work utilizes the theatre, but also at that of form. As in the "Midnight, Forecastle" chapter of *Moby-Dick*, which takes the form of a dramatic script, Melville's work for magazines often collapses an artificial, critical distinction that has divided orality from textuality. In one short work from this period, "The Fiddler" (anonymously published in *Harper's New Monthly Magazine* in September 1854), Melville makes reference to a seemingly obscure figure from British dramatic history, the child actor Master William Henry West Betty. In a curious piece of dialogue the author grants this figure a crucial role in the reader's interpretation of the story, which seems outwardly to concern a chance meeting on Broadway between a failed romantic poet and a violin player. Melville writes:

> "Did you ever hear of Master Betty?"
> "The great English prodigy, who long ousted the Siddons and Kembles from Drury Lane, and made the whole town run mad with acclamation?"
> "The same," said Standard . . .
> I looked at him perplexed. He seemed to be holding the master-key of our theme in mysterious reserve; seemed to be throwing out his Master Betty too, to puzzle me only the more.
> "What under heaven can Master Betty, the great genius and prodigy, an English boy twelve years old, have to do with the poor common-place plodder Hautboy, an American of forty?" (Melville, 261)

Master Betty appears here as a cipher, whose meaning is a "master-key" that not only unlocks "The Fiddler" but offers us new perspectives on the wider aesthetics of Melville's fiction. The question upon which the plot rests is given to the narrator and speaks to Melville's own literary exercise: "why cross the ocean, and rifle the grave to drag his remains into this living discussion?" (261). Critics have offered readings of Hautboy that have varied from seeing him as "an exemplification of Melville's view of the ideal man" (Gupta, 437) to seeing him as a mirror of Melville's artistic failures. None, however, have sought to seriously probe the significance of the "ghost" of Master Betty that haunts the text and informs the narrator's vision of his new acquaintance.

In this chapter, I show how Melville's story resurrects the transatlantic history of William Betty as a means to explore his own search for an aesthetic that he might perform in order to serve both the demands of the spectacular world of antebellum magazine publishing (into which he had been forced by his dire financial situation) and his own higher literary ambitions. In "The Fiddler," the author uses the child actor as a conduit through which the reader (and the narrator) come to comprehend "an American of forty" (Melville, 261), the "eternally blessed" (260), "overgrown boy" (258) Hautboy, whose ability to "hit the exact line between enthusiasm and apathy" (260) in conversation, and whose "off-handed, dashing and disdainfully care-free" (262) style of violin playing, strike the narrator as "miraculously superior" (262) forms of art. Like the "dashing" manner of his performance, the man-child Hautboy skillfully balances the middle-class ideal of sincerity with a playful childishness that serves as a model for ideal literary relations in antebellum New York.

In choosing the theatre as his ostensible subject in a New York–based publication in 1854, Melville was cutting close to the bone by deliberately engaging with the preeminent site of contemporary disputes concerning class politics and cultural authority in the city. I see this story, long regarded as a secondary work in Melville's oeuvre, as central to recent debates in American studies concerning class relations and performance culture. In particular, many critics have sought to question the validity of Lawrence Levine's assertions concerning "culture" in America after the Astor Place Riot of 1849, in which class conflict over performances of Shakespeare by the English William Macready and the American Edwin Forrest resulted in the deaths of twenty-five people.[2] Indeed, Melville had a personal relationship to the events at Astor Place, having been one of the so-called "elites" who publically supported Macready over Forrest at a time when he was also seeking popular success in the marketplace. This points to his continuing attempts to find a cultural middle ground within an increasingly divided antebellum New York. Levine's narrative linking Astor Place to the antebellum schism between "high" and "low" cultural forms, which were in turn a reflection of ossifying class divisions in mid-nineteenth-century America, breaks down if one adopts a more nuanced and less obviously bifurcated approach to class. In its place, critics have begun to propose a model of "middlebrow" professional authorship, in which, through carefully selected cultural references and what Michael Denning would call "accents," antebellum writers sought to balance the competing aesthetic and class-based demands of their audiences.

Furthermore, readings of Melville's work benefit from locating it within a transatlantic critical tradition in which national cultures are not assumed to have stable or fixed meanings. By consistently locating the "elite" within the terms of "British" cultural production (or that of the American Whigs who prized it) and "low" art within "American" performance cultures such as minstrelsy, Levine's arguments not only inadvertently reinscribe a potentially misleading notion that has attached prestige exclusively to European culture, but they also miss the history of performances of Shakespeare before Astor Place that often highlighted the tensions and fluidities between market-oriented and elite theatre. It is this history to which Melville returns in "The Fiddler" as a means to generate a "middlebrow" aesthetic that was appropriate for the new magazines, and so question emerging narratives that located cultural authority as a possession of a disembodied, romantic intellect. Before coming to a close reading of the story, it is worth recounting some incidents in the peculiar life of Master William Betty.

From 1804 to 1806, between his twelfth and fourteenth birthdays, Master William Henry West Betty, the only son of a bankrupt Irish country gentleman, began to play Shakespearean roles such as Hamlet and Richard III alongside adult actors to full and hysterically enthusiastic audiences in the great London patent theatres of Covent Garden and Drury Lane. Grown men rioted outside theatres demanding to see him. A whole industry developed around him, as merchandise from expensive crockery sets to cheap pamphlets and broadsides depicting the boy in classical theatrical poses flooded stalls and shops. Prices were vastly inflated at his performances, and he was invited by the Prince of Wales to have his portrait painted by the royal artist John Opie. Judith Plotz has suggested that even that paragon of conservative elites William Wordsworth referred obliquely to the child actor in Book Seven of *The Prelude* (1805 text) in the figure of "the lovely boy . . . embalmed by Nature" (272). Puzzling as the phenomenon is, it is worth noting that Betty rejuvenated a theatre industry that had been hit hard by the pressures of the Napoleonic wars and an economy in decline. In particular, Betty was able to draw both patricians and laborers to his performances, greatly adding to both a much-needed sense of national unity and London theatres' account books. As Giles Playfair remarks of a run of Betty appearances at Drury Lane, "the gross return from a total of twenty-five performances amounted to more than £15,000 . . . [the manager] found himself, for the first time in a long while, operating in the black" (120). The greatest of Master Betty's income, though, came from tours of provincial stages, where, free from the high prices and elite status of the London patent theatres, he was able to play to packed crowds of artisans and rural laborers.

Although it may seem that enthusiasm for the boy's acting was merely a felicitous moment in the history of British fashion, his talent seemed to captivate even those among the cultural elites who made it their business to question the value of whimsical popular movements. In a short time Master Betty had become so famous that the notoriously exacting romantic critic William Hazlitt was said to proclaim him, in the terms of an idealized romantic pastoralism, "some gay creature of the elements," while the painter James Northcote stated that his cultural fame reached the heights of emperors and kings: "He and Bonaparte now divide the world" (quoted in Playfair, 79). In his time he became something of a poster boy for popular English (and Irish) romanticism, "a wonder of the age" whose talent

Fig. 2. "William Henry West Betty," James Northcote.
Reproduced courtesy of the National Portrait Gallery, London.

expressed the political power of Napoleon and the oratorical skill of the famed Roman actor Roscius. Consequently, Betty's freakish appearance on the London stage embodied characteristics that are both opposites and analogies: the timelessness of an ideal romantic Nature and the fleetingness of spectacle and fashion.

There was even a market for Bettymania in New York City. In a pamphlet of November 1806 (printed and circulated in New York by an anonymous fan of the child actor), the author writes, "Whatever was properly presented to his mind, he could immediately lay hold of and seemed to seize, by a sort of intuitive sagacity, the spirit of every sentence, and the prominent beauties of every remarkable passage" (16). As a description of his art, this passage resonates simultaneously with a broadly Platonist conception of natural genius that was favored by the romantics and a focus upon the more artisanal elements of learning and mimicry. Cheap London and provincial newspapers aimed at the working and lower-middle classes carried daily updates of Master Betty's relationship with his tutor, Mr. Hough. Reports focused on what he was learning and how he was progressing, establishing a relationship between acting and craft that appealed to those who were establishing themselves through apprenticeships in the trades. To his fans, Betty was supposed to possess an ideal balance between romantic "intuitive sagacity" and a skill at quick learning that could unite the diverse elements of the theatrical audience. In this way, the boy's appearance on the stage blurred an artificial line that situated elite culture within the terms of "high" romantic drama and labor within the "low" world of the marketplace.

The story of William Betty did not end happily. The physical exertion that was required of him on the stage endangered his young body and at various times he was hospitalized for fatigue and injuries stemming from a gruelling acting schedule. Dropped from the roster of actors at the theatres that had once supported him (after his voice had broken around the summer of 1807), Betty was never able to regain his fame in the remainder of his life, and, in 1821—forced into retirement after an unsuccessful come-back tour—he attempted suicide. Although Betty had a popular appeal that also resonated with the aesthetic concerns of the cultural elites, this was rooted in the temporariness of his preadolescence. Anne Varty has remarked that Master Betty was the origin point of a phenomenology of childhood acting that developed throughout the century. Betty was one of the origin points for the peculiar nineteenth-century vogue for child actors in adult roles, which helped to establish the careers of notable thespians such as Ellen Terry in Britain and John Howard Payne in the United States. Unlike the majority of actors in this period, nineteenth-century audiences came to see children as incapable of deception or deceit. Varty states:

> The child's spontaneity generated a special intimacy between audience and performer. When an audience witnessed the act it was allowed invisibly to participate in the "make-believe" of the child's world . . . The child's paradoxical exhibition of absolute sincerity on stage invited scopophilic attention. (14)

When British and American audiences watched children perform in adult roles they were engaged in a voyeuristic act that had its root in the belief that children, as opposed to adults they aped, were unable to distinguish between acting and playing. To inhabit the world of the child actor was, however briefly, to witness in their play-performances the ultimate expression of the oft-sought ideal of sincerity. While adult actors were continually treated with suspicion and mistrust by the middle classes in both Britain and America, children became oddly exempt from these strong antitheatrical prejudices. Betty's career depended on his childhood, which allowed him to access the hallowed space of sincere performance favored by elite romantic and popular audiences alike.

To the romantics who idolized him, his very growth into a man was portrayed as a tragedy that destroyed his "natural" talents and beauty and set into motion a chain of events that was to be his downfall. Growth, for the British romantic mind, annihilated the divinely ordained and sublime power of the child as, ironically, the reality of natural changes became anathematic to the "child of nature" myth. Judith Plotz has even argued that the romantic conception of childhood constitutes a form of violence against the child. Indeed, Wordsworth's selection of the term "embalmed" to describe the "lovely boy" of *The Prelude* courts the Gothic. Plotz writes,

> The male Romantics practice a kind of forcible repatriation of childhood, a patriarchal kidnapping that wrests children away from the female sphere . . . and sequesters them in a paternally circumscribed realm of permanent difference. (xvi)

Wordsworth's "natural" does not describe processes of transition and change so much as a realm of fixity separated from the realities of everyday life: a "realm of permanent difference" and transcendent power that relies upon the interiorization of the subject and their appropriation by a patriarchal order. Indeed, the image of the child that prevails in *The Prelude* is contiguous with what Paul Giles sees in *Atlantic Republic* as the general purpose of the poem as a whole: "an epic narrative about recentering . . . re-establishing the rooted and the commonplace at the centre of poetic consciousness" (35). For the English romantics the aesthetic fixity of English childhood also helped to define a national consciousness and character as similarly fixed and static: as clarified, reified, and ultimately antisocial. In fact, asociality was a key value of early nineteenth-century English romanticism since nature was perceived to be an entity that existed beyond the realm of human experience and sociality. For the romantics to access nature required one to abandon the man-made world.

Consequently, William Betty came to serve the needs of a British nationalist and romantic project of self-definition that rested upon a supreme form of individualistic solitude. Russ Castronovo has noted that in nineteenth-century literature attempts to define the ideal citizen of a single nation often rest upon the presentation of that figure as dead to the real world of chance, incident, and exchange. He refers to this as "necro ideology," the killing of a thing to make it politically and socially stable. Castronovo writes, "necro ideology . . . not only annihilates historical consciousness, thereby immobilizing possibilities for political change; it also generates entities clumped about the nation-state who leave in their wake social corpses" (14). Betty may be envisaged as one such corpse: a child metaphorically killed by the political unconscious of English romantic thought, which sought to capture him forever as a symbol of idealized boyhood. It is the complex ironies of Betty's cultural power and his position as an icon of "high" and "low" art that interests Melville in "The Fiddler."

"Would they applaud the poet as they applaud the clown?"

"The Fiddler" is narrated by a man named Helmstone, who first appears to the reader as a disembodied voice of shame and despair. Melville opens with his narrator's fury at his inability to write a successful poem, mocking his own literary frustrations after the publication of *Mardi*. The author writes, "So my poem is damned, and immortal fame is not for me! I am nobody forever and ever. Intolerable fate!" (Melville, 258). Unlike the rest of the dialogue, Melville elects not to have the first words of his narrator within speech marks. However, the statement does not take the form of a direct address to the reader. Indeed, the reader's presence is not felt, as Helmstone's statement is internally directed rather than externally expressive. In framing the story, this internally directed statement serves the purpose of locating the narrator within a romantic literary tradition that focuses upon the internalized language of the soul whose realm is the eternal: "Intolerable fate!" (258).

Elaine Hadley has provided an interesting account of the competition between romantic poetic language and the embodied performances of working-class melodrama that is useful for engaging with the terms of Melville's fiction. Hadley notes, "The romantic subject's internalization of feeling . . . results in a form of identity that is seen to be private and essential, the exclusive possession of the individual" (*Melodramatic Tactics*, 33). In Hadley's Foucauldian terms, the romantic subject's form of address is spatialized to reflect the political sovereignty of the individual over the collective. In the work of the transcendentalists, this egoistic individualism was becoming sutured to a liberal tradition of self-reliance, in which political sovereignty and an "original vision" were the fruits of one's intellectual labor. As Melville had showed previously in *Moby-Dick*, through his characterization of Ahab, this egoistic individualism always ran the risk of becoming tyrannical when self-reliance was coupled with a dangerous desire to wield power over others. There is an ironic reversal at play in the fate of Melville's narrator. Unlike the transcendentalist authors, Helmstone is unable to map this subjectivity onto political or economic self-reliance, because to do so would require an initial "investment" of cultural capital by others, namely critics. Melville presents a world in which to be self-reliant, one must first be praised.

The spatial dimensions of romantic expression are expanded in the following line and further enhance Melville's privatization of the narrator's identity: "Snatching my hat, I dashed down the criticism and rushed out into Broadway . . ." (Melville, 258). The preposition "out" situates the narrator within an internal environment that reflects the internally expressive nature of the opening statement. The passage then continues to note "enthusiastic throngs were crowding to a circus in a side-street near by, very recently started, and famous for a capital clown" (258). Mediated by the temporary embodiment suggested by the gesture of "snatching" up his hat, the internality of the opening statement is exploded by Melville's shift of perspective to the street, which the narrator designates as the realm of the crowd. Furthermore, the statement "capital clown" connects a term that denotes the performer's skill and cultural capital (as in "capital fellow") with the terms of financial investment (literal "capital"). It is here that we see the significance of Melville's choice of the actor as the ideal model of identification for the writer. Like Master Betty, whose critics praised his talent at original *and* emulatory forms of expression, the stage requires of actors that they demonstrate their professionalism through publically ratified performances of internal sentiments. Theatre therefore highlights the fantasy of romantic subjectivity by showing that under market conditions no "successful" professional identity could ever be purely the "private and essential . . . possession of the individual" (Hadley, 33).

The first two paragraphs of the story establish a dialogue between romantic authorship, associated with the internal world of the intellect, and the dynamic space of the street, associated with the marketplace and the carnival. It is worth following the work of Isabel Lehuu in seeing his reference to the circus in terms of contemporary discourses surrounding print culture. When Melville speaks of the circus, he is drawing parallels in the mind of his contemporaries with the literary marketplace with which he had become associated. The seemingly insatiable desire of the antebellum middle class for depictions of street life, which tradition and etiquette compelled them not to experience firsthand, fed a concern that the middle-class intellect would become degraded by overconsumption of low-grade cultural products. For Lehuu, the sheer abundance of print in antebellum New York posed a challenge to older sources of cultural authority and frequently drew comparisons to the carnival. Unlike the upper-middle-class salon, which was designated as a space of objective truth telling, the street was frequently coded as a site of deceit and subterfuge. Lehuu remarks that antebellum print culture might be productively understood in the terms of Mikhail Bakhtin's sense of the "carnivalesque." Lehuu writes,

> The period often described as the golden age of print was in fact a period of unstable cultural order. To the amazement of contemporary critics and enthusiasts alike, the printed word *staged* a carnival, in the twofold sense of both staging a dramatic representation and entering a phase within the maturing of American culture. (4)

Unlike Bakhtin's carnival, however, the antebellum carnival of print did not only serve as a counterpoint to the world of capitalist acquisition, or even as a rare outpouring of cultural pluralism in the face of fixed hierarchies and traditions, but was an embodiment of the free market's appeal to the values of abundance and choice. Even the most elite journals (like *Harper's* and *Putnam's*) were susceptible to critiques of this kind. Since the magazine form relied upon a heterogeneity and diversity of content, there was always an implicit possibility that the new public sphere would lose its assumed moral center of republican virtue and become carnivalesque in character. As Jean-Christophe Agnew asserts in relation to *The Confidence Man*, a work that similarly explores the intersections between authorship and marketable performance, "Melville's literary carnival adamantly refuses to reveal or to redeem the world it turns upside down" (*Worlds Apart*, 200). In antebellum society, to write of street life as a carnival was not necessarily to present an alternative to the advancing world of the capitalist marketplace but rather to offer the reader a hyperbolic representation of a future world that seemed unavoidable.

The language of class marked the fusion of carnival with the marketplace in the antebellum mind. In mid-nineteenth-century New York, class affiliations were often couched in terms of the Cartesian duality between body and mind. Most famously, popular journals and broadsides treated the Astor Place affair as the violent outcome of a transatlantic, professional rivalry that began after Edwin Forrest—whose appeal to working-class, Tammany Hall Democrats was largely rooted in what Evert Duyckinck and Walt Whitman saw as the muscular, "oxlike" physically of his acting style—took offense against William Macready's "cerebral" performance of Hamlet in Edinburgh, particularly the "excessive" wafting of a handkerchief, designed to illustrate a certain, effete intellectualism in the character.[3] This dynamic between mind and body reflected the new conditions of antebellum society, especially in relation to questions over New York's financial and industrial future. While the Whig elites of New York were directly involved in the complex financial and mercantile practices of international speculation and trade, at sites like the Astor Place Opera House and the American Art Union they cultivated artistic practice as a disembodied space of neutrality free from the influences of the very market society they had helped to create. By contrast, working-class artistic practices often made recourse to the working body as a sign of their desire to retain an older artisanal relationship between labor and individual creation in the face of growing proletarianization and alienation in the emergent industrialized marketplace.

Melville's language in this opening passage reflects his theme. By juxtaposing the narrator's ahistorical, transcendental vision of "immortal fame" with a transitory dynamism suggested by the words "snatching," "dashed," and "rushed," Melville demonstrates his command of two competing spatio-temporal registers that would have resonated within antebellum social hierarchies. The first signals a conservative version of the romantic sublime that attached a condition of timelessness to power. This would have spoken to the elite Whig conception of conservative stewardship and romantic providence. The second undercuts this by highlighting the temporary, conditional nature of life. Like Master Betty, whose style was both natural and artificial, the realm of the soul and that of fashion, Melville's style inhabits both fixed and mobile versions of experience. As Andrew Lawson has shown in regard to Whitman (whose *Leaves of Grass* was to appear in New York less than a year later), "at stake in Whitman's heteroglot style is the issue of cultural authority: the social power implied by the possession of literary language and the challenge to that power implied by other less legitimate language" (Lawson, xiv). Helmstone's deployment of the "high-flown, Emersonian language of the soul" (xvii) reflects his desire to locate himself within the terms of the literary elite that is frustrated by the demands of the author's position as an agent within a newly emergent market society.

In this way, Melville suggests that Helmstone's romantic subjectivism—frequently associated with the patrician, neoclassical values of the older New York Whig elites—is untenable in the context of the emergent market economy. Indeed, Melville even suggests that such a perspective may actually be unethical. When Helmstone meets his friend Standard in the street, the latter remarks, "Ah! What's the matter? Haven't been committing murder? Ain't flying justice? You look wild!" (258). The connection between Helmstone's elite romantic pretensions and violence is established at several points in the story, particularly in relation to Helmstone's poetry, which includes a "sublime passage . . . in which Cleothemes the Argive vindicates the justice of war" (259). Historicized in the context of the Astor Place Riot and Melville's deployment of theatrical imagery, statements connecting "murder" and "the justice of war" with the romantic language of the "sublime" would have resonated strongly with Melville's readership in terms of class conflict.

In the numerous pamphlets and broadsides that circulated in response to the Astor Place Riot, there was much speculation over whether the state police fired into the crowd at the direct request of the patrician, opera-going elites. In one such pamphlet, entitled "Account of the Terrific and Fatal Riot," the author notes that "the private boxes were taken by the season" (5) before immediately shifting register to a discussion of the National Guard's "attempt to charge with the bayonet" (6) into the amassing crowd outside the theatre. In the pamphlet, the textual slippage between privately owned theatrical space and state violence is not accidental. The culture of theatre boxes was a hotly disputed issue in New York at the time, as their cost and the view they afforded were taken as broader symbols of elite power and control. In "Account of the Terrific and Fatal Riot" the author correlates the opulence of the theatre box with the power to command the army against the poorer elements of the city.

Since Foucault's groundbreaking work *Discipline and Punish*, the most common critical tradition in theatre studies has been to read boxes in terms of Bentham's panoptic prison. Critics have seen the architectural structures as affording the owners an invisibility that was synonymous with the unverifiable and unimpeachable exercise of power in the modern, liberal state. However, theatre boxes differ from the panopticon in several key ways that are crucial to the relationship between sight and power that Melville explores in "The Fiddler." While the view from the central tower of Bentham's panopticon allowed the invisible viewer to survey the differentiated and individuated subjects beneath him, theatre boxes operate by offering the owner a choice to be either visible or invisible. Seated behind the curtains of the box, the viewer could see without being seen. However, sitting forward would enhance both the owner's view of the stage and the visibility of the viewer to other patrons, while largely screening off many of the audience members in the cheapest seats either above ("the gods") or directly below the boxes (the pit). Theatre boxes are not strictly panoptic machines, since they actually function by asserting the owner's right to choose visibility in contrast to the anonymity forcibly inflicted on the poor. Those that owned the boxes could be seen as subjects whose individuality was affirmed in the context of Astor Place by their right of access to the state power of the National Guard, while those that could not afford such luxuries came to be seen as an embodied collective whose right to individuality (which in the context of Jacksonian America often meant access to state power) was placed in question. In effect, theatrical boxes reflected a power based upon visibility *and* invisibility. Elite patrons could, in effect, benefit from both the power associated with being known and, as the aftermath of Astor Place would show, an invisibility that would allow them to avoid prosecution or culpability for the violence committed in their name.

The forms of visible, theatrical protest undertaken by groups such as Mike Walsh's Spartan Band of building occupation, the ebullient, theatrical, public personhood of the Bowery B'Hoys, and the Tammany Hall tradition of street-based political oratory, point to the fact that in New York during the 1840s and 1850s, working people such as those that were killed at Astor Place tended to see their political future as lying in a hopeful, possible reconciliation of embodiment with political power. The Jacksonian politics of individualism pursued by Tammany Hall expressed the desire of the antebellum working class for *both* access to state power when required and the option to be left alone to live self-determining lives. The working public loathed outward displays of prestige such as the Astor Place Opera House's boxes not because they imposed a surveillance regime that individualized them—after all, individuality was partly the point—but because they were an affront to the Jacksonian democratic ideal of a socially egalitarian space of visible class admixture and interaction.

As previously noted, Melville would also explore this theme in "The Two Temples" (1854), in which, after the narrator climbs the spire of the new Grace Church, the congregation beneath him become a "standing human mass" (Melville, 303). In effect, his regime of vision operates counter to the panoptic principle by turning them into an undifferentiated group rather than individuated subjects, a perspective he calls "sovereign." By contrast, the English theatre of the story's second section is a location of comparatively peaceful mixing between classes that is packed with differentiated figures and social types whose expressions are transparently readable: "quiet, well-pleased working men, and their glad wives and sisters, with here and there an aproned urchin, with all-absorbed, bright face" (310).

If we read Melville's short fiction as deliberately invested in the language of theatre, then rejecting the poststructuralist approach to the class politics of theatrical space has greater implications for interpreting Melville's aesthetics. At the level of form, "The Fiddler," like "The Two Temples," resists the kinds of perspective that Sheila Post-Lauria has identified with *Harper's Magazine*, the very periodical that published it. Post-Lauria has remarked that submissions to the magazine often focused on "aloof, spectator-narrators representing the privileged middle class isolated . . . from the events . . . to observe less fortunate characters from above" (168). By contrast, Melville's work associates this kind of detached aesthetic with an elite power that in its desire for objectivity ultimately screens off, or distorts, the real working-class presence. Instead, the story is structured around a dialogue between the knowable and unknowable, and between vision and invisibility, which reflects the dynamics of Melville's search for literary recognition in the antebellum marketplace. Like the politics of individualism demonstrated by theatre boxes, which operated around a vacillation between visibility and anonymity, Melville's story exhibits a radical uncertainty on behalf of its narrator about whether to participate or to remain distant from events. What might be rendered as uncertainty, or liminality, should be understood as the analogue of the right of the individual to freedom of choice—to not being bundled together into a mass by economic hardship—that was being fought for by figures like Mike Walsh at Tammany Hall.

To possess both individuality and a sense of the power of collective class-based solidarity is one of the key functions served by Hautboy in the text. Described as "juvenile," "animated," and wearing a "bunged beaver," Hautboy is styled on the preeminent, much-loved—and feared—social type of 1850s New York, the Bowery B'Hoy. Indeed, the phonetic possibilities of his name suggest a direct connection. In contemporary works such as Benjamin Baker's popular melodrama *A Glance at New York* (first staged in 1848), the B'Hoy was less an image of degeneracy and gang violence than an "incarnation of republican virtue in an urban setting—fiercely independent, self-reliant, and free" (Lawson, 5). In their theatrical self-fashioning, the Bowery B'Hoys represented an ideal, individual negotiation of class politics in public space. Never fully losing their identity to the mob yet able to retain a certain appealingly raffish aura of the street, Bowery B'Hoys suggested the possible future direction young manhood would take under the conditions of the expanding urban marketplace. The importance of the visual realm of the theatre is asserted when the three figures go to watch the aforementioned clown. In contrast to the stratified and "classed" regimes of vision at "elite" sites like the Astor Place Opera House or within the internalized intellect of the romantic subject, the circus reflects the more egalitarian visuality of the street. As the clown performs, Helmstone's eye is drawn to Hautboy, registering a sentimental connection between his new acquaintance and the performer. The narrator remarks:

> Hautboy was the sight for me. Such genuine enjoyment as his struck me to the soul with . . . the reality of a thing called happiness. . . . Now the foot, now the hand, was employed to attest his grateful applause . . . In a man of forty I saw a boy of twelve; and this too without the slightest abatement of my respect. (258–59)

Against the backdrop of the circus, Hautboy's responses to the show come to resemble the gestural performances of the clown. When Helmstone says, "Now the foot, now the hand was employed to attest his grateful applause" (258), it is as if Hautboy's gestural manner of being in the world mimics the clown's tumbling and expressive performance. To the eye of Helmstone and the reader, the spectator himself becomes a spectacle. A ritual is being enacted in which the viewer and the viewed subject are equally involved in the performance, challenging Helmstone's prior commitment to the power that comes from a purely internalized and detached romantic intellect. For Helmstone, Hautboy is radically embodied through his act of viewing. By viewing the scenes unfolding before him, Hautboy registers the certainty of his position in the world and the sincere pleasure he takes in it. Melville establishes within a theatrical setting the relationship between the spectator and the performance that Ralph Waldo Emerson found in the natural world. In *Nature* (1836) Emerson writes that the "lover of Nature" becomes a "transparent eyeball," "whose inward and outward senses are . . . truly adjusted to each other" (*Nature*, 38). Like Melville, Emerson was concerned about the politically conservative implications of a total disembodiment that sought to transcend nature and removed one wholly from engagement with an ever-changing world. Since for Emerson "God" and "Nature" were part of the same universal essence, to remove oneself from a relationship with the natural world was a hubristic attempt to exceed the reach of God. In Melville's story, Helmstone's evocation of Hautboy's gestural mimicry of the clown highlights the way that in viewing the world one might also interact sincerely with it. Hautboy is, in effect, a participant observer.

Consequently, so as to critique the detached perspective that Post-Lauria associates with *Harper's*, the "most politically conservative and sentimental monthlies of the decade" (165), Melville posits the filial relations of visible and embodied subjects as a radical form of democratic association. Not only is the "rurally ruddy" (258) Hautboy watching the clown, but also Helmstone is watching Hautboy. Additionally, through the use of the first person, the readers of Melville's story are themselves positioned as viewers. The matrix of gazes between the characters serve to draw the reader of the short story into a voluntary, shared experience of viewing not unlike the theatre, undermining the ideal of a disembodied and detached romantic consciousness that had often been designated as the preserve of the elite individual. As a facet of Melville's broader search for a place within the literary marketplace of 1850s New York, this "participatory" form of reading was a perfect aesthetic for the new magazines as they attempted to build national audiences. The ritual of participation in the shared vision of the clown in "The Fiddler" is a synecdoche of the larger project of the antebellum magazines. In the story, as with his diptychs and selected works from *The Piazza Tales*, reading becomes a performative, ritual act among individuals that possesses no immediate or personal means of association.

By historicizing the story in relation to the material culture of its production we see that Melville takes a Rousseauist line with "The Fiddler" in demonstrating how the surrender of individual agency to the participatory realm of the social theatre generates democratic potential through the positive relations of affect. When the story first appeared in *Harper's New Monthly Magazine*, like the majority of antebellum magazine fiction, it contained no attribution to any one author. This has led several critics of "The Fiddler," most notably David R. Eastwood in a 1976 edition of *American Transcendental Quarterly*, to wonder whether Melville was in fact the writer of the tale, seeing in it too little of Melville's supposedly "signature" romantic irony. By a strange process of empirical analysis—there are eight charts and graphs in the article that seek to illustrate "a statistical test of authorship based on Mendenhall's characteristic curve of composition" (Eastwood, 40)—Eastwood finally concludes that it is Melville's story and not Fitz-James O'Brien's, and we can all breathe a sigh of relief. Read through a lens of ritual and social theatre, wherein individual agency is surrendered to the democratic world of affect in the public sphere of transnational print culture, this study of authenticity seems absurd. There is an enticing irony in that this kind of study of authenticity is precisely the target of the narrative of the tale, in which Melville's critique of Helmstone partly rests upon the coupling of his romantic individualism with his desire for personal fame: "I am nobody for ever and ever. Intolerable fate!" (Melville, 258). It is an interesting parallel that Melville himself, famously angered by the cult of individual self-fashioning and celebrity that dominated antebellum print culture, refused to have his image etched onto the frontispiece of his own books, claiming that the individual creator should play second fiddle to their technical accomplishments. In *American Romanticism and the Marketplace* Michael Gilmore claims that Hawthorne and Melville differ considerably in their ideas about the position of the author in relation to their work. Whereas for Hawthorne self-fashioning and personal history was essential (as can be seen in works such as "The Old Manse" and the decision to perform his romantic rejection of the past by changing his name from Hathorne to Hawthorne as a protest against his Puritan ancestors), for Melville it detracted from the truth-telling exercise of literature.

 The narrative ends with a conclusion that "genius" can exist without "fame" in the collective exchanges of music: "Next day I tore all my manuscripts, bought me a fiddle, and went to take regular lessons of Hautboy" (263). Hautboy (whose name is itself an old French name for an oboe) is a conduit, literally a tube for making pleasant sounds. Although this makes him, in effect, an incomplete human being, the author implies that his incompleteness also makes him capable of genius or a form of cultural heroism. Such a treatment of the heroic potential of Helmstone recalls Thomas Carlyle's perspective in his widely read and influential lectures *On Heroes, Heroworship, and the Heroic in History* (1841). In this work, Carlyle noted that the hero must always present an incomplete picture of himself in order that he act as an inspiration to others. The complete human being of the kind that later-century realist literature would find so appealing as a subject, Carlyle reasoned, is weak, fallible, and unsuitable for heroism.

The inevitable brevity of the magazine short story, like the thin characterizations of popular stage melodrama, were therefore powerful forms for the expression of nineteenth-century attitudes to the hero, since the characterization of a person had always to be incomplete so as to make psychological depth secondary to the effects of incident and exchange. This exploitation of the possibilities of short fiction for treatments of the modern hero can be seen in the work of Melville's contemporary Frederick Douglass. Douglass dedicated much of his life to the narrative exploration of heroism inside and outside the condition of slavery, but despite frequent calls to write long-form prose narratives chose the form of the short story/novella to express himself in fiction. *The Heroic Slave* (1852) is a testament to the power of partiality and incompleteness as a requirement of the heroic individual. Madison Washington (Douglass's hero) is not the narrator of the tale and is only encountered at intervals in the story, which serve to highlight his symbolic actions without focusing too considerably on the conflicted nature of his mind beyond that which is expressed through dramatic dialogues to another individual.

Yet this very partiality and the traditional association of the short story with the stage raised unique problems for black authors speaking to white audiences. For Douglass, one of the difficulties of using a black narrator in short fiction was that, unlike with his life-writing, the association of short prose fiction with performance (especially in the context of a post–*Uncle Tom's Cabin* moment) and the complex forms of identification it mobilized always raised the spectre of blackface minstrelsy. For Douglass, in *The Heroic Slave* the partiality of the narrator's vision of Madison Washington allowed him to avoid the problematic forms of identification that were frequently mobilized in fictional works by abolitionists like Lydia Maria Child. In "The Black Saxons" of 1841, Child's repentant slave-owner hero Mr. Duncan is forced to disguise himself in blackface in order to obtain clarifying knowledge about the reality of his slaves' lives. Child's narrative follows Duncan closely, generating a sympathetic identification between a presumably white, presumably racist reader assessing the pro- and antislavery debates in the dominant culture and the fictional slave owner. Consequently, when Duncan dons "a complete suit of negro clothes, and a black mask well fitted to his face" (195) so as to follow his slaves to a Methodist meeting in the woods that serves to cover a conspiracy, the readers too are drawn into participation in this performance, enacted in the skewed pursuit of knowledge about African American culture. What for Child serves as a means to radical sympathy, for Douglass would have only operated within demeaning racial stereotypes and forms. For white abolitionist authors like Child, possessing full knowledge of black experience required possessing blackness in the only form that was socially acceptable, the debased racial parody of minstrelsy.

It is these very concerns that motivate the narrative of Melville's own short story "Benito Cereno," whose final image of the black leader Babo's direct, incomprehensible gaze as his head, that "hive of subtlety," rests on a pike resists the full identification of the reader with the rebel slave. In that story Melville refuses to offer internality precisely because to do so the writer would have had to enact a blackface minstrelsy of his own that would be abusive to the humanity of his African subject. Race is not a key element of "The Fiddler," yet the fundamental logic of partial identification still applies to the form of "otherness" Melville choose to consider: childhood. Instead of offering a full picture of a man, or trying to possess his consciousness, Melville presents Hautboy as a fragment whose power lies in his inspirational affect for Standard and Helmstone. Full identification with Helmstone in the story is, as I will show a little later, ultimately rejected as a mimicry that is, at best, demeaning, and, at worst, unethical. Eastwood's survey mentioned above, and others like it, respond to a residual mid-twentieth-century valorization of individual acts of resistance that inform the earliest texts in the discipline of American studies (like Matthiessen's *The American Renaissance*) and see American literary culture as always opposed to totalitarianism, both left- and right-wing. Such claims are patently ahistorical and say more about the twentieth century's fears of the collective than nineteenth-century print culture's treatment of the body politic. However, "The Fiddler" fits more within a republican culture that prized partial ritualized union than a mid-twentieth-century culture that prized autonomous individualism. In the context of mid-nineteenth-century magazine literature, what is important is not the individual per se but their observation of and participation in a ritual process that establishes that individual as an intersubject shaped by dissemination and a wider collective culture but not wholly absorbed by it.

In fact, so crucial is viewing to the meaning of "The Fiddler" that Helmstone himself remarks, "[I] needed the optical sight of such a man to believe in the possibility of his existence" (Melville, 260). By specifically defining the required "sight" as "optical," Helmstone alludes to the romantic, visionary tradition that had previously dominated his view of the role of the American author. Unlike the fantasy landscapes of the romantic visionary poet, the "ambitious dreamer" (261) Helmstone must confront the force of the real: an "optical sight" and not a speculative one. Indeed, Standard mocks the "visionary" powers of his friend when he says, "Doubtless your own masterly insight has already put you in possession of all" (263). Through Standard's attachment of "insight" to "possession," the author draws attention to Helmstone's own earlier connection between individual vision and individual ownership: "the internalisation of feeling" that is essential to elite conceptions of romantic literary authority. For Helmstone, everything he is able to perceive, he imposes his authority upon. Indeed, the term "insight" perfectly connotes the internalized and ratiocinative form of visual and cultural authority traditionally favored by readers of *Harper's Magazine*. In its place, Melville posits a model of cultural authority that is derived from a playful relation with, rather than critical distance from, unfolding events. It is this desire for "proximity" that returns us finally to Master Betty, whose success as a cultural practitioner was largely dependent upon assumptions about the "honesty" and "purity" of his acting and the sense of participation his performances offered the audience.

When Helmstone remarks, "In a man of forty, I saw a boy of twelve . . . without the slightest abatement of my respect," Melville is connecting embodied performance with "respect" and "respectability." Hautboy is able to perform "successfully" in the world because he is not quite an adult in manner. Helmstone and Standard's attribution of the characteristics of Master Betty to Hautboy derive from his capacity to balance competing registers of experience without self-consciousness, the absolute sincerity of his responses to the world. Hautboy is, in effect, the living embodiment of the nineteenth-century child actor, whose inability to distinguish between acting and playing was the source of his cultural power. Ironically, what should be most contemptible in him—the excessive pleasure he derives from the carnivalesque consumption that associates him with a much-maligned underclass—makes Hautboy the ideal arbiter of cultural authority and literary prestige in antebellum New York. As the narrator says:

> What was sad in the world he did not superficially gainsay; what was glad in it he did not cynically slur; and all which was to him personally enjoyable, he gratefully took to his heart . . . his extraordinary

cheerfulness did not arise either from deficiency of feeling or thought. (Melville, 260)

The liminal position of playful sincerity that Hautboy represents—between childhood and adulthood, the market and the street, English cultural prestige and American democracy—reflects Melville's own search for a workable aesthetic for his magazine fiction. In the narrator's acknowledgement that this liminality is like childhood in its transience, we see Melville confronting the possibility that the varying aesthetic demands placed upon him are untenable in the long term. As a model for literary authorship, Hautboy is ultimately insufficient because, like the music he plays on his violin, he only establishes his claim to cultural authority in the very moment in which it is expressed. However, like the clown's show at the center of the text, it is to these fleeting, ritualized moments of coalescence only possible within a performed medium that the author attributes the status of great art. At the same time, the transience of the experience reflects the demands of the short story genre, upon which Melville had begun to depend financially. By its very nature short and fleeting, reading a short story for Melville resembles the kind of theatricalized and collective experiences venerated in "The Fiddler."

Melville ends the story on a note of irony, which reflects the fact that for all the positive potential embodied in the new magazines, Melville would not find total aesthetic contentment in the form, turning to the religious poetry of pilgrimage in the latter part of his career. After eating lunch at "Taylor's," the group returns to Hautboy's home "in the fifth storey of a sort of storehouse, in a lateral street to Broadway" (262). The very location of Hautboy's house marks him as an embodiment of liminality, a storehouse being both a site of market exchange and a temporary holding place for goods. Upon hearing him play "Yankee Doodle," Helmstone remarks that he has become "a charmed Bruin" under Hautboy's guidance. Rather than precipitating Helmstone's development as an artist, Hautboy transforms him into a dancing bear: carnivalesque, infantilized, and devoid of soulfulness.

Ultimately, Melville's art would move in the direction of a search for more permanence than was possible within both the magazines and the antebellum culture of "sincere" performance that is depicted in "The Fiddler." In the story's final lines, in a passage that seems to modern readers like a foreshadowing of Melville's own pilgrimage to the Holy Land in 1856, Helmstone evokes the exile of Cicero to the East: "If Cicero travelling in the East, found sympathetic solace for his grief in beholding the arid overthrow of a once great city, shall not my petty affair be as nothing" (263). In this short story, Melville confronts the paradox at the center of his art. In Ishmael's conflicted views of Ahab in *Moby-Dick*, as in the pilgrim's response to Christ in *Clarel*, the tension between the growth of the individual that is possible under the guidance of another, and the loss of individuality when one completely emulates their guide, is an ever-present theme in Melville work.

"Bartleby, the Scrivener": Performance, Professionalism, and the Romantic Child

In "From Wall Street to Astor Place: Historicizing Melville's Bartleby," Barbara Foley neatly paraphrases the two dominant critical perspectives that have been taken to the story since interest in it emerged in the mid-twentieth century. Foley notes that critics have either tended to interpret it autobiographically "as an allegory of the writer's fate in a market society, noting specific links with Melville's own difficult authorial career," or as an essentially Marxist "portrait of the increasing alienation of labor in the rationalized capitalist economy that took shape in the mid-nineteenth-century United States" (87), with recent interest in the tale being given over to a discussion of spectrality and the role of the commodity.[4] In addition to these groups it is important to note the continuing recent interest of "Bartleby, the Scrivener" to philosophers (most especially Deleuze and Agamben) who see within Bartleby's signature phrase "I would prefer not to" a study in the possibilities of individual resistance to appropriation by the law. Furthermore, in recent years (following the poststructuralist and feminist turns in literary studies from the 1970s onwards) increasing numbers of critics have sought to approach the text from gendered, psychoanalytical, New Historicist, and other standpoints, with specific attention having been recently placed upon Foucauldian discourses of spatiality.

Despite the overwhelming body of scholarship on the tale, few have attempted to engage with it in a transatlantic context as an experimental study of the limits of romantic and sentimental modes of expression as forces of dissent in mid-nineteenth-century literature. As an exercise in synthesizing these as yet comparatively disparate traditions in scholarship, by situating "Bartleby, the Scrivener" within the context of "The Fiddler," the tale may be reconceived as a satire on the ideological blindnesses and assumptions created by sentimental, romantic, and Gothic traditions in the short story. In their place, Melville proposes a form of melodramatic or theatrical expression, of a type more commonly associated with Charles Dickens, as a means to create collective affect and a positive model of social exchange between individuals. This offers an alternative reading of Bartleby's supposed dissent that highlights his desire to be seen, as opposed to the desire for privacy. Read in this way the story may be understood as enacting the tension between visuality as an individuating and hierarchicalizing discourse of power and the simultaneous importance of public expression to theatricalized dissent against such modern technologies of capitalist control in the mid-nineteenth-century United States. But the story also participates in the discussion conducted more broadly across Melville's short fiction of the hazardous slippages in the transatlantic mind that Elisa Tamarkin has charted between the republican discourse of "deference" and the liberal perception that any ritualized treatment of the body always courts the condition of "dependence."

The story concerns a dramatic conflict that passes between two figures within a legal office over one's decision to refuse, or rather to "prefer not to," fulfil his mandated role to copy important documents. The motif of the law operates in several ways in the text, referring to the historical rise of a class of men with whom it is associated (whose work had moved away from a domestic situation of patronage and towards more corporate structures of capitalism in the nineteenth century) as well as the Rousseauist conception of a society based upon contract rather than familial structures of descent. However, the contractual relationships constituted by the common law do not apply fully in courts of chancery like those in which the narrator is proclaimed to have worked. Chancery courts operate on a judgment of equity by the jurisdiction of a third party (in England the king, in America the Supreme Court). This means that chancery courts are not bound by due process in the same way as other courts. That the narrator is "one of those unambitious lawyers who never addresses a jury, or in any way draws down public applause" (Melville, 18) makes sense in this context. The jurisdiction of a master of chancery is absolute, patriarchal, and privatized. It emerges not from the open discussions of a republican polity but from the will of an individual whose judgment is made on behalf of a divine, or semidivine, ruler. As Charles Dickens shows in *Bleak House*, the Court of Chancery is a profoundly undemocratic institution, operating by precedent without debate. In addition, and as Graham Thompson notes, the importance of the office as a spatial arena "with the power to organize and structure personal and social relationships" (5) cannot be overstated, as it is within the context of a controlled environment that Bartleby's coded performance takes on its meaning.

The two primary combatants in this drama are a lawyer-narrator who is "a rather elderly man" (Melville, 18) coming to the end of his life and who has been notable for his "profound conviction that the easiest way of life is the best" (18), and Bartleby, a young man supposedly at the start of his career who refuses to copy, move, and then eat, resulting finally in his death in prison. When encountering a dead Bartleby in jail at the end of the story, the narrator comments that he was "strangely huddled at the base of the wall, his knees drawn up, and lying on his side . . . nothing stirred" (50). As Pearl Solomon remarks of this passage in *Dickens and Melville in Their Time* (1975):

> [F]aced by the dead walls of brick and flesh which surround him, he chooses to assert his personality and die; and not even to die as a man, but as an unborn child . . . He regresses backward into the womb of time . . . back, also, into the foetal position. (84)

Melville establishes two temporal trajectories in the story that run in opposite directions. The lawyer's narration is focused upon his own aging, while his description of Bartleby's passage through life highlights a non-teleological regression into a childlike state that the narrator perceives as dependence, ending eventually in his death in the "foetal position." Indeed, that the narrative unfolds in the first person (a frequent device of gothic storytelling) is all-important as it excludes Bartleby's own subjectivity from the account at the same time as it renders questionable his position within a larger world of incident and exchange. In effect, the series of causal relations that prefigure the world of the story are left to the conjecture of the narrator as he speculates on Bartleby's past life. This places the focus of the work upon moments of exchange between the narrator and his clerk, the only thing out of which any meaning can be derived. Consequently the story operates within the dramatic tradition of the nineteenth-century American short story that I have sought to define across this book: an economy of spectacle rather than internal coherence, of events and not reflections.

The lawyer-narrator's insistence upon constancy and teleology mark his relationship to a rationalized form of historical, liberal consciousness, while Bartleby's actions render him as meaningful only within the moment of exchange. The narrator's attempts to "write a biography of [Bartleby]"

(Melville, 18) are ultimately flawed because the clerk's meaning is radically embodied, instantaneous, performed, and momentary rather than coherent, rational, and absolute like the life of the narrator. As an experiment in the limits of literary modes in nineteenth-century America, Melville sets these two trajectories against each other in competition for meaning. In the section of the story that precedes "the advent of Bartleby" (Melville, 19), much is made of the theme of age and aging, both through the narrator's admission that he is getting old and the clerk Turkey's defense of his subpar copying by suggesting that "Old age—even if it blot the page—is honorable . . . we *both* are getting old" (21). As the narrator presumably ages in the normal way he comes to read Bartleby as increasingly akin to a child, regressing into a state that is read by the narrator in the way that nineteenth-century British and American audiences read the child actor, as a timeless expression of truth or an outward sign of a "paradoxical exhibition of absolute sincerity" (Varty, 14). Crucially, like the British romantics who when they looked at Master Betty saw an "aesthetic fixity" or sublime truth, Bartleby is always discussed in the narration in terms of his resolute immovability and finally (in the last line of the story) his relationship to a universalized, transcendental humanity: "Ah Bartleby! Ah humanity!" (51).

The narrator of "Bartleby, the Scrivener" is the opposite of Helmstone in "The Fiddler," who comes to see the sublime romantic child as nothing more than a performance. To historicize "Bartleby" sufficiently, one must reconstruct the discourses around literary modes in which the figure of the child plays an important part. It is my contention that Bartleby's resistance ultimately fails because the narrator, informed by romantic and sentimental assumptions with a cultural history, wrongly conflates Bartleby's resistance with discourses surrounding the sublime nature of childhood in the nineteenth century. The lawyer-narrator's subjective individualism renders Bartleby as a figure outside of the political realm of experience and action, the child of the office family that is ultimately seen as dependent upon the narrator himself. This creates an ontological confusion in which it becomes impossible for the narrator to locate Bartleby's actions as those of an equal responding to the immediate effects of his own historical moment and results in a form of social death similar to that which the British romantics unconsciously subjected Master Betty.

Beginning in the 1980s, developments in scholarship on childhood in America by such figures as Karen Sánchez-Eppler and Priscilla Ferguson Clement have sought to demonstrate how the invention of "childhood" as a discrete life stage owes much to the conditions of developing industrial modernity in the nineteenth-century United States, with its associated divisions between "work" and "play." Indeed, Sánchez-Eppler has suggested that changing meanings of childhood even contributed to a broader midcentury challenge to the Jacksonian political order and its conventional interpretation of liberal, autonomous selfhood. She writes:

> Children's dependent state embodies a mode of identity, of relation to family, institution, or nation, that may indeed offer a more accurate and productive model of social interaction than the ideal autonomous individual of liberalism's right discourse ever has. (xxv)

The child's right, so nineteenth-century reformers would argue, was not to a liberal selfhood synonymous with political enfranchisement, work, and, ergo, adulthood, but to dependence—to be looked after, live as though they were loved, and be "free" from the pressures of individual autonomy. Despite attempts by romantic and sentimental thinkers in the nineteenth century to draw clear demarcations between childhood and adulthood around notions of work though, the reality was that the move from individual and artisanal modes of labor to more corporate forms in the middle of the century forced people into forms of association with their employer that resembled, awkwardly, the kinds of dependence that were coming to be seen as the possession of the child in relation to their family, even as the law of contract and free labor asked that associational bonds be more fraternal than paternal. In "Bartleby, the Scrivener," Melville vectors models of political order (republicanism and liberalism), and various interpretations of work (individual and collective), through concepts of childhood and dependence, demonstrating their interrelatedness in the antebellum era. In short, Bartleby's wish to be considered as an autonomous, free-thinking, political subject clashes in the tale with the lawyer-narrator's concept of his workers as a surrogate family—an ideal that is proved to be inseparable in the antebellum imagination from the potentially infantilizing discourse of dependence.

Yet there is even more at play here, since the office is not just a site of familial love but also a site of desire. Graham Thompson notes that the narrator's dream "to protect [Bartleby], to be close to him, to have him for his own, and then to retell the story of their relationship, needs to be considered in relation to sexual desire" (4). The possibility that the lawyer-narrator's scopophilic desire for Bartleby also constitutes a form of unconscious nineteenth-century pedophilia is intriguing. Desire certainly figures centrally in the narrator's relationship to his clerk and this becomes even more troubling when that desire is thought of as pederastic. Extending this logic further, if Bartleby is considered part of the family, an adopted child, then the narrator's desire is not only pederastic but incestuous. It is at the moment that Bartleby dies (also the moment that he is at his most childlike) that the lawyer manifests his desire for him in material terms: "Something prompted me to touch him . . . I felt his hand, when a tingling shiver ran up my arm and down my spine" (Melville, 50). The touch of a dead child elicits a paroxysmal response from the narrator, which constitutes a critique of romanticism's necrophilic child-love. If, as in Russ Castronovo's understanding, the attempt of romantics to fix forever in a sublime state the subject of their gaze unconsciously enacts a form of patriarchal violence against that subject, then the desire of the narrator for his clerk results in a form of social death, which in Bartleby's case becomes the *ne plus ultra* of Gothic transgression (pederasty, necrophilia, and incest all at once). There is at the heart of Melville's story a queer affect, reliant upon the narrator's confusion of childhood and adulthood, mastership and apprenticeship, autonomy and dependence, possession and desire, life and death, and power and love.

The anonymous lawyer-narrator of "Bartleby, the Scrivener" possesses characteristics often associated with the benevolent patriarch of the sentimental genre and the preference of the romantic poet for a peculiar form of child-love. As a master, his clerks appear to him as a surrogate family whose peculiarities he tolerates so long as power ultimately rests with him in matters of importance. The narrator remarks, "at the period just preceding the advent of Bartleby, I had two persons as copyists in my employment, and a promising lad as an office boy" (Melville, 21). Despite the inefficiency of both of his clerks (Turkey and Nippers) at various points every day, the lawyer-narrator's treatment of them is benevolent, Christian, tolerant, and at times even charitable: "One winter evening I presented Turkey with a highly respectable-looking coat of my own" (22). While this does little to alleviate the condition of their poverty through increased wages or structural changes in the nature of labor relations, it demonstrates an affective bond of sorts. The narrator's response to his clerks more closely resembles the filial bonds of the eighteenth-century apprenticeship system than the nineteenth-century condition of wage labor. According to the narrator, the "advent of Bartleby" is sanctioned by an increase in workload resulting from his appointment to a new position of master in chancery. While this results in more clerical and copying work, the narrator does not dismiss his inefficient clerks and employ two more fitting for the level of work newly required, even though the speed at which Bartleby answers the advertisement suggests that there are plenty of unemployed clerks in the city. Instead, perhaps out of this filial loyalty, the lawyer keeps Turkey and Nippers on (still presumably only operating at the level of efficiency of one good man) and employs another: Bartleby. The excess wages required to keep on an inefficient clerk, or not promote the "lad" that is so bright and "promising" to fill the position on a lower wage, does not suggest uncaring, utilitarian capitalism but the affection of a master for his apprentices or a father for his children. A purely pragmatic, if somewhat callous, nineteenth-century employer would have merely relied upon child labor. But the lawyer-narrator is not that callous. He actually suffers, much like Amasa Delano in "Benito Cereno," with a certain form of blindness reliant upon his liberal politics and emotional sentimentalism. The arrangement of the office is not (like the factory in "The Tartarus of Maids") that of a ruthless capitalist institution in the mid-nineteenth-century mold. In fact, rather than resembling the American model of capitalist labor relations, as Michael Gilmore notes, "the lawyer's chambers . . . have a distinctly English flavor" (133) that is a patriarchal ideal of master and apprentice. Indeed, Turkey's submissive responses to his master when confronted about his frequent errors play upon the lawyer-narrator's patriarchal sense of entitlement: "With submission, sir, it was generous of me to find you in stationary on my own account" (Melville, 24).

In Pearl Solomon's reading of the story:

> [T]he master-workman relationship is almost as important in the nineteenth-century as that of father and son . . . the relationship between Bartleby and his master is unconsummated, almost non-existent, each one living enclosed in his own identity or will; the master not in any way paternal, nor the clerk filial. (11)

Solomon's critique of "Bartleby, the Scrivener" rests upon assumption that alterations in the structure of capitalist relations in the nineteenth century came to the exclusion of all bonds of affection. I would argue that it is rather that new forms of affect were established that sought to replace the purely hierarchical modes of association with more corporate forms of affiliation between men. In other words, fraternalism, with its more egalitarian bond of brother to brother, replaced the patriarchal order of the eighteenth century. At the point at which Bartleby enters the narrative there is a strong sense of filial affection operating in the "chambers at No.—Wall-street" (Melville, 19). In fact, the lawyer-narrator's attitude to labor relations is an oddly outmoded paternalism that is stifling, not for its lack of affection but for its peculiar commitment to constancy, regularity, and order organized around a central father figure.

When Bartleby arrives in the office the lawyer immediately performs two actions that mark him as an archetype of an outdated form of sentimental patriarchy. Firstly—and immediately following a description of Bartleby as he first appears—the narrator remarks that dividing his office from the workspace of his clerks are "ground glass folding-doors" (21). It is the narrator's decision to specify that the doors are only partially transparent that is interesting in this claim. Graham Thompson reads these doors as instituting a regime of visibility that "is not entirely equivalent to the forms of visibility instituted in the Panopticon" (7) but is reliant upon an institutionalized discourse of surveillance among workers in an office: the assumption of surveillance rather than its actualization. The ground-glass doors suggest that visibility to the lawyer is not especially important to his model of an ideal working environment, while also implying a form of partial sight or ideological blindness that results from his assumptions. Instead, the lawyer prefers control to be maintained by an aural regime, an exercise that in the nineteenth century carried a worrying association with the monarchical proclamation and assumed power of tyrannical rulers. The lawyer-narrator "prefers" to holler for his clerks when they are needed, rather than have them always visible. He remarks, "I resolved to assign Bartleby a corner by the folding-doors, but on my side of them, so as to have this quiet man within easy call" (Melville, 24). The lawyer's control of his clerks is not implemented through vision but through sound, or else by means of paper decrees.[5] Through this process his clerks become increasingly invisible to him, especially since the location of Bartleby's desk and screen interrupts the lawyer's visual field. His clerks are his children but, unlike the popular proverb, they are neither seen nor heard.

This also has the effect of disembodying the narrator, turning him into an anonymous force to his clerks. As Elizabeth Barnes remarks of eighteenth- and early nineteenth-century political culture, "rhetoric habitually locate[d] patriarchal authority in the disembodied unspecific male who stands for both the individual and the collective at once" (8). The lawyer appropriates his clerks and becomes synonymous with the office itself, which is an extension of his subjectivism; it is *his* office as if no one else works there. That the lawyer-narrator is never named is therefore appropriate to the form of power he typifies. Taking Hautboy in "The Fiddler" as an example of Melville's ideal mid-nineteenth-century cultural hero (one whose body becomes centrally implicated in his exchanges with the world), in the context of Melville's fiction the lawyer-narrator's actions regress him into an older model of power. In effect the lawyer-narrator becomes a tyrant/patriarch, albeit one reliant upon an assumed familial affection for him among his employees. In this way he resembles Old Bach in "The Tartarus of Maids" in his assumption that his laborers work for him out of love rather than necessity. Furthermore, if we take the New York office of "Bartleby" as akin to the ships of his other fiction (that is as a partial reflection of a larger state structure) then the lawyer-narrator's actions turn his office into a model of eighteenth-century sentimental political culture: paternalistic, hierarchical, and reductive in its confusion of the complex exchanges of democratic culture with a sense of familial affection. Love is not in abeyance in the office of the master in chancery—it is, for the author, merely the wrong kind of love.

Unlike the fear associated with surveillance in the twentieth and twenty-first centuries, visibility emerged in mid-nineteenth-century literature as the preferred form of sensory engagement with the world. In theatre's ritualized use of gesture and socially ratified performance in the creation of meaning, visuality becomes less a subject of distrust than a force for progressive social change. Vision for the dramatist, unlike Foucauldian and other poststructuralist discourses, has a modality that at once allows for registration and its functional opposite, a performed self. However, both enact the most important purpose of the dramatic aesthetic: the visibility of one body of people to another. Registration is less a fear in drama than invisibility, which always results in some manner of social death through the exclusion of the subject from a world of exchange and contact. There is, though, one important caveat. The romantic mode that developed out of sentimentalism in the late eighteenth century, even though it tends to be reliant on a form of vision, causes social death by turning the body into a sublime force of perpetual serenity and isolating it from Enlightenment concepts of free exchange with the world. The lawyer-narrator oscillates within the story between these two discourses, either refusing to "see" Bartleby and the other clerks (hiding them behind a screen) or seeing them as sublime, such as when he equates the young man with his "pale plaster-of-paris bust of Cicero" (Melville, 26). This may also be said of other of *The Piazza Tales*, especially "Benito Cereno" and "The Piazza," both of which deal with the modality of the visual—the power of surveillance and the power afforded the observed subject through the performance of identity. In "Benito Cereno," Babo's power lies in the fact that Amasa Delano's liberal form of individualism forces him to perceive Babo's relationship with Cereno as one of dependence, when in fact he is performing the expressive actions of a dependent individual to cover his tracks. Babo affords especial comparisons with Bartleby as both manipulate visibility in interesting ways: Babo through his performance of a slave's subservience and Bartleby, as I will show, through his theatrical desire to be seen. Both of these figures constitute a critique of romantic or sentimental discourses of the visual that assume ownership of the subject of the gaze by the viewer, or, at least, their internal coherence. Considered from the point of view of theatre and ritual, however, in which selfhood is constituted through socially ratified performance, visibility can also offer opportunities to the viewed subject to manipulate the viewer's gaze.

The internal world of the office is doubled in the outside world of Wall Street when Bartleby denies the lawyer-narrator access to his office later in the tale. He states "of a Sunday, Wall-Street is deserted as Petra; and every night of every day it is an emptiness" (33). As Michael Gilmore remarks of "Bartleby, the Scrivener,"

> Melville's tale is concerned, then, with the invisibility of one class to another . . . The New York of Melville's narrator evidently permits a prosperous resident to travel from his home to his place of work without ever encountering a working-class neighbourhood or even setting his eyes on a workman outside the office. (140)

This "invisibility" does not always simply mean absolute exclusion from sight but might also be taken to suggest a form of vision that turns a historically contingent body in motion into a fixed object of transcendental individuation. Like Irving in his appeals for an embodied form of social exchange to overcome Revolutionary cultural amnesia, or Poe's calls for transparency in class relations through gesture, the author's ultimate appeal is towards a new spectacular and embodied form of political protest for the working and lower-middle classes that moderates between the invisibility they had under the benevolent patriarchy of eighteenth-century political culture and the devastating sublime of nineteenth-century romanticism.

Historicizing the story, Barbara Foley shows that the 1840s and 1850s were a time in which labor activists in New York were performing acts of passive resistance as a protest against the unfair capitalist practices of figures such as John Jacob Astor, the very man through whose good grace it is implied that the lawyer obtains his position in the chancery in "Bartleby." Through squatting and what would in another age be called "sit-ins," prominent activists like "Mike Walsh, an omnipresent radical of the 1840s" (91), attempted to resolve labor disputes without resorting to the kinds of mob violence that characterized the frequent nativist attacks on immigrant Irish laborers. In the context of his response to the Astor Place Riot, through Bartleby's "theatrical" actions Melville depicts an ideal form of protest that modulates between the sublime political violence of a rioting mob and the absolute neglect of the working and lower-middle classes by the highest echelons of elite New York patrician culture. Melville's ideal elites are not disembodied but rather complicit in a theatricalized social ritual that binds man to man and class to class. Because of his continual fears of mob violence and his turn towards forms of elite cultural leadership, "respectability" is crucial to Melville's aesthetic. Bartleby's "pallidly neat, pitiably respectable" (Melville, 24) self-presentation makes him an ideal figure for enacting Melville's preferred form of social protest. Melville's art therefore comes close to the project of mid-nineteenth-century British authors, who, as Gilmore suggests "commonly saw their role as one of bridging the gulf of separation through literature . . . they felt that they could restore a spirit of trust and caring among the classes" (141). In the case of Charles Dickens, Edward Bulwer-Lytton, and to a lesser extent Benjamin Disraeli, this caring spirit relied upon overt and theatrical performances of character that marked one as a clearly "readable" entity in the wider social world.

It is following the lawyer's actions, which render partially invisible Bartleby and the other clerks, that Bartleby enacts the first stage of his resistance. The author's description of events is worth quoting at length:

> One object I had in placing Bartleby so handy to me behind the screen, was to avail myself of his services on . . . trivial occasions. It was on the third day, I think, of his being with me, and before any necessity had arisen for having his own writing examined, that, being much hurried to complete a small affair I had at hand, I abruptly called to Bartleby. In my haste and natural expectancy of instant compliance, I sat with my head bent over the original on my desk, and my right hand sideways, and somewhat nervously extended with the copy, so that immediately upon emerging from his retreat, Bartleby might snatch it and proceed to business without delay . . . Bartleby in a singularly mild, firm voice, replied, "I would prefer not to." (Melville, 25)

Commanding Bartleby with his voice (the first time this has been required), the lawyer has his eyes down as he tries to hand the paper to his clerk. This implies that Melville's narrator wishes to deny Bartleby's right to be seen. In the context of a culture that prizes the visual and the external and in which self is constituted through a series of socially ratified performances, the lawyer effectively denies Bartleby's condition as human by his refusal to see him. In turn, Bartleby's resistance forces the lawyer to "ris[e] in high excitement, and crossing the room with a stride" (25) come behind the screen and look at his clerk. Following this act the narrator's description of Bartleby is fascinating in its attention to detail: "His face was leanly composed; his grey eye dimly calm . . . not a wrinkle of agitation rippled him" (25). The lawyer looks at Bartleby in this moment and Bartleby, we can assume by reference to his own calm, fixed gaze, looks back. At this moment the two figures are involved in a shared act of viewing and being viewed that resembles the ritualized exchanges of the drama.

Gilles Deleuze and Giorgio Agamben have both read Bartleby's phrase "I would prefer not to" as a powerful act of ambivalence. For these critics Bartleby holds up the action of power in a capitalist system by refusing to resort to the binary logics that are the philosophical bases of modern power. However, this form of deconstruction bequeaths a legacy similar to the ideal sublime state of European romantic thought, focusing on suspension rather than a process or a physical act of exchange. Instead, Bartleby's actions have meaning precisely because they have particular historical resonances that are both real and literary: Mike Walsh's labor activism and the theatrical traditions of the mid-nineteenth-century short story. As Alexander Cooke has recently noted:

> Neither Agamben nor Deleuze adequately considers the process of a constituted figure *saying* to the law: "I would prefer not to" . . . Neither addresses the question of the conditions for the *event* of resistance performed in "Bartleby, the Scrivener." (87)

Rather than consider the tale as a philosophical treatise on the possibilities, or impossibilities, of a language of dissent, Cooke considers the importance of Bartleby's actions *as* resistance. Bartleby's act of resistance is ultimately theatrical, corresponding more closely to drama's valorization of spectacle than to modern deconstruction's resistance to binary logics of control. To "prefer not to" is more powerful than to "refuse" for Melville because, even as it channels a spirit of resistance, it does so under the auspices of oft-sought middle-class republican ideals of politeness and courtesy. At several points the narrator remarks that Bartleby's effectiveness results from the respectable and well-mannered execution of his protest: "it was his wonderful mildness chiefly, which not only disarmed me, but unmanned me . . . Bartleby was an eminently decorous person" (Melville, 32). What motivates Bartleby is less a transcendental model of philosophical protest than a historically contingent desire for a form of visibility that recognizes the validity of deference as an expression of political selfhood. In addition, he wishes to see the body of his employer and thereby enact a ritual of exchange in which the performed bonds of republican brotherhood can replace the structured hierarchies of sentimental paternalism.

This pattern is repeated several times in the course of the narrative. Each time the narrator hollers for Bartleby he is confronted with an act of resistance from his clerk: "I would prefer not to." In turn, each time this happens the narrator looks again at Bartleby and considers the importance of what he has done, either insofar as it relates to the clerk's assumed mental or physical state, or what the narrator feels he has done to deserve such dissent. Up to a certain point the protest works and the lawyer-narrator recounts his disturbed state and the additional time he has to take away from his work to personally carry out the tasks that Bartleby is paid to do.

The interruption to this process comes when the lawyer-narrator discovers that Bartleby lives in his office. Following this discovery, the narrator states, "revolving all these things, and coupling them with the recently discovered fact that he made my office his constant abiding place and home . . . a prudential feeling began to steal over me" (34), before remarking that this feeling "disqualified me for the time from church-going" (34). As Thompson notes, "the nature of these 'special thoughts' and 'strange discoveries' would seem to be tied up intimately with this desire the lawyer-narrator is directing towards Bartleby" (16). What disqualifies the lawyer from churchgoing is a pederastic desire that stems from his simultaneous equation of Bartleby with the figure of the boy-child in the fraternal space of the office and the sublime, otherized, dependent object of desire. If, as I have suggested, the clerks function as a surrogate family for the lawyer-narrator, then the new scrivener destabilizes the family unit by adding another child. However, unlike Nippers, Turkey, and Ginger Nut, who have all been legitimized by the process of time and experience, the legacy of that child is questionable. The uncanny horror that comes from Bartleby's refusal to move is the horror of an old man who discovers he has taken possession of an unknown child for whom he has a peculiar desire. Such a fear reflects the destabilizing effect of the short story form upon preexisting antebellum hierarchies of reading. Bartleby, like Hautboy and the short story form itself, possesses something of the aura of the culture of the street: unverifiable, partially anonymous, and potentially illegitimate. Much as the short story was something that emerged from the market but was increasingly being found in the middle-class home, so too does Bartleby take up residence in the lawyer's private space. After discovering that Bartleby has taken up full residence in the private familial space of the office, the lawyer-narrator decides to question his scrivener about where he was born—in effect, his legitimacy within the family. The lawyer asks, "Will you tell me Bartleby, where you were born?" (Melville, 35) and is confronted with a further statement of "I would prefer not to."

Bartleby's refusal to acquiesce to this request and recount his history places him in a new relational discourse with the narrator; he becomes a troubling, illegitimate child within the office family. Not long after this, and following a further bout of refusals to work, the narrator remarks, "he seemed alone, absolutely alone in the universe . . . a bit of wreck in the mid-Atlantic" (38). The narrator's reference to solitude and to Atlantic crossing suggests that Bartleby is understood in terms of migrancy and orphanhood, but it also raises the question of how the meaning of English-like deferential, theatrical expressions of connection might be misread in the new liberal, individualistic American context. This infantilizes him further and renders his protest null and void, since the tactics of his theatricalized dissent requires the lawyer to recognize him as a fellow man, not a foreigner, child, or sublime other. The orphan child, Elizabeth Dill reasons, "is the ultimate democratizing force that challenges the superiority of family in a republic as one who only ever elects a family" (716). But Bartleby's right to choose his own family, the ultimate democratic act of agency, is scuppered by the narrator's desire to either possess him or render him as an unrepresentable other. At the point that Bartleby is constituted by the narrator's conscience as a sublime, orphan child and placed into a representational space of transcendent otherness, the scrivener's fate is sealed. Despite the narrator's attempt to tear himself away from the object of his desire, the horror of that desire will haunt him, forcing a recurrence of the event through the act of writing and then publishing his story. The desire of the narrator for this sublime child resembles the desire of Wordsworth and Hazlitt for Master Betty, which resulted finally in the boy's inability to fulfil their expectations and his social death.

In "Bartleby, the Scrivener" the narrator's mind oscillates between two modes of discourse in relation to Bartleby, which reflect the sentimental and romantic modes in mid-nineteenth-century literature. Firstly, Bartleby is rendered as a child by the conflation of office hierarchy with familial and domestic structure. Secondly, he is rendered as a sublime orphan and captured in a static state that is, as Castronovo suggests, the transformation of the political subject into a social corpse. In the narrator's slippage between these two forms, what Melville proposes is a third, more democratic, representational space that does not assume the ownership of the viewed subject by the viewer, either through the assumption of patriarchy or the annihilation of their historical contingency, but instead recognizes each man as a social being whose humanity rests upon performances that render them as subjects in relational discourse to others.

CHAPTER 5

"*Contending for an Empire*"
Performing Sincerity in Hawthorne's New England

> Bright were the days at Merry Mount when the Maypole was the banner-staff of that gay colony. They who reared it, should their banner be triumphant, were to pour sunshine over New England's rugged hills and scatter flower-seeds throughout the soil. Jollity and gloom were contending for an empire.
>
> —Nathaniel Hawthorne, "The Maypole of Merry Mount" (1837)

> On the one side we have critics who, like Melville, respond at least metaphorically to the Calvinist language and overtones in Hawthorne; who judge that Hawthorne in some sense really believed in the ideas which order (or disrupt) the lives of his characters. On the other side are those who, like James . . . interpret Hawthorne's "play" with Puritanism as a sign of the distance between literature and reality or belief. Thus two rather different Hawthornes have competed for critical empire.
>
> —Michael Colacurcio, *The Province of Piety*

In "The Maypole of Merry Mount," the fifth story of *Twice-Told Tales* (1837) (a collection whose very name evokes the performative, oratorical qualities of short story narrative), Hawthorne presents the reader with a dramatized account of two distinct forces competing for "the future complexion of New England" (32) in the seventeenth century. The first community the author introduces are the "the lightsome hearts of Merry Mount" (29), a colony not far from the austere Puritan-controlled Boston and an embodiment of the "old mirth of Merry England" (30), an imaginary time before the Puritan ascendancy. The people of Merry Mount live in a perpetual state of festivity in which "May, or her mirthful spirit, dwelt all the year round ... sporting with the summer months and revelling with autumn and basking in the glow of winter's fireside" (29). Hawthorne renders Merry Mount as a site of perpetual license "where jest and delusion, trick and fantasy, kept up a continual carnival" (31) and in which revellers unendingly dance around a maypole in a range of elaborate masks and costumes. "On the shoulders of a comely youth," writes Hawthorne, "uprose the head and branching antlers of a stag; a second ... had the grim visage of a wolf; a third ... showed the beard and horns of a venerable goat" (30). The Merry Mount celebrations are presented as a strange fusion of Catholic carnival, English folkdance, Anglican wedding service, and Native American ritual, in which "Gothic monsters" wearing "red noses pendulous before their mouths" (30) are mixed together with "Grecian" cross-dressing rites of Comus and Indian celebrations of the hunt. Hawthorne presents the dance of the Merry Mounters around the maypole as evidence of the community's commitment to a philosophy of pleasure. However, as two of the Merry Mount community (Edith and Edgar) come to realize, the confused nature of their festivities renders this philosophy "vague and unsubstantial" and the "shapes of our jovial friends ... visionary and their mirth unreal" (31). Within the context of their battle with the Puritans, the mixed nature of their rituals and the centripetal effect of their maypole dervish establishes the revellers as an image of the pure immanence of the body bound to the earth: festivity without higher meaning.

Into this sketch of Merry Mount several antagonists are introduced: a "band of Puritans who watched the scene, invisible themselves [who] compared the masques to those devils and ruined souls with whom their superstition people the black wilderness" (30). By positioning them within the woods and making them "invisible themselves," Hawthorne makes Endicott and the other Puritans' perspectives correspond to the panoptic critical distance imagined by the nineteenth-century sketcher or the official state investigator: to see and yet remain unseen. As Elaine Hadley characterized Wordsworth's poetry, the romantic intellect (synonymous in Hawthorne with the Puritan imagination) casts the subject "in the position of a spectator, potentially encountering that position's unique obstructions to the operation of sympathetic recognition" (26). In this way Hawthorne alludes to a tradition of Puritan resistance to the immanence of the body as the prison of a transcendent soul that Ralph Waldo Emerson later typified in his desire in "Nature" (1836) for disembodiment: to become a "transparent eye-ball ... part and particle of God" (39). Gazing through the woods at the maypole dance, Hawthorne presents the Puritans as so committed to subjectivity and internal reflection as to become an "invisible" force: transcendent, disembodied, and unverifiable, while the Merry Mount community becomes, conversely, immanent and bound to earthly or animal forms. Eric Voegelin notes of the seventeenth-century Puritan revolt against the Church of England in *The New Science of Politics* (1952) that it emerged from an impatient desire for disembodiment—a "Gnostic," vainglorious, and radical will to force the earthly world of man to correspond with the transcendent world of God.

Although Puritans preached the New Testament "Covenant of Grace," which argued that salvation was justified by faith alone and Christ's sacrifice was for all human sin, in reality many Puritans actually practiced a "Covenant of Works" in which salvation was conditional upon obedience, and punished on earth those who transgressed against God. The "Antinomian Controversy" of the mid-seventeenth century revolved around Anne Hutchinson's claims that most Puritan ministers actually preached a modified form of the "Covenant of Grace," which was politically motivated to preserve hierarchical power. In place of the "Covenant of Works," which required subservience to the laws of the church rather than those of scripture, Hutchinson professed to have a personal relationship with God that more closely resembled the commitment to individualism over collective or hierarchical church worship that Puritans doctrinally professed but seldom, in actuality, abided by. Like the Quakers, who similarly rejected hierarchy in favor of the inward movement of the spirit, Hutchinson was banished from Boston for her radical views.

This confusion of Covenants is described by Eric Voegelin as a "Scriptural camouflage" that

> cannot veil the drawing of God into man. The saint is a Gnostic who will not leave the transfiguration of the world to the grace of God beyond history but will do the work of God himself, right here and now, in history. (147)

The Puritan Gnostic impulse toward disembodiment and the conversion of earthly matter into transcendental spirit resulted in a form of identity that Elaine Hadley characterizes as typifying the elite vision of the later "romantic mode." "The romantic subject's internalization of feeling and virtue," writes Hadley, "still results in a form of identity that is seen to be private and essential, the exclusive possession of the individual" (33). As for the transcendentalists who followed them two hundred years later, individualism, disembodiment, and radical reform shared a crucial mental space in the Puritan mind.

In the epigraph to the tale, Hawthorne writes, "the grave pages of our New England annalists have wrought themselves almost spontaneously into a sort of allegory" (29). As myth-and-symbol critics like Richard Chase and Yvor Winters have adduced, the Puritan origin of American experience is often manifested in literature by means of a heightened sense of the allegorical dimensions of storytelling. Reflecting on this tradition, Russell Reising summarized this position in *The Unusable Past: Theory and the Study of American Literature*. "Since human conduct is predetermined by God as either all good or all evil," writes Reising, "experience is reduced to an allegory in which moral choice is lacking" (59). In fact, from the earliest critiques of Hawthorne there has been a belief that his use of allegory is "evidence" of his Calvinistic mind. In Edgar Allan Poe's famous remarks on *Twice-Told Tales*, he states that:

> [W]e find [Hawthorne] monotonous at decidedly the worst of all possible points—at the point which, having the least concern with Nature, is the farthest removed from the popular intellect . . . I allude to the strains of allegory which completely overwhelm the greater number of his subjects. (*Essays and Reviews*, 225)

For Poe, the domination of allegory established Hawthorne as at odds with the popular taste and sentiment: an anachronistic marker of the "elite" culture that typified Puritan attitudes towards the world. In his famous review of Hawthorne, Poe suggests that the central flaw at the heart of Hawthorne's work in the short story is a didactic moralism that was quite unlike Poe's own emphasis on purely aesthetic elements such as unity of effect and tone. As G. R. Thompson has noted, Poe's attention to emotion, sensation, and "dramatized tension or suspense" ("Literary Politics and the 'Legitimate Sphere': Poe, Hawthorne, and the 'Tale Proper,'" 178) in the story, over and above moral purpose, was specifically directed against Hawthorne's own religiously inflected allegorism. Yet in rendering Hawthorne as the heir of Calvinist New England didacticism, Poe was engaging in a very deliberate and self-conscious misreading designed to set his own theory of fiction in direct opposition to the emerging "Northeastern literary establishment . . . [and] Boston and New York cliques" (179). As a friend of James Fields and James O'Sullivan, Hawthorne was damned in Poe's eyes by association with what the Whiggish Southern author saw as the taint of "Young America's" idealism and Concord transcendentalist mysticism. Indeed, Poe even sharpened this critique between 1842 and 1847. In his third review of Hawthorne's work (written after the publication of *Mosses from an Old Manse*), Poe "pronounce[d] Hawthorne still to be a man of 'genius' but limited by a narrowness of theme and mode that derives from the undue influence of the quacks of the literary establishment" (183). Poe's own critical attitude, then, which might have more comfortably brought Hawthorne into the fold of his theory of the short story in America, draws distinctions between his stories and Hawthorne's based on personal vendettas and bugbears, despite some similarity in aesthetic techniques. What Poe misses deliberately in "The Maypole of Merry Mount" is that Hawthorne's tale is an allegorical reworking of the biblical story of Adam and Eve's expulsion from the Garden of Eden, but with a central caveat that takes the story away from the Puritan, moralizing tradition in which good and evil are judged against a sublime, universal standard. In Hawthorne's rendering, Adam and Eve, reimagined as the "Lord and Lady of May," Edith and Edgar, are innocents punished by harsh Puritans who believe they are enacting the will of God on earth. The role of judgment upon transgression is passed to Endicott, whose Puritan philosophy resembles Eric Voegelin's image of the Gnostic: an elite figure whose desire to make heaven correspond with earth results in a utopian campaign of violence towards the material world. From the first, Hawthorne's allegory is morally ambiguous, a challenge as much to the Puritans as an Old Testament God whose judgment was swift and vicious. Hawthorne uses an allegorical framework to denounce all impulses towards violent reform. As Amy Schrager Lang convincingly argues of Holgrave in *The House of the Seven Gables* (1851) in *The Syntax of Class*, Hawthorne ultimately rejected all utopian schemes, religious, moral, or social, as weak masks of a vulgar desire for revenge against history. Lang writes:

> Holgrave reveals in his radical reformism a naïve rejection of history, a desire to free the present from the domination of the past, to make everything anew . . . But desire to erase the past is in him inextricably and paradoxically bound to a desire to avenge it, the impulse toward utopian reform is compromised by the impulse toward revenge. (39)

Indeed, Hawthorne's tale is not just a critique of Puritan violence, it is also a challenge to a history of New World writing to which the Puritans were absolutely wedded. As Sacvan Bercovitch and others have shown, Puritanism has been overdetermined in readings of American history because of, among other things, their high levels of literacy and preference for writing and documenting events from their own religious perspective. If one pronouncement might be made about the *Twice-Told Tales*, it is their profound discomfort with written history—which is always undercut in the stories by an appeal to a competing logic of the performing body—what people do, not merely what they say or write. As such, Hawthorne's urge to dramatize history (to make history histrionic) in his tales corresponds to the tradition of resistance to written language I have argued is a pronounced tendency in the short story in America after Irving. By suggesting that these events from New England history "wrought themselves *spontaneously* into a sort of allegory," the author implies that little force had to be applied to history to make it correspond with his desire for "a philosophic romance." While the Puritan vision of allegory was writerly and involved a violent reshaping of human experience into symbols and moral absolutes, Hawthorne applies little force, suggesting that the story is a product of the felicitous processes of human history; it is a "*sort* of allegory," not a true allegory, precisely. In so doing, Hawthorne distances himself from the elitist, Puritan desire to impose the will of God, as they imagined it to be, upon human experience—a desire commensurate with the traditional practices of writing history. Hawthorne's narrative voice is that of a cataloguer of events, but yet not an imposer of transcendental, moral frameworks upon reality. In this way Hawthorne's narration chimes with the central concerns of drama, which always situates "law and morality in a public performative space inhabited by social and familial feelings rather than within the private spaces of individuals or in God" (Hadley, 71). Like Irving before him, history for Hawthorne becomes a force in which to locate fluid and mutable forms of identity, rather than something that must be reworked through text in order that one might fix "truth" for all time as transcendent and inviolate.

Rather than imagining authorial identity as constructed through the individual labor of a single, coherent, imaginative subject, as in much romantic art, Hawthorne's use of history places the author within a collective narrative space of incident and exchange. Indeed, Hawthorne presents the tale as the product of a natural creative process achieved in history without undue struggle or force. Unlike the broader romantic and transcendentalist tradition, which transformed the intense individual experiences of the Puritan conversion narrative into secular forms of literary epiphany and sought to remove the individual subject from the material concerns of human history, Hawthorne replaced vigorous moral reflection with a fluid process of creation crucially dependent upon the ephemeral moments within that human history. In making reference to his source materials "Strutt's Book of English Sports and Pastimes" and "pages of New England annalists" (29) Hawthorne establishes his authorial identity not as a true original making everything in his image but as a semiprofessional historian of New England culture. As Michael Colacurcio has usefully argued in *The Province of Piety*, Hawthorne saw himself, firstly, as a historian whose "most original insights were more empirically historical than speculatively moral or theological" (14).

Much as Irving saw the romantic elevation of the mind, and the epistemological power of writing, as a potential source of nationalistic violence in Jefferson, so Hawthorne in "The Maypole of Merry Mount" equates Puritan resistance to the body with both a destructive urge to annihilate life and with the act of the author imposing moral frameworks upon reality. Enraged at what they imagine is a demonic masquerade, resembling both the rural spring rites of the England they had abandoned and the "perversions" of Catholic carnival, the Puritans, led by the "Puritan of Puritans . . . Endicott himself" (32) attack the colony, strike down the maypole, and brand and crop the ears of several of their enemies. The Puritan reaction to the revellers is presented as a continuation of Puritan resistance to most forms of ritual activity. Favoring internal subjectivity and deep reflection on the nature of the sublime over outward, embodied expressions of sentiment, Puritan culture, and the culture of New England well into the nineteenth century, opposed most forms of ritual activity and theatre, seeing in gesture and theatricality traces of the "vulgar" Catholic Old World. As Karen Halttunen notes:

> The sixteenth-century Puritan revolt against the Anglican Church was established on the pulpit and the Bible against the altar and the Eucharist—on the articulate power of the word as opposed to the inarticulate power of symbol and ceremonial ritual. The English Puritans were drawn largely from the rising middle classes, and pagan rituals were the cultural earmarks of English peasantry and the urban lower classes. The Anglican Eucharist, the courtly masque, and the Dionysian peasant revel were all linked together in the Puritan mind. (156)

Although at first reading "The Maypole of Merry Mount" seems to be a simple story fictionalizing a genuine, historical instance of Puritan brutality, when read with an eye to the contemporary circumstances of its production, the tale dramatizes Hawthorne's self-conscious, aesthetic negotiations with literary production in antebellum America. Embedded within this seventeenth-century battle is a history of transnational, religious, and class conflict that can be seen to influence Hawthorne's own literary production in the nineteenth century. Antiritualistic and antitheatrical attitudes remained prevalent among the New England upper-middle classes in the nineteenth century, even as other northern cities like New York and Philadelphia, as well as the southern cities of Richmond, Baltimore, and Savannah, were developing complex and rich cultures of theatre. This was especially true of many of the New England literary elites who, after the publication of Emerson's "Nature" in 1836 and the emergence of transcendentalism on the national scene, underwent a renewal of interest in a similar concept of the sublime that had motivated their Puritan ancestors. However, as Odai Johnson has suggested, it was not that Boston was inherently antitheatrical. Indeed, theatre and performance of all sorts were well known in New England from colonization onwards. It was rather that the historiography of American literary history has presented a skewed picture of events. Because legal documents and official histories were often written by elites, who often opposed performance so as to assert their power and influence over the populace, and these documents were selected for preservation in archives, the record is biased in favor of a narrative of Massachusetts's antitheatricalism. Consequently, "The Maypole of Merry Mount" does not tell a universal truth about New England attitudes across all time, so much as perform an antielitist rewriting of New England history that includes space for the experiences of performing bodies. It demonstrates that antitheatricalism was often a product of a desire for control of space—of "contending for an empire" that was not intellectual alone but very physical and very real. Indeed, the true history of Merry Mount involves nearby Boston attempting to assert its power over a dissenting neighbor. Additionally though, in presenting the Puritans as middle-class interlopers into the festivities of an English peasantry, Hawthorne alludes to the class status of Puritanism's nineteenth-century literary inheritors, the Boston Brahmins and New England transcendentalists, who were in the process of aligning nationalism with the upper-middle-class impulse towards moral reform.

This "Gnostic" character of Puritan faith to which Hawthorne alludes in the tale would find its most vocal exponent in Ralph Waldo Emerson, whose individual-focused interpretation of transcendentalism, after the publication of "Nature," was increasingly being seen by critics as something of an orthodoxy. Although it was not fully developed until *Essays: First Series* in 1841, the most "Gnostic" of Emerson's theories was the concept of "Compensation"—the idea that the universe was shaped by a cosmic balance and every internal thought was equally matched by an external force: "[the] soul, which within us is a sentiment, outside of us is a law" (*Essays*, 86). At the core of this philosophy was a similarly elitist attitude as that of Puritan Gnosticism, which had two possible effects: either it resulted in certain political quietude attendant upon a belief in the status quo as the expression of a natural order, or else cultivated a sense that the movements of the spirit *must* have earthly effects or else face the disruption of the cosmic balance.[1] In either case, it was a confusion of the spiritual with the material. What "Compensation" ultimately amounted to though was a theory of history without a corresponding theory of hegemony, which either vindicated the elites for their historical role or demanded that those elites force history to correspond to their pattern. At its heart, the theory of compensation is inherently elitist in its assumption that individuals who can shape reality are assisting in the revelation of God, or Nature's, overall plan—an imperative moral duty towards reform of the earthly world. This inevitably (and perhaps unconsciously on Emerson's part) privileges those with the historical power and influence to act and regards those who cannot as, to use Emerson's slightly troubling term, "defects" that it was the duty of the reformer (who is part of the unfolding of natural law) to correct. However, "The Maypole of Merry Mount" undercuts this "Gnostic" tendency in New England thought and culture by engaging with the class politics of writing itself. It, and many of the other *Twice-Told Tales*, shows how history is not only written by the victors but, perhaps somewhat obviously, is written by the writers: that text has dominated in narratives of New England history in a way that ultimately came to misrepresent that history. By presenting the Merry Mounters as a peasantry marked by carnival, festivity, and the pleasures of the body, Hawthorne alludes to the lower-class print culture that characterized the wider marketplace into which his work emerged: a site rich in sensationalism, playfulness with identity, and performances of all kinds.

As Isabelle Lehuu shows in *Carnival on the Page*, the climate in which Hawthorne's work entered the public sphere was one in which there was a great explosion of literary works dealing with carnivalesque themes directed to the tastes of the increasingly literate, urban, lower and lower-middle classes. Lehuu writes:

> From the miniature gift-books to the massive papers, all the new reading materials shared a festive and somewhat transgressive quality.

They performed a collective spectacle in which producers and consumers, publishers and readers came to participate.... To the amazement of contemporary critics and enthusiasts alike, the printed word staged a carnival. (4)

While the explosion of literary material in this period facilitated the inclusion of artisans and the working classes within the traditionally refined spaces of literary culture, it also produced a reactionary response from the upper-middle classes, who saw in the new literature's celebration of spectacle a transgressive, proletarian threat to traditional order, a degeneracy or primitivism. Hawthorne had written for these gift books and story papers himself in the years prior to *Twice-Told Tales*, yet it was with the publication of his stories in book form (constricted in binding and safe behind a cover) that the author attained elite literary status among the Concord set and a degree of fame—the very thing that Poe found suspicious. In describing the maypole festivities in his story Hawthorne conflates peasant ritual in the seventeenth century with contemporary debates concerning the dangerous potential of the emergent market culture. Hawthorne's long description of the mixed nature of the Merry Mounters' ritual practices, where rites of Comus appear alongside Indian hunting rites and the like, resonates with nineteenth-century views concerning the dangerous capacity of a heterogeneous, market-based economy for deception. The carnivalesque character of the people of Merry Mount closely resembles descriptions by middle-class reformers of the lifestyles of the urban poor in the nineteenth century as a confusing and undifferentiated mass of revellers nurtured and provided for by an emergent market of penny dreadfuls, sensationalist newspapers, music halls, and mass entertainments. Lehuu remarks, "during the second quarter of the nineteenth century the daily newspaper became the epitome of both carnivalesque ritual and market fair, where boundaries were crossed and the private made public" (37).

By contrast, the sanctified realms of the intellect that characterized literary romanticism nominally resisted the publicizing impulses of the marketplace and provided a means of celebrating the middle-class privatization of identity. As Hadley shows, "the romantic subject . . . is what one might be tempted to describe as a romanticized version of the private identity of class society" (32). While such a view of authorship was acceptable in the eighteenth and early nineteenth centuries, as the market revolution of the antebellum period restructured society, the new middle classes increasingly came to demand a literature that reflected their own negotiations between a market-based public identity and the private realm of the intellect. Indeed, since the Reformation the public world of the market and ritual's external expressions of the body had been rendered in the middle-class Protestant imagination as comparable forces, a process that allowed Protestants to conflate "perverse" pagan and Catholic practices with the urban lower classes. As Jean-Christophe Agnew remarks:

> Puritanism embraced representational strategies aimed at righting a world that money (among other things) appeared to have upended, a world that threatened to become, in effect, a permanent carnival. (54)

In following Protestants during the Reformation in ontologically fusing in their imaginations ritual and festivity with the market culture of the urban poor, the American upper-middle classes (for Hawthorne the main inheritors of older Puritan attitudes) underwent a process of negative self-definition through which they could represent themselves as separate from that world. In the story it is implied that both the Merry Mounters and Endicott's Puritan army require one another for self-definition. When the Puritans first attack the author writes:

> The Puritans played a characteristic part in the Maypole mummeries. Their darksome figures were intermixed with the wild shapes of their foes, and made the scene a picture of the moment when waking thoughts start up amid the scattered fantasies of a dream. The leader of the hostile party stood in the centre of the circle, while the rout of monsters cowered around him like evil spirits in the presence of a dread magician. (32)

As the Puritans come to play a part in a mythic drama that the Merry Mounters are enacting, so too does Endicott come to resemble "a dread magician"—that is, the very thing that Puritan austerity and antimysticism sought to destroy.

As I have remarked earlier in this book, the short story as a form that appeared in what Lehuu characterizes as the "carnivalesque" public world of print in the nineteenth century possessed a greater (or rather less easily denied) relationship to market culture than did the novel, the romantic lyric, or the essay, whose aesthetics established romantic distance as a preferred model of engagement with the world and reflected the need to satisfy a more private readership at home. As a genre, the strengths of the short story, and the magazine short story especially, initially lay in how its thematic engagements corresponded with its position as an essentially public art form with roots in the eighteenth-century culture of display. In fictions that dealt with how identity could be formed within a social space of exchange, the short story responded to the need of the new middle classes to negotiate between the public world of the market and the private realm of the intellect and the home. Consequently, in choosing to write short stories Hawthorne was involved in a complex balancing act that involved a negotiation of the class and religious politics of nineteenth-century literary culture. In depicting a conflict between a heterogeneous, revelling peasantry representative of the culture of the nineteenth-century marketplace and austere Puritan elites that resemble the upper-middle-class reformers of antebellum America, "The Maypole of Merry Mount" theatricalizes Hawthorne's aesthetic dilemma. In addition, the story shows how the Puritan inheritance of antitheatricalism and antiritualism in prose, and of favoring a transcendent vision of the soul in opposition to the world of the body, is in tension with the origins of the short story tradition, from Irving onwards, in ritual and drama. Just as the Puritans and the Merry Mount community are "contending for an empire," so too is Hawthorne in seeking to balance competing intellectual forces in the short story. In doing this Hawthorne was also rejecting the transcendentalists' conflation of the Puritan mind with a stable American national character by showing that subjectivity was always in the process of negotiation and could not be pinned to fixed correspondences such as Nature, God, or Imagination.

"The Maypole of Merry Mount" therefore helps us explore what numerous critics have called the "Hawthorne Question": "where he *stands* on various philosophical, moral-ethical, religious, and political issues—as if he were one of those nineteenth-century reformist lecturers he despised" (G. R. Thompson, 1). Of especial significance to the debate is how much his own Puritan ancestry, and that of New England as a whole, affects the aesthetics of his work. In conflating Hawthorne too easily with New England Puritanism, critics over the years have attempted to present him as similarly committed to a project of romantic self-definition that chimes with the concerns of literary nationalism in imagining American character as separate from the historical patterns of the Old World: a new history or "errand into the wilderness." As Colacurcio frames the "Hawthorne Question," it rests upon how much we countenance Herman Melville's early account in "Hawthorne and His Mosses" that the New England writer was motivated by a "great power of blackness . . . that Calvinistic sense of Innate Depravity and Original Sin" (238) over Henry James's view of Hawthorne as an aesthete testing the limits of several fictional and historical methods of representing reality. Indeed, the debate between Melville and James might be categorized as a tension between what James called "showing" and "telling" (dramatization versus didacticism). On one side we have Melville's claim that Hawthorne "showed" the world his moralizing, Calvinist vision of history, versus James's sense that Hawthorne dramatized and played ironies off against one another and so developed a more "legitimate" form of literary fiction. Indeed, this same tension is implicit in Poe's categorization of Hawthorne's short stories as inherently didactic and allegorical in tone, as opposed to his own, aesthetically more "advanced," fictions.

Embedded in this debate is a restatement of the broader issues that have framed this book. Within the dialectic Colacurcio establishes between Melville and James lies the question of the extent to which Hawthorne reinscribes New England transcendentalist and romantic conceptions of the deep and eternal sublimity of nature, linked in his work with Puritan Gnosticism, over a performative ontology in keeping with the concerns of the short story tradition in America. In other words, if the American short story from Irving and Poe onwards sought to establish a ritualized, embodied, and theatrical conception of experience, how does this interact with what many critics have assumed is the antitheatrical legacy of Puritanism in Hawthorne's work? Furthermore, the battle between James and Melville's "Hawthornes" has an implicitly nationalist subtext. Melville's Hawthorne is presented as the inheritor of the same Puritan attitudes towards life that were reworked by the New England transcendentalists in the nineteenth century into a uniquely "American" national mindset in opposition to British culture. By contrast, James's Hawthorne is more skeptical of a literature that corresponds directly with a nationalist agenda. For James, such a prostitution of talent to base nationalism would be, frankly, embarrassing. Instead, James presents Hawthorne as operating within an Anglo-American tradition of letters in which the formal experimentation of aesthetics plays a more important role than grim, Calvinistic soul-searching.

To come to some answer to the "Hawthorne Question" it is worth looking at the conclusion of "The Maypole of Merry Mount." In the story Hawthorne neither inherits wholesale nor wholly rejects the Puritan traditions of New England but balances that inheritance with the demands of a changing literary audience. In effect, like many middle-class authors in the mid-nineteenth century, Hawthorne settles finally on a conclusion in which sincere, public expressions of feeling are rendered as a counterpoint both to the anonymity of the carnivalesque market world (symbolized by Merry Mount) and the antisocial impulses of the romantic intellect (symbolized by Endicott's religious utopianism). Hawthorne suggests that the possibility of reconciliation between competing forces lies with the young couple Edith and Edgar.

When the author first introduces Edith and Edgar he situates them "within the ring of monsters," describing them as "the two airiest forms that had ever trodden on any more solid footing than a purple-and-golden cloud" (30). Neither "invisible" like the Puritan spectators nor inhabiting the monstrous forms of the other revellers, Edith and Edgar suggest a possible reconciliation between immanence and abstraction, a form of embodiment that reflects the interests of the new Anglo-American middle classes by mediating between the "deceptive" public world of the lower-class carnival and the privatized, intellectual space of the Puritan elite. As Andrew Lawson remarks in *Walt Whitman and the Class Struggle*, these transitional figures reflect the experiences of the increasingly literate and significant antebellum lower-middle classes that were marked out from "the unskilled, less respectable, and wholly dependent working classes" (8). Reliant upon the market and yet educated and articulate enough to resist its deceptions, the lower-middle classes typified the ideal social subject, which found its voice in the complex negotiations of short fiction. Hawthorne establishes Edith and Edgar as the only people among the assembled crowds of Puritans and Merry Mounters whose "hearts glowed with real passion" (31). Furthermore, and unlike the rest of the Merry Mount community, Edith and Edgar resist Endicott's patriarchal tyranny through publicized expressions of feeling by which their love is theatricalized in the public world rather than in the exclusive mental spaces of their individual subjectivities. As such, Edith and Edgar are physical manifestations of Hawthorne's aesthetic design, which seeks through the genre of the short story to present the mind as constituted within a public space of exchange.

True to the designs of the dramatic stage heroes of the nineteenth century, Edgar "entreats" Endicott to back down, combining resistance with a deferential mode of social exchange. He states majestically, "Stern man . . . how can I move thee? Were the means at hand, I would resist to the death; being powerless, I entreat" (34). Edith, like the heroine of a stage melodrama, places her body in the way of violence, relying upon conservative attitudes concerning the sanctity of the female body to make her protest: "'Be it death,' said Edith, 'and lay it all on me'" (34). In this way, through their highly theatrical utterances, the "heroes" of the piece correspond with the nineteenth-century middle-class desire to make inner feelings correspond directly with outward expressions. The effectiveness of their actions lies in how these performances of deference or theatrical pleas to sympathy rely upon the recognition of the actor and the respondent as mutually constituted social subjects. By appealing to Endicott in this way, he too becomes embodied. Through their resistances the two lovers force a change in Endicott as his austere, patriarchal forcefulness, which is based in a transcendent vision that separates him from the material world, weakens. "Yet the deepening twilight," writes Hawthorne, "could not altogether conceal that the iron man was softened. He smiled at the fair spectacle of early love; he almost sighed for the inevitable blight of early hopes" (35). In response to their emotional expressions of resistance, Endicott preserves Edith and Edgar, incorporating them into the Puritan society rather than murdering or punishing them as he does the others.

While the Puritans exist in a purely mental space in which the earthly world is fallen and damned, and the Merry Mount community in a vapid delusion of constant festivity, Edith and Edgar share a bond of common feeling that is an antidote both to the anonymity that was the nightmare of a purely public world of the marketplace and the privatized identity of the romantic intellect. Furthermore, through their bond of love, Hawthorne implies, Edith and Edgar come to resemble one another. Hawthorne writes of the pair:

> One was a youth in glistening apparel with a scarf of the rainbow pattern crosswise on his breast. His right hand held a gilded staff—the ensign of high dignity among the revellers—and his left grasped the slender fingers of a fair maiden not less gaily decorated than himself. Bright roses glowed in contrast with the dark and glossy curls of each . . . (30)[2]

By making them near-identical reflections of one another, Hawthorne's story resonates with a crucial problem in nineteenth-century American literature that Leslie Fiedler first identified in *Love and Death in the America Novel*: the inability to imagine democracy in a form that goes beyond an essentially desexualized, homosocial bond. In presenting them as more or less identical, the author converts the ritualized sexual union of the marriage of a young man to a young woman into a bond of fraternity between equals that denies "mere" sexual impulses in favor of the "higher" values of love and companionship. By this process, differences of gender or sexuality are denied in favor of what Dana Nelson refers to as "that 'privileged spot' where commanding men can be rightfully recognised and known by like-minded/bodied/propertied men" (4), which is the limit of sympathetic exchange. As Nelson suggests, the possibility of transatlantic community lies in the maintenance of this fraternal relation. The fraternal sympathy that Edith and Edgar embody differs from the oedipal relation to power that Frederick Crews suggests typifies Hawthorne's aesthetic in his classic study of his short fiction, *The Sins of the Fathers* (1966). For Crews, Hawthorne's early provincial tales often depicted the violent rebellion of sons against their fathers so as to symbolize the American revolt against Great Britain. In "The Maypole of Merry Mount" it is rather that through their theatrical displays and sympathetic appeals Edith and Edgar force Endicott into a fraternal relation in which each subject is publicly constituted through intersubjective exchanges. Like Irving, Poe, and Melville, Hawthorne shows that the possibility of reconciliation between competing forces lies in theatricalized expressions of equality in the public sphere.

Edgar and Edith's hearts glow with the kind of love, more the sympathy of equals than the passion of sexual partners, that Michael Gilmore sees as the antebellum writer's ideal relationship with their audience. Gilmore writes of Hawthorne and Melville:

> [T]hey attempted to forge some kind of human bond with their readers: to deny or circumvent the impersonal relation of [purely economic] exchange. Melville's companionable first-person narrators, appealing to a circle of fraternal listeners; Hawthorne's dreams of encountering "the one heart and mind of perfect sympathy" . . . essentially artisanal versions of author-audience relations. (17)

Gilmore's reference to the artisanal elements of Melville and Hawthorne's writing is crucial as it fuses the politics of nineteenth-century class structure to literary aesthetics. Rather than favoring a form of authorship that emphasized the writer's social division from his audience through an aesthetic of detached observation, Hawthorne and Melville adopted a literary technique of attachment. Hawthorne's art is that of the idealized artisan who in the mythologies and popular narrative of the time possessed an emotional connection to the products of his labor that was not possible within the mechanized spaces of working-class factory production. Skilled, respectable, and able to balance individual labor with the demands of a sympathetic community, the artisan was Anglo-American popular literature and drama's favored subject. Hawthorne embodies this relation through his characters' negotiations between elite literary romanticism (Boston Calvinism) and the market fair (Merry Mount).

In concluding the story Hawthorne has Endicott reestablish the differences of gender between Edith and Edgar as part of his project of "civilising" the Merry Mount community. Endicott states, "there be qualities in the youth which may make him valiant to fight and sober to toil and pious to pray, and in the maiden that may fit her to become a mother in our Israel, bringing up babes in better nurture than her own hath been" (Hawthorne, 35). In referring to "our Israel" Endicott equates the providential project of nation building with the gendered division of labor between the public and private spheres. True to the tenets of Puritan culture, always for Hawthorne synecdochic of a later nineteenth-century American society, Edgar's future identity lies in the "masculine" world of soldiering, while Edith's is to become a mother in the domestic sphere. Against the grain of popular nineteenth-century attitudes, Hawthorne presents the gendered division of labor not as a "natural" force but an imposed one. The corollary of Hawthorne's tale is that the Puritan project of fusing American nationhood to religious Providence is an unnatural imposition upon a far more "natural" Anglo-American fraternity.

The story initially seems to chronicle a victory for the Puritan mind (symbolic for Hawthorne of a wider American worldview) over the "decadent" Old World, though by the end several ironies have been exposed. Firstly, to symbolize their incorporation into the Puritan society Endicott crops Edgar's hair "in the true pumpkin-shell fashion" and both the lovers are dressed in "garments of a more decent fashion . . . instead of their glistening vanities" (35). Recalling God's command to Adam and Eve to clothe themselves as they left the Garden of Eden, Endicott assumes the position of the Godhead and reestablishes the moral law commanded by the Old Testament Covenant of Works. Since the Boston Puritans were meant to preach the Covenant of Grace (the last covenant with man in which Christ's sacrifice was meant to redeem all sin and justification for heaven was by faith alone), Endicott's command to Edith and Edgar to do duty to the community by following their laws is a perversion of the Puritan religion that brings it closer to the hierarchies of Catholicism. Endicott's perverted version of Puritanism is symbolized in what the author marks as his final act in the story:

Endicott the severest Puritan of all who laid the rock-foundation of New England, lifted the wreath of roses from the ruin of the Maypole and threw it with his gauntleted hand over the heads of the Lord and Lady of May. (35)

A figure whose entire worldview is rooted in resistance to the ritualized acts of the theatre and the Eucharist performs a symbolic gesture that marks Edith and Edgar's new position within the Puritan community of Boston. Through the symbolic act of throwing the wreath over their heads, Endicott "transubstantiates" the roses into a symbol of a new bond. The outward expressions of sincerity by the two lovers have so profoundly affected Endicott as to puncture his stern and austere Puritan vision, forcing him to commit a symbolic act that is fundamentally at odds with the antiritualism of the dominant strain of Puritan theology. In effect, it is Endicott, not Edith or Edgar, who undergoes a conversion, while such an act renders questionable Endicott's position as one of the Puritan elect.

Secondly, the egalitarian, mutual support that characterized Edith and Edgar's relationship with one another earlier in the story persists, even as they are incorporated into a Puritan religious worldview that preached the importance of individual faith and self-interest. The author states that "in the tie that united them were intertwined all the purest and best of their earthly joys" (35). Unlike the sentimental mode, which located these positive emotions in the private spaces of the family and the home, Edith and Edgar, through their implicit similarity and public declarations of sincere feeling, represent the complex, embodied negotiations of nation, religion, and class that typified the nineteenth-century American short story. Read with a view to the transatlantic implications for the American mind of Edith and Edgar's fraternal love, Hawthorne suggests that the Puritan worldview does not constitute a totality. In encountering the people of Merry Mount, Endicott becomes a partial convert to an "Old World" culture that the "modern" philosophy of the Puritans can never quite annihilate. This culture, then, like Irving's, Poe's, and Melville's, is a mnemonic remembered by the body, indestructible by means of written history, and easily transferred between individuals. This has inevitable implications for Hawthorne's resistance to the New England transcendentalists' conflation of Puritan conversion narratives with romantic nationalism. As Edith and Edgar come to exist within the heart of the Puritan community, so embedded within the American Puritan mind is a relationship with the history of the Old World that disrupts the dangerous claims of nationalism. Indeed, rather than offering up a ready, hermetic, and intellectually unproblematic tradition to the American mind, Hawthorne's theatricalization of Puritan history in his work presents that mind as constituted in relation to the competing forces that it would seek to deny or refute. The incorporation of Edith and Edgar into the community works to disrupt the teleological narrative that marked Puritan attitudes towards history. In this way Hawthorne uses the aesthetic of the short story in a manner that renders "national" consciousness as consistently unstable and adaptable. As Paul Giles states in *Transatlantic Insurrections*:

> Hawthorne's . . . major work, apprehends its peculiar vision of American national destiny through a comparative structure of transnationalism. It is precisely such processes of comparison that Emerson, with his idealization of individualism and self-reliance, found so disturbing. For Emerson, such comparative consciousness could prove psychologically disorienting and intellectually debilitating, liable to cloud the philosopher's primary focus upon his own integral vision. (181)

In forcing the Puritan mind to undergo a process of theatricalization in the public sphere through the form of the short story, Hawthorne holds their traditions of self-reliant individualism and soulful meditation up to the light of public scrutiny. In so doing, Hawthorne establishes a space that at once mediates between the deceptive culture of the market and the romantic intellect *and* renders unstable the Puritan equation of national providence with written history and individual self-interest.

"Life figures itself to me as a festal or funereal procession": Pageantry, Mourning, and Sincerity in "The Christmas Banquet" and "The Procession of Life"

From the earliest examples of his art in *Twice-Told Tales* Hawthorne uses the body to register his authorial negotiations of the politics of nation, religion, and class in antebellum America. "The Maypole of Merry Mount" theatricalizes an experience that runs counter to the logical order of things. In it a wedding becomes a massacre and the attempt of the Puritan elites to convert others to their theological purview goes awry as Endicott, the figure who typifies that community, undergoes an ironic conversion of his own. In the next part of this chapter I propose that in order to synthesize competing forces in his fiction, many of Hawthorne's short stories adopt a technique of inversion. In his work appear rituals, like the kind found in Poe and Irving's work, therefore appealing to the needs of an audience accustomed to a certain established tradition in American literature. However, in much of Hawthorne's short fiction, particularly that which appears in his second collection, *Mosses from an Old Manse* (1846), weddings become funerals and processional civic pageants become dances of death. Unlike in Poe's "The Cask of Amontillado," where the reversals peculiar to Catholic carnival expose unequal class relations and destabilize Montressor and Fortunato's brotherhood, inversion for Hawthorne ultimately functions to allow the creation of an imaginative bond of community by offering the conditions necessary for clear and unambiguous communication.

In *The Art of Authorial Presence: Hawthorne's Provincial Tales*, G. R. Thompson adopts a similar approach to Hawthorne's work, coining the term "negative romanticism" to describe his aesthetic of inversion. Thompson defines "negative romanticism" as "the conscious embodiment of the indeterminate and conflictual as opposed to a subconscious (re)enactment of unresolved oppositions" (13). By ignoring Hawthorne's use of theatrical expression, suggesting instead that the author adopts romantic perspectives based in his provincial New England Calvinist heritage, Thompson circumvents the politics of class inherent in Hawthorne's aesthetic. Consequently, where Thompson's reading and mine differ is in the relative importance we afford market culture and the popular taste in the development of Hawthorne's style. Rather than seeing Hawthorne's use of inversion as a way of expressing provincial attitudes at odds with the prevalent nationalist perspectives of a wider American literary culture, it is better to see Hawthorne's preferred technique as a way of reconciling romantic and Puritan sensibilities with the carnivalesque spirit of the dominant antebellum print culture.

By adopting such a perspective, Hawthorne's work participates within the culture of the transatlantic middle class. Through a technique of inversion Hawthorne engages with a major force in nineteenth-century Anglo-American culture, the rituals of mourning that were imagined as the zenith of sincere social performance. Consequently, Hawthorne's work in short fiction chimes with the broader concerns of nineteenth-century Anglo-American literature in imagining a third space of representation between romantic transcendence and a deceptive world of carnivalesque immanence in which theatricality can be reimagined, not as a fraught site of potential deception but a ritualized pattern of action in which outward performances are made to correspond with sincere inner feelings.

In "The Procession of Life" (1846) Hawthorne engages with how the politics of class are bound up with discourses of representation. The author begins by describing the kind of civic procession that could be found in any British or American town on days of celebration or remembrance during the nineteenth century, in which representatives of each trade marched through the streets in an order decreed by the town elites. The author writes:

> Life figures itself to me as a festal or funereal procession. All of us have our places, and are to move onward under the direction of the Chief Marshall . . . Its members are classified by the merest external circumstances, and thus are more certain to be thrown out of their true positions than if no principle of arrangement were attempted . . . In this manner, it cannot be denied, people are disentangled from the mass and separated into various classes according to certain apparent relations; all have some artificial badge which the world, and themselves among the first, learn to consider as a genuine characteristic. (Hawthorne, *Mosses from an Old Manse*, 161)

The author then proceeds to imagine other types of classification that might surpass class and position, "assuming to myself the power of marshalling the aforesaid procession" (162) and restructuring it along the lines of feeling and earthly experience rather than the "artificial badges" of class and position. As structuring principles the author suggests the following experiences respectively: "Physical Diseases," "gifts of intellect," "the sacred bond of sorrow," "the brotherhood of crime," and "Love," before finally concluding that "Death" is the only force to ultimately overcome false and artificial distinctions. In attempting to balance the public taste for "carnivalesque" representations of rituals and performances with the demands of a romantic high culture, Hawthorne suggests that the only acceptable form of external presentation is that which directly responds to a genuinely felt emotion. While the external displays of the rich bespeak their position in society, they are ultimately deceptive because that position is based on material wealth alone and signifies no internal emotional state.

For the author the only experience that is capable of eliciting the genuine emotional state of universal brotherhood is the experience of death. While all other emotions and experiences are open to corruption and the allure of hierarchy, death alone can "assume the guidance of a procession that comprehends all of humanity" (172). For the author even "Love" and "Truth" present their own difficulties. The author remarks:

When a good man has long devoted himself to a particular kind of beneficence—to one species of reform—he is apt to become narrowed into the limits of the path wherein he treads, and to fancy that there is no other good to be done on earth but that selfsame good to which he has put his hand, and in the very mode that best suits his conceptions. (169)

In a similar manner to how Endicott is presented as a Gnostic whose individual conception of truth and right force him into violent relation with the material world in "The Maypole of Merry Mount," so those that suffer from a transcendental conception of the universal power of love or truth are likely to become tyrannical.

The author's solution to the problem of conceiving of a universal humanity is to incorporate the experience of death into the physical processes of life by imagining both as operating in continuity as a procession. Hawthorne writes, "breathe thy wail upon the earth's wailing wind, thou band of melancholy music . . . There is yet triumph in thy tones. And now we move!" (172). The presence of death acts as a force that mobilizes the procession, whereas all other ideas gradually lead to stasis. For Hawthorne, death must be ever present in life to create motion and a communal bond. Indeed, the short story was the perfect form for evoking this idea. Public by virtue of its circulation in journals and newspapers and naturally abridged by virtue of its length, the short story always raises the spectre of death or incompleteness by means of its very form.

In this way the author typifies Mary Louise Kete's observation in *Sentimental Collaborations* that the experience of constant mourning was frequently seen as an essential condition for the construction of middle-class subjectivity in antebellum society. Kete sees mourning as replacing "conversion as the primary spiritual and social event of the American's life" (57). Unlike the Freudian conception of mourning as a period of time that allows the individual to psychically overcome the experience of loss, returning finally to the desired state of possessive individualism and coherent ego identity, Kete interprets the process of nineteenth-century mourning through material and performance studies as a means of establishing a connection with the dead that was unending: a productive melancholia not dissimilar from John Keats's sense of negative capability. "The cultural practices of mourning," Kete writes, "[are] not interested in autonomy or liberation but in the restoration of constitutive bonds, which make subjectivity possible" (62). For Kete, nineteenth-century mourners came to see the formation of a collective bond that fused the living to the dead as preferable to the construction of a coherent individual identity that, in time, overcame the breach of death.

The desire to establish a communal bond between subjects living and dead expressed itself in the complex negotiations between romantic and theatrical modes of literary expression. While Kete's vision of mourning expressed the need for ritualized social bonds, constitutive ties, and communal affect, the romantic mind tended to imagine death as a force beyond the capacities of the human world to comprehend. Kete's vision of the role of death and mourning differs from the "necro ideology" that Russ Castronovo sees as a defining characteristic of the romantic mind in the manner by which it treats life and death as an ongoing process in human history. By contrast, the "necro ideology" of romanticism evaluated the confusing motion and incidents of life against a standard established by death as an idealized and fixed point outside of time: a sublime moment of perfect order that transcended human history. In Kete's understanding, embodying death through the performance of mourning became an essential process of middle-class identity formation as death and mourning became ontologically inseparable from one another. It is in this spirit that Hawthorne imagines the "procession of life" in his story. Hawthorne presents death as implicated within the external processes of the social world and embodied in performance, not, as in the case of the romantic deathly imagination, a moment of perfection whose meaning lies outside the comprehension of that social world.

In addition to the task of fusing death and life into an unending bond, mourning also symbolized the ideal conditions for the expression of sincere middle-class social performances of respectability. As Karen Halttunen shows, across the nineteenth century "mourning ritual increasingly was coming to resemble a form of public theatre, in which the performances not only of the mourners but of the corpse itself became the object of open and unabashedly theatrical concern" (157). While much theatre culture was still affected by Bostonian skepticism towards theatrical presentation, mourning retained its position as a more respectable form of public ritual. Unlike the feeling of grief that it theatrically embodied, mourning operated through public expression and made its claims to identity in a social space of performance. Like many forms of middle-class culture in antebellum America, matching the internal feeling of grief to the external expression of mourning was both a desirable and potentially fraught process. As the author writes in "The Procession of Life," "Grief is such a leveller, with its own dignity and its own humility . . . If pride—the influence of the world's false distinctions—remain in the heart, then sorrow lacks the earnestness which makes it holy and reverend" (Hawthorne, 165). The ideal state, as with the outward demonstrations of inner love that typified Edith and Edgar's behavior in "The Maypole of Merry Mount," was to find a theatrical expression that perfectly mapped onto a feeling.

Although it takes the initial form of the literary sketch, through the use of the writer's disembodied narrative voice, the direction of the narrative in "The Procession of Life" has the effect of including the author within the processes he describes. By making death the universal condition of humanity, the ironic implication is that the author's disembodied narration is a paradox that cannot hold steady. In Hawthorne's story the romantic "neutral space" of disembodied narration is destabilized by the very process of that narration. Through this Hawthorne implies that even the romantic imaginative author must be involved in the process of connecting life and death together through the material embodiment of constant mourning.

Hawthorne's project in "The Procession of Life" is similar to the funereal processes of the circum-Atlantic world that Joseph Roach describes in *Cities of the Dead*. The kind of theatre that Hawthorne imagines is a public display in which death and life are fused and which operates as a link between the transient, artificial displays of individuals and nations and the larger arc of human history. In the story Hawthorne takes mourning and death out of the private sphere of sentimental domesticity and reinscribes it onto a festive, public world. As Roach shows, such a world, in which performance is the key to identity, is always saturated with memory. "Living memory," writes Roach, "remains variously resistant to . . . forgetting . . . through the transmission of gestures, habits and skills" (26). The "one great brotherhood" (Hawthorne, 172) to which the author of "The Procession of Life" refers is hostile to nationhood, because it is based upon a memorialization process in which all human life, historical or contemporary, is bonded together as an imagined community of the living dead. The story suggests that through death, and the "living memory" of performance, a fraternity is established that destabilizes national fantasies.

In "The Christmas Banquet" Hawthorne adopts a similar technique of inversion to that which transformed a festive procession into a funeral march in "The Procession of Life," but does so to comment upon the nineteenth-century cult of mourning and its elevation of grief as the most sincere form of feeling. The story begins with a writer called Roderick (a thinly veiled characterization of Hawthorne himself) who is reading a story he has written to his wife. From the first, Hawthorne has Roderick confess that he has in his own past had a "sad experience," which "has gifted me with some degree of insight into the gloomy mysteries of the human heart, through which I have wandered like one astray in a dark cavern" (225). Through the implication of an earlier period of mourning or depression and Roderick's sincere expression of feeling, Hawthorne establishes how crucial sincerity and mourning are to the structure of the proceeding tale. To highlight this, Hawthorne has Roderick announce that the story is essentially a sketch of an individual who longed to "exchange his load of ice for any burden of real grief that fate could fling upon a human heart" (226).

The story that follows revolves around a Christmas party, established as a yearly concern by "a certain gentleman's last will and testament . . . for ten of the most miserable persons that could be found" (226). Hawthorne implies that the gentleman's success in life was not due to an ebullient optimism but a commitment to a life of constant mourning that was the ideal of sincere middle-class expression. Roderick writes, "it seemed not the testator's purpose to make these half a score of sad hearts merry, but to provide that the stern or fierce expression of human discontent should not be drowned, even for that one holy and joyful day" (226). By presenting the Christmas banquet as an endowment by an old gentleman, Hawthorne takes the cult of mourning out of the sentimental sphere of domesticity and situates it as an ongoing concern within a nineteenth-century world of charity and public works. Like the many public funds that were established to aid the needy around Christmastime in nineteenth-century Britain and America, the banquet potentially has an educating function in inculcating within the assembly the manners of sincere social feeling, the expression of which was essential to achievement among the nineteenth-century middle class.

Appropriate to the cause of middle-class mourning in establishing life and death in continuity through all of time, "the arrangements and decorations of the banquet were probably intended to signify that death in life which had been the testator's definition of experience" and were "accurately copied from those . . . of ancient mourners" (227). In particular, it is the ancient Egyptian cults of Anubis that provide the most definitive model for the party's décor. The decorators are said to have "seated a skeleton at every festive board, and mocked their own merriment with the imperturbable grin of a death's head" (227). As Dana Nelson has shown, in addition to functioning to "prove" racialist discourses of polygenesis that separated "civilized" descendants of the Nubians from "barbarous" primitive tribes, Egyptian culture was much prized in the antebellum era because of the way its mourning practices chimed with Anglo-America's own. For instance, much in the same way as Egyptians placed the skeletons of ancestors at the head of the dinner table during festival time, Kete describes how the desire to make an unending connection with the dead in the 1850s engendered a craze for making decorative pictures and ornaments out of dead children's hair or clothes to be displayed in the public rooms of middle-class homes.

The author then provides a list of social types who find their place among this party. Roderick presents a series of depressives and misanthropists to transcendental reformers who, like Ralph Waldo Emerson, "had gone astray from the firm foundation of an ancient faith, and wandered into a cloud region, where every thing was misty and deceptive" and "a theorist, who had conceived of a plan by which all the wretchedness of earth, moral and physical, might be done away with" (Hawthorne, 239). In each case what defines and groups them is the sincerity of their feelings, with which their external self-presentation perfectly corresponds.

The tension of the story relies on a figure called Gervayse Hastings, who, much to the continuing puzzlement of the assembly each year, seems to have no outward sign of grief or sadness except a certain vague "coldness" of manner. Because his outward manner seems to bespeak no internal suffering or grief, each year the group attempts to imagine the reason for his attendance at the party. At the dénouement it is finally revealed that Gervayse Hastings represents "a want of earnestness — a feeling as if what should be my heart were a thing of vapor—a haunting perception of unreality . . . I have really possessed nothing, neither joy nor grief" (241). Following this announcement he ceases to cast a shadow—that is, he undergoes a strange partial disembodiment. Unable to mourn or express any real emotion, Hawthorne imagines Gervayse Hastings as an absolute pariah within a culture committed to sincerity and social feelings. As Roderick finally remarks to his wife Rosina after completing his reading of the story, "we do meet with these moral monsters now and then—it is difficult to conceive how they came to exist here . . . They seem to be on the outside of everything; and nothing wearies the soul more than an attempt to comprehend them within its grasp" (241).

In "The Christmas Banquet" Hawthorne alludes to the dangers of an absence of sincerity within the culture of the antebellum middle class. It is valuable to see such dangers as Hawthorne's meditations on the difficulties inherent in his own artistic negotiations of romantic and theatrical culture. Unable to emote appropriately and sufficiently to inhabit the symbolic order, and yet not typifying the romantic individual who is absolutely disembodied through transcendentalist meditation on the sublime, Gervayse Hastings becomes the peculiarly "hollow and feeble" (241) counterpoint of the ideal social type of republican convention. While Edith and Edgar in "The Maypole of Merry Mount" were able to express a bond of mutual feeling that set them apart from both the Puritan elites and the "carnivalesque" masses, Hastings's negotiations of competing forces effectively render him as a dead signifier. In this state none are able to completely understand him, "not even those who experience the like" (241).

Hawthorne's short fiction is often marked by his constant fear that the meaning of his works would be lost in the motion between the author's intentions and the literary marketplace. In his reading of a story from the same period as "The Christmas Banquet," "Rappacini's Daughter" (1844), Michael Gilmore suggested that "Far from inviting misunderstanding, Hawthorne presents himself as its innocent victim, a writer deprived of an audience because the public persists in mistaking his grim exterior for his inner character" (68). Even while he challenges the limits of sincerity as a force for social cohesion by presenting a figure that is unable to embody the conditions necessary for sincere social performance in "The Christmas Banquet," Hawthorne still, ultimately, expresses a wish to be able to communicate unambiguously within the social world. Hawthorne's aim is not just to document a culture objectively but to participate within it.

It is the fear of his art being unable to communicate sufficiently that motivates Hawthorne in one of the last short stories he ever wrote for adults, "Main Street" (1849). In "Main Street" Hawthorne reflects upon the short story itself as a genre by presenting public expression and the artistic imagination as centrally highlighted formal concerns. The story also prophesies a possible limit to republican expressivity, and therefore a certain kind of short story that typifies its concerns, in a new demand for realistic representation in the years preceding the Civil War.

Embodying the Authorial Dilemma in "Main Street"

"Main Street" takes the form of a panorama or puppet show, like the kind increasingly seen in cities and towns during the mid-nineteenth century, "illustrating the march of time" and "call[ing] up the multi-form and many-colored Past" of Salem Town (Hawthorne, 41). It is narrated by a flamboyant and verbose showman whose "pictorial exhibition" is designed to "elicit generous approbation" (41) from a crowd of spectators whose frequent interruptions punctuate the narrative. Beginning in Enlightenment France, the craze for puppet shows and automata was an important feature of nineteenth-century theatrical culture. As Simon During remarks in *Modern Enchantments*, "Now that automata have dropped out of stage show business . . . it is easy to underestimate their power to attract, amuse, and amaze" (120). During shows how the increasing interest in automata and puppets across the nineteenth century demonstrates that, even at the supposed height of romantic Neoplatonism in Europe and America, the majority of people were more attracted to "a light materialism . . . than to the creativity . . . that characterised Romantic shows" (123).

Critics as diverse as Charles Swann and Michael Colacurcio have noted that the story serves to recall to the reader the material of Hawthorne's own early provincial and Puritan tales. In fact, Colacurcio has, rather disparagingly, suggested that the story is a weak précis of more intellectually ambitious earlier work that "reads like a table of contents of Hawthorne's Puritan tales of the 1830s" while seeking to serve the author "as a sort of finger exercise in preparation for the symphonic form of *The Scarlet Letter*" (32). While it is certainly true that "Main Street" occasionally appears to be a summary of other fiction, reading the story through Hawthorne's engagement with the performative nature of short story authorship places it centrally within the author's literary attempts to reconcile competing forces of influence in his short fiction through embodiment and social performances of sincerity in the public sphere.

The publication history of "Main Street" reflects the story's overall project of reconciling the historical influences of Puritanism and romantic textualism with dramatic embodiment. The story was published in Elizabeth Palmer Peabody's *Aesthetic Papers* (1849), the publication of which was Peabody's attempt to respond to critics of transcendentalism that found its focus on the imagination too otherworldly. As Paul Gilmore states in "Romantic Electricity, or the Materiality of Aesthetics" (2004),

> Peabody's selection of essays and sketches . . . indicates that she views the aesthetic not as a withdrawal into consciousness and form but as a particular kind of engagement with the world. She describes this engagement as "the unpersonal," a kind of experience that "sinks and subordinates the observer to the object,—which, by putting my personality aside, enables me to see the object in pure uncolored light." (468)

Unlike Thoreau or Emerson (whose only works to appear in *Aesthetic Papers* were the more politically and socially grounded essays "Resistance to Civil Government" and "War," respectively), Peabody's philosophy drew upon her categorization of "the aesthetic" and subordinated the concerns of the self-reliant individual to those of "an ideal sphere" (Gilmore, 468) or a space in which romantic energy could infuse earthly matter and act as an impetus for the embodied exercise of sympathy. While Emerson and Thoreau were attempting to generate an imaginative space in which the individual ego could exercise itself unbound by the concerns of the public, a form of thinking that, at times, courted the dangers of political entropy, Peabody saw the future direction of transcendentalism in expressions of universal brotherhood within the public sphere. Peabody's attempts to "subordinate the observer to the object" have clear parallels with Hawthorne's intentions in "Main Street," where identities are constituted by means of intersubjective exchanges of ritualized deference.

It is important to Hawthorne's artistic exercise in "Main Street" that the story begins with a gesture, a ritualized, deferential code that functions to establish a fraternal or sympathetic link between the showman and his audience. Hawthorne writes:

> A respectable-looking individual makes his bow, and addresses the public. In my daily walks along the principal street of my native town, it has often occurred to me, that, if its growth from infancy upward, and the vicissitude of characteristic scenes that have passed along this thoroughfare, during the more than two centuries of its existence, could be presented to the eye in a shifting panorama, it would be an exceedingly effective method of illustrating the march of time. (41)

Through this opening action Hawthorne shows how the role of gestural and ritualized patterns of behavior are central to the meaning of the story as a whole. The physical act of deference that the showman offers to his audience establishes the communicative link between his inner character and its nature as a socially contrived performance. As Charles Swann states, "In 'Main Street' the showman moves to center stage to generate a narrative, to represent the story of the history of Salem" (53). The showman's position within a public space of exchange is registered typographically in Hawthorne's fluid motion from a description of the showman's action ("a respectable-looking individual makes his bow") to his own narrative ("In my daily walks"), which is presented without speech marks.

Like the heroes of nineteenth-century stage and print melodramas, the showman's thoughts and action are presented as ontologically inseparable from one another. By placing command of the historical narrative of Salem within the realm of an embodied author-showman, Hawthorne presents a third space between the Puritan/romantic intellect and the carnivalesque world of the sideshow spectacle that serves to reconcile these competing forces. Furthermore, the bow serves to acknowledge the felt presence of the audience within the following tale. In this way Hawthorne's narrative included the role of the public in the creation of artistic meaning. While romanticism and sentimentality sought to establish a site purged of the influences of market culture, either through the intellect or in the space of the middle-class home, it is the relationship to the market that gives the theatrical short story many of its most vital meanings.

That the showman is "respectable-looking" equates this third space of representation between romanticism and the market with the nineteenth-century politics of class. The showman represents the semirespectable artisan of the nineteenth-century Anglo-American imagination in the manner by which his intellectual labor ("I have often thought") is mediated through his craft in a public space of exchange and contact ("I have contrived"). Consequently, the showman-narrator embodies the ideal social type of the lower-middle-class author that Hawthorne saw as the best exemplar of author-audience relations. Hawthorne's showman is, at once, a historian, an orator, and an engineer, whose attempts to balance the demands of mental and physical labor are seen in his melodramatic rhetoric, which, in Andrew Lawson's terminology, constitutes the "middle register" of the antebellum middle classes. The showman's rhetoric comprises references to "the little wheels and springs" of machines in the same sentence as the "brilliancy in a November cloud" (42). Like Lawson's Walt Whitman, the showman-narrator's speech "carries a sign of . . . [a] bid for cultural distinction" in its semantic fluctuations between the language of the mechanic and the "high-flown, Emersonian language of the soul" (xvii), beauty and Nature .

This rhetoric is bound up with Hawthorne's own project of attempting to establish a medium of pure, unadulterated communication that balanced competing, often directly contradictory forces of influence. By exposing the mechanics of the diorama, Hawthorne also exposes the mechanics of his own literary technique in short fiction. Through embodiment in the character of the showman, the author ceases to be the unaccountable force of the romantic narrator, as his creations are shown to be just "a complicated piece of mechanism" (Hawthorne, 41). Present within Hawthorne's desire for an open exposition of his literary machinations in "Main Street" is a utilitarian logic of disenchantment: to represent all thought and action as accountable within a public world of exchange. Indeed, the mechanical contraption that drives the procession of scenes serves as an artfully contrived synecdoche of Hawthorne's own negotiations of economic necessity and the Puritan/romantic intellect. The showman's "pictorial exhibition" fuses the market-oriented spectacle of the puppet show with a Puritan vision of providential history, presenting them as mutually dependent forces within Hawthorne's own art. Hawthorne's use of puppets transforms real historical figures into embodied images whose identity and meaning are literally connected to the environment in which they are placed, reducing thought and feeling to actions within a public space of exchange. According to the showman-narrator, the mechanism operates "with no greater trouble than the turning of a crank" (41). The narrative that he then presents removes all tension from the historical process as the "ancient and primitive wood . . . ever-youthful and venerably old" (42) peopled by "Squaw Sachem" and "Wappacowet" gives way to an image of "Roger Conant, the first settler of Naumkeag" planting "the germ of a city" (43). This image, in turn, resolves into a scene from the Puritan settlement. As the showman-narrator remarks, "marvel at the deep track that he makes . . . the wild woods, the wild wolf, and the wild Indian, will alike be trampled beneath it. Even so, shall it be. The pavements of the Main Street must be laid over the red man's grave" (45).

The sense of inevitability that marks the showman's rhetoric eerily imitates the Puritan vision of history. As Sacvan Bercovitch remarks, the Puritan mind was marked by a peculiar disposition towards a belief that all events "pointed forward to something grander still: the imminent renovation of all things in a 'new heaven and a new earth'" (68). As every historical event was imagined as a predestined stage of a providential mission, so was it conceived as one more step towards the ultimate, apocalyptic rebirth of human history. "A new beginning," writes Bercovitch, "and a newly urgent sense of an ending; an intermediate between these, at once linking them in time and confirming the overall design . . . was the story of New England" (68). Like the Puritan vision of providential and revelatory history, the narrative of "Main Street" accounts for its own ending, when a wire snaps, stalling the machine on an apocalyptic image of "the Great Snow of 1717" (62), even before the exhibition has really begun. The showman states:

> Unless something should go wrong, as, for instance, the misplacing of a picture . . . or the breaking of a wire, which would bring the course

of time to a sudden period . . . I flatter myself, ladies and gentlemen, that the performance will elicit your generous approbation. (41)

In his spirited defense of Hawthorne as a romantic author Charles Swann has remarked on how the "conclusion is prepared for at the beginning" (53). However, this observation ignores the tale's play with Puritan historiography suggested in Hawthorne's technique, instead reading it as a romantic statement about incompleteness. To see "Main Street" in this way would be to read the story within a tradition of the romantic sketch rather than, more correctly, within a tradition of short story writing that connected form with various modes of performance and expressivity. Swann is right to say that "Main Street" resists "any revolutionary or utopian perspective" (73) in its image of annihilation, but Hawthorne's decision to stop the mechanism at the Great Snow does not come from a passionate belief in the sublime power of nature or the feebleness of man's mimetic art before God. Rather, in doing this Hawthorne is ironically and self-consciously burlesquing the traditions of Calvinist thought with which he had become associated.

In "Main Street," the irony of the showman's representation of Puritan historiography (the easy and inevitable march towards a Protestant utopia predesigned along a schema) is made possible by a technology that finds its value within the marketplace, a common site of distrust to the very Puritan elites whose providential vision it mechanically renders. Like Hawthorne's own early narrative attempts to represent Puritan history through the market-oriented form of the short story, the showman uses modern technologies of theatrical representation to enact the process imagined in the Puritan religious mind. Consequently, by showing that the process of providential history can only be fulfilled by artificial representations of that history, Hawthorne cleverly destabilized the fixed correspondences of the Puritan imagination that came to see Indian extermination and European colonization as "natural" or "transcendent" processes. The effect of this is to pose a challenge to contemporary romantic categorizations of experience that were typified by the transcendentalist nationalisms of certain upper-middle-class elites in New England literary culture. In so doing, Hawthorne sets up the possibilities of ritualized embodiment in opposition to the Puritan nationalism that had taken on the secular, contemporary guise of Emersonian, self-reliant individualism.

In "Main Street," as in earlier tales of Puritan life such as "The Gentle Boy," "The Maypole of Merry Mount," and "Endicott and the Red Cross," Hawthorne shows how the surety of the Puritan mission is based upon the systematic abuse of Indians, Quakers, and women. Many of the juxtapositions of images in "Main Street" involve the removal of female influence by a Puritan patriarchal culture. The initial superimposition of Roger Conant building his house over "the great Squaw Sachem, whose rule . . . extends from Mystic to Agawam" theatricalizes the patriarchal usurpations of power that will be seen in later dioramas within the show. The showman's narrative is packed with images of women being punished at the hands of the Puritan elite, such as "Dorothy Talby . . . chained to a post at the corner of Prison Lane . . . for no other offence than lifting her hand against her husband" (52), Cassandra Southwick's imprisonment, and "Ann Coleman, naked from the waist upward . . . dragged through main street, while the constable follows with a whip of knotted cords" (55).

While a simple representation of this history would fix meaning, only serving to replicate the Puritan imagination that saw patriarchy and national providence as stable and resolute "natural" facts, Hawthorne includes the voice of the audience in "Main Street" and so opens the showman's artistic expression of history to debate within a space of exchange. Hawthorne's aesthetic in "Main Street" renders art and history as dialogic entities that are always potentially subject to intervention or rupture. The interruptions of the "acidulous-looking gentleman in blue glasses, with bows of Berlin steel" (43) serve to disrupt the showman's narrative and force him to constantly reconsider the effectiveness of his art as a means through which to represent history. In this space of debate and exchange the "natural" correspondences between religion and patriarchy, or history and the Puritan mission, are invalidated or, at least, rendered as another artifice among many.

In his reading of "Main Street" in *The Temple and the Forum* Les Harrison posits that Hawthorne's position within "a Boston literary market that conceived of itself as the nation's intellectual capital" (xxii) allowed him to burlesque the reified demands of "high art" made by the elites of his city. For Harrison, the late 1840s saw "Hawthorne's recognition of the artistic power of the cultural artefact when it is allowed to circulate freely in the marketplace" (63). Such power lay in the potential of a circulating commodity to destabilize fixed readings and produce debate at a time when the New England author was increasingly tasked with defining the role of the national author. However, even as it generated new energies in art, the production of such a space of exchange and the opening up of authorial meaning to the *demos* was also a potential frustration for the artist, whose negotiations of the market and the imagination would never be quite adequate to the varied demands of a diverse national audience. In particular, much of the narrative tension in "Main Street" finally comes to rest upon the "gentleman in blue glasses" and his increasingly hostile demands for "realism," a literary endeavor that Hawthorne (who found such value in high artifice and theatricality) found decidedly questionable. Indeed, Hawthorne explicitly referred to his distrust of what he saw as blandly descriptive forms of realism in the preface to *The House of the Seven Gables* (1851). In the preface Hawthorne attempts to present his work as "Romance" rather than a "Novel," the latter being a form that he views as traditionally associated with "the realities of the moment" and a description "of local manners" (xvii). This distrust of the realistic urge in fiction is also present in "Main Street." At salient points in the narrative the gentleman interjects with such claims as "the trees look more like weeds in a garden" (Hawthorne, 43) or "these historical personages could not have possibly met together in the Main Street" (50) and states that "it is my business to see things just as they are" (46). It is possible to see the gentleman as the embodiment of older Puritan attitudes towards theatrical representation, but it is far more valuable to see him as a prophetic voice that registers the changing demands of antebellum audiences. In riposte to the attacks on the verisimilitude of his representations made by the man in blue glasses, the showman calls for more rose-tinted spectacles: "we must now and then ask a little aid from the spectator's imagination" (43). But such imaginative investment is not what is demanded. Instead, the gentleman calls for the authority of realism and not the collective participation in fantasy or playful dialogue between author and audience called for by a more overtly theatrical, ritualized conception of the artist's role.

Discussions about realism in the middle of the nineteenth century had an importantly gendered dimension also. By the late 1840s, realism and local color writing of the kind Hawthorne courted, and parodied, in "Main Street" was developing an association with writing by women. The realist novel, as Phillip Barrish notes in *The Cambridge Introduction to American Realism*, partly began its life in female writers' attempts to use the sentimental mode, which had drawn its aesthetic energy from a claim to depict real experience. Such a crisis of masculinity, as Michael Davitt Bell has famously argued, would lead writers such as William Dean Howells to recast literary realism, and later naturalism, as masculine pursuits appropriate as expressions of the "virile" nation. Consequently, the argument against realism in "Main Street" can be seen as part and parcel of Hawthorne's critique of women's fiction more broadly, his famous denunciation of Susan Warner and others as a "damned mob of scribbling women." Hawthorne's claim to speak for New England had, by the time of his turn to writing novels in the 1850s, new challengers in the form of successful figures such as Rose Terry, whose local color realism traded off its use of regional dialect of specific localized detail.

"Main Street" shows that by 1849 Hawthorne was reflecting upon the limits of the style that had marked his earlier short fiction. By this date, as Daniel Walker Howe shows in *What Hath God Wrought*, the use of Samuel Morse's telegraph to report the recent Mexican-American War was beginning to occasion a heightened demand for more "realistic" representations of historical events, transforming the desire for sympathetic exchange in the public sphere that had motivated antebellum sensationalism into a utopian dream of rational "objectivity." In an age in which technologies like photography and the telegraph were mobilizing this new public demand for "realism," Hawthorne's story questions the limits of the theatrical short story's artificial and ritualized exchanges of republican sympathy. What finally comes to mark the puppet show is the failure of communication through embodied and ritualized social exchanges and not the transparency of class and cultural relations Hawthorne had imagined in 1837 in the figures of Edith and Edgar at Merry Mount. While Les Harrison sees the conclusion of the tale as evidence that "the showman has deliberately stopped his machinery, or exhibited it in an unfinished state, in order to present exaggerated descriptions of 'wonders' that his display could never have delivered" (68–69), the regretful tone of the final passages may tell a different story. To read the story as Harrison does is to typify the "Puritanical" concern that theatre is a deception, over the possibilities of the form for the generation of feeling and sympathy. It is possible to see the conclusion as Hawthorne's final abandonment of the short story as a genre sufficient to the demands of the new age. Crucially, the image that the showman "chiefly regret[s]" being unable to show is "a representation of the street in its whole length, from Buffum's Corner downward, on the night of the grand illumination for General Taylor's triumph" (63) in the recent Mexican-American War. In this way Hawthorne implies that traditional forms of representation have become insufficient to the demands of the new nationalism in the age of "manifest destiny" and the acceleration of information that came with the expansion of the telegraph. The final voice in the piece is the voice of the gentleman with blue glasses, whose claim that "I said that your exhibition would prove humbug and so it turned out. So hand over my quarter" (63) sounds a prophetic note. Hawthorne fears that in the new age of American empire, the negative forces of objectivity, capitalist exchange, and the individual ego will triumph over collectivity, emotionality, and transparent social relations.

What the debate between realism and drama in "Main Street" ultimately signifies is an antebellum crisis of authority. As fears over hypocrisy marred the possibilities of sentimental domesticity to provide a unifying force in culture and the problem of elitism troubled the romantic mind, so a new expectation of realism would pose a significant challenge to the authority of the traditional republican, performing subject. This realist impulse registered at once a new demand for a detached form of authorship that would impose no moral framework upon events yet remain, paradoxically, free from accusations of elitism. Unfortunately, Hawthorne would never fully explore this intuition in the medium of the short story. Instead this task would fall to the generation that followed him, who would find this authority by the new nineteenth-century science of anthropology and institutionalized practices of data collection and description that transformed a long-standing tradition in American letters of paying attention to the manners and behaviors of the American populace from what Washington Irving saw as an amateurish, "sauntering" pastime into a fully fledged professional discourse. In doing so the essential presupposition of the antebellum short story that gesture and ritual were transparent forms of social relation that allowed for the creation of collective national, or transnational, political bodies was supplanted by a sense that manners and behaviors were group based, exclusive, and pluralistic and could only be decoded by those in possession of specialist or local knowledge.

Epilogue
Louisa May Alcott's Theatrical Realism

I am very well and very happy. Things go smoothly, and I think I shall come out right, and prove that though an *Alcott* I *can* support myself. I like the independent feeling; and though not an easy life, it is a free one, and I enjoy it. I can't do much with my hands; so I will make a battering-ram of my head and make a way through this rough-and-tumble world. I have very pleasant lectures to amuse my evenings . . . and, best of all, a free pass at the Boston Theatre. . . . My farce is in the hands of Mrs. W.H. Smith, who acts at Laura Keene's theatre in New York. She took it, saying she would bring it out there.

—L. M. Alcott, "Letter to Her Father," Boston, Nov. 29, 1856

Went to see Forrest as Othello. It is funny to see how attentive all the once cool gentlemen are to Miss Alcott now she has a pass to the new theatre.

—L. M. Alcott, "Journal—Monday 14th November 1856"[1]

Across this book I have shown how through careful allusions to embodied forms of performance and ritual nineteenth-century American authors developed the short story as a distinct literary form defined by its particular embeddedness within the increasingly theatrical antebellum public sphere. Beginning with darkly comic depictions of rural folk performances, through fraternity hazings and sacred dramas, to child actors, death cults, and historical reenactments, the antebellum short story utilized gesture and symbolic action to respond to a world of print and performance in which external behaviors were beginning to take precedence over philosophical reflection in defining patterns of reading. Rather than seeing the short story as emerging from within the privatized and tortured intellectual spaces of the romantic liberal subject, I have suggested that the short story took shape in full view of the public and courted the emotions of its diverse audiences by means of gaudy exteriors and expressive gestures that reached beyond the individual to participate in a variety of forms of collective action and behavior. From this perspective the short story looks quite different from the romantic/modernist form organized around epiphany, alienation, and radical subjectivity that Frank O'Connor first described in the middle of the twentieth century. Instead of private readers, the short story sought out the public collectivities that only theatre and ritual were capable of making perceivable, speaking in registers that crossed class and cultural lines often as a means to ameliorate conflict during a time of increasing sectarianism and division.

Nathaniel Hawthorne's prophesy in "Main Street" that an end to this expressive, republican tradition of the American short story would come with the rise of realism and the desire for "objectivity" in fiction came true only in part. In making this claim Hawthorne missed the fact that even as it challenged the melodramatic style of antebellum short story writing, the rise of the local color and high realist genres that Henry James saw as a bulwark against sentimentalism in the postwar period would also allow room for the work of another writer—his Concord neighbor Louisa May Alcott—to continue the tradition of theatrical short story narrative that he, Irving, Poe, Melville, and others had helped to shape.

Alcott's reputation as a writer has undergone a significant renovation in recent years. No longer perceived as merely a quaint author of domestic narratives aimed at children, the discovery of a body of anonymously or pseudonymously published work in the 1970s has led to Alcott being lauded by critics for her special capacity to construct works that drew readers from across the spectrum of American political and social life by means of the artful cross-fertilization of numerous styles, genres, and forms of popular prose fiction. This same capacity to cross genres though has also led to accusations that Alcott led something of a literary double life that reflected a particularly tortured and conflicted artistic consciousness. At once the writer of salacious gothic melodramas such as "Behind a Mask" and "V. V. or Plots and Counterplots" (works Alcott herself self-deprecatingly disavowed by referring to as her "blood and thunder" or "necessity" stories) and moralizing tales for young audiences, Alcott has been treated as *the* preeminent female romantic in the American canon (at least in prose) through a critical focus on her as an internally divided figure that was, like Melville, Poe, and Hawthorne, unable to find her particular niche. Alcott's perceived "dilemma" has also been read as synecdochal of the problems facing all women writers in the nineteenth century who sought to live by their pen. Where consensus has developed it is around the idea that Alcott's work serves as an important bridge between the dominant forms of sentimental authorship that defined much antebellum women's writing and the local color or domestic realism of the Gilded Age.

Alcott's own complex shuttling between melodrama and something like a "literature of manners" has come to exemplify what is often seen as a wider cultural shift in American letters that critics have frequently organized around the locus of the Civil War. Certainly, the rise in popularity of realism and new forms of local color writing that Amy Kaplan and others have observed in the years following the war significantly altered the landscape and cultural work of short prose fiction. The popular critical narrative suggests that by the later nineteenth century the antebellum era's focus upon expressivity, emotionality, and participation had largely been supplanted, at least in higher literary circles, by what Michael Elliott has called the "valoriz[ation] [of] the first-hand observation and textual representation of group-based difference" (*The Culture Concept*, xiii) seen in the work of figures like William Dean Howells, Rose Terry Cooke, Sarah Orne Jewett, and Henry James. Informed by a developing popular interest in ethnography and the institutionalization of science, in the Gilded Age writers became less interested in utilizing fiction as a means to organize a ritual of participation and rather more concerned with describing difference or seeking out particularities, giving rise to both the regionalism of the local color writers and the deeply descriptive forms of high realism. Such authors came to abandon melodrama and turned their backs on festive, heterogeneous public life of the antebellum era, which was disavowed as a distinctly lowbrow, lower-class form of writing. Instead realism sought out a special position for the author as a semiprofessional observer of the group-based differences that American anthropologists would eventually come to label "culture."[2] Such a conception of the literary marketplace is reminiscent of both Lawrence Levine's comments about theatre as a site in which people increasingly came to define their class status and position in the later nineteenth century and Pierre Bourdieu's famous discussion of distinction and the consumption of "high art" as markers of cultural difference. If melodramatic or sentimental fiction from the age of abolitionism had sought to speak across divides, realism in the age of *Plessy vs. Ferguson* sought only to further refine and clarify them, often making difference seem static and intransigent or, as in texts like *The Rise of Silas Lapham* or *Daisy Miller*, dramatizing the folly of any individual who attempted to rise in status or "pass" as an insider to another culture or social group.³ At the same time, the new realism gave readers access to the rich internal worlds, particularly of women, that had in the past often been excluded from popular narrative forms.

Locating Alcott within traditions of realism has also affected how readers have perceived her politically. Richard Brodhead and others have seen in Alcott's "move" from gothic fiction to domestic realism an aesthetic decision based around her increasing complicity in the rise not just of local color writing and its associated reification of regional difference but also of the repressive disciplinary regimes of the late Victorian period that tried to curb the expressive emotionality of Jacksonian sensationalism. This shift of perspective, Brodhead argues, is rooted in Alcott's urgent desire to preserve a sense of middle-class respectability in the face of a culture that was increasingly coming to associate sensationalism with a lower-class sensibility, especially when such work was the product of a female author. I would argue the contrary. While concerned about the access to middle-class audiences that came with "respectability," Alcott never fully embraced it. Instead, as can be seen in the samples from her journals and correspondence I have quoted above, Alcott drew personal and aesthetic energy from her position on the borders of gentility that shaped her prose fiction. In the late 1850s, Alcott was a regular attendee at the Boston Theatre, part of the vanguard of women who were beginning to assert their claims to enjoy the spectacles and publicity of the drama on an equal footing with male audiences. Interestingly, Alcott's 1856 letter home to her father, the Concord transcendentalist Bronson Alcott, does not shy away from admitting that for all the worthy lectures and athenaeum events she attended by luminaries such as Theodore Parker, E. P. Whipple, and R. W. Emerson, "best of all" her entertainment came by way of a "free pass to the Boston Theatre," only recently built in 1854 on Washington Street. In her private journals Alcott confessed that it was this fact, and her brief, largely unsuccessful career as a playwright, that allowed her to enter society fully. Alcott took evident pleasure in going to the theatre, even with its associated dangers to her respectability. She enjoyed the ambiguities of being seen, even desired, by the "gentlemen" audience members at one moment, only to then be discussing high art with Boston Brahmins at another.

By way of a conclusion to this book, I will offer brief close readings of three texts from the beginning of Alcott's career that suggest how her work in short fiction might best be understood as a late flowering of the republican tradition I have described earlier that sought to combine the world of sensation with the new vogue for description and subjectivity that have frequently been understood under the terms of "high realism." I argue that Alcott's early experiments in popular gothic short fiction, the prize-winning "Pauline's Passion and Punishment," which she wrote for *Frank Leslie's Weekly* in 1862, "Behind a Mask" of the *Flag of Our Union* from 1866, and one of her tales for children, "The King of Clubs and the Queen of Hearts," from the 1864 collection *On Picket Duty*, should not be read as wholly distinct intellectual projects in which her radical, lower-middle-class sensationalism gradually gives way to a more conservative local color or domestic realist vision. Rather, these three texts reveal her attention to the same question that motivated the other writers considered in this book: how the performing body participated in the public sphere yet also served as a means for the construction of personal identity. Considering Alcott as a participant in this tradition helps to us to reconsider the move from antebellum melodrama to Gilded Age realism less as consequence of a radical breach or sea change in American literary culture in response to the national tragedy of the Civil War, and more as a gradual process of adaptation that demonstrates the interlocking of one mode with the other. Furthermore, seeing Alcott in this way helps to challenge the narrative of realism's abandonment of an aesthetic of democratic participation in favor of a newly specialized and refined form of detached, or objective, vision of the kind that Hawthorne found so dangerous and repugnant. Finally, I suggest that Alcott's attention to the somatic and theatrical elements of reading draws her work into the orbit of philosophical pragmatism, specifically the equation of body and mind made in the work of her contemporary William James, psychologist and brother of the "master" of psychological realism Henry James. It is my contention that across her career Alcott's work in the short story embraced the focus on theatricality begun by early national and antebellum authors such as Irving, Poe, Melville, and Hawthorne, while subverting the gendered assumptions underpinning much of that work so as to develop a platform within the genre for a feminist renovation of republican expressivity that could be utilized in the development of a structured critique of dominant, essentialist, Gilded Age nationalisms. This approach would pave the way for future feminist short story writers (especially Kate Chopin and Charlotte Perkins Gilman) to embrace performativity and the pleasures of the body in the shaping of their more fully developed critiques of traditions of liberalism, racial whiteness, and manhood as the necessary conditions for full US citizenship.

"Pauline's Passion and Punishment" was Alcott's first attempt to move beyond the Concord circles of her youth and construct a "blood and thunder tale" that would court popular audiences. Published anonymously in the first two 1863 issues of *Frank Leslie's Weekly*—a popular New York "story paper" known primarily for its lavishly illustrated accounts of Civil War campaigns and crime reports—the tale begins with a typical melodramatic tableau of a "handsome woman, with bent head, locked hands, and restless steps" whose "wreaths of hair that had crowned her with a woman's most womanly adornment [are] disordered upon [her] shoulders" (Stern, 107). This woman, later revealed to be the eponymous heroine Pauline, is presented against the backdrop of "the green wilderness of a Cuban *cafetal*" (107). In the context of the American Civil War, which raged so visibly on the pages of *Leslie's*, Cuba serves the role of a surrogate space for Alcott's plantation drama that deliberately evokes, yet also charts a course that runs clear of, a traditional locus of antebellum sentimentalism, the Old South. This translocation of the plantation drama to Cuba (a slaveholding country the United States had repeatedly attempted to buy or annex throughout its history) served an important function in preserving the sympathetic economies of the narrative since, as Madeleine Stern has suggested, *Leslie's* readership included a considerable number of Yankee soldiers and their families who would likely have rejected a story that directly referenced the newly seceded South. By initially locating her narrative in Cuba, Alcott constitutes the imperial imagination as a potential site for a utopian renovation of the project of national sympathy upon which antebellum sentimentalism had frequently relied. Appearing in *Leslie's* allowed Alcott access to a national readership that had to be approached with tact during a time of such open hostility and division between the states. However, Cuba does not just serve a utopian function. It also operates as a circum-Atlantic space that is the backdrop to a drama of performed identities and "surrogations" that aimed to destabilize fixed nineteenth-century correspondences between national, gendered, and racial characteristics or behaviors. In other words, her version of nationalism is filtered through an implicitly transatlantic mode—much as Washington Irving had engaged with British history to discuss contemporary American realities in *The Sketch-Book* at the beginning of the century.

Much like the melodramas that Karen Halttunen describes the young Alcott writing for her family and attending "in Boston whenever she could" ("The Domestic Drama of Louisa May Alcott," 239), the opening scene of the story is framed in such a way as to dramatize or make public a private moment of personal anguish and despair. When the tale first appeared, it was introduced by a headline denoting its status as a "Prize Story," followed by a large lithograph of a young woman on what appeared to be a veranda holding a letter and weeping. The woman's face is covered by her hand, suggesting either a deliberate refusal or unawareness of the viewer's gaze and so transforming the disembodied act of reading into an embodied act of voyeurism. Indeed, such an approach demonstrates Alcott's awareness of the panoptic aesthetic of *Leslie's*, a paper whose rich visuals and claims to special access to the hidden "stories" behind events were its main selling point. So as to elucidate the clear relationship between the story and the accompanying visual materials that were *Leslie's* main selling point, the picture of the woman bleeds into the text of the story as a large "T" drawn onto the hem of her dress serves as the first letter of the opening phrase, "To and fro." From the first moments of the tale, Alcott enacts the same logic of participation and cultural embeddedness that had motivated her literary forebears' own work in the short story form. Alcott elaborates upon this deliberate connection between the textual act of *reading* and the voyeuristic act of *looking* by creating a network of linked gazes through which the reader's act of reading is performed by Pauline's Cuban lover, Manuel, who, like the reader of *Leslie's*, is introduced as "an alien presence" who is "watching that other figure [Pauline] as it looked into the night and found no solace there" (109). In the first scene of the story Alcott dramatizes the act of reading in a way that gently satirizes her readers' own desire for sensational narratives that exposed to public view the inner passions, disappointments, and, crucially, bodies of women as being an element of *Leslie's* broader aesthetic of vision. Manuel's act of voyeurism in looking at a disgraced and erotically dishevelled Pauline with her "lace rent to shreds on the indignant bosom that had worn it" (107) is the reader's own and renders the democratic transparency aimed at by *Leslie's* in the terms of pornographic violation. Indeed, these theatricalized acts of looking have a distinctly sexualized character since, as Shelley Streeby has suggested in *American Sensations*, the description of Manuel as a "Southern" man of "warm coloring" would have resonated within the racial hierarchies of *Leslie's* as a sign of a characteristic foreign sexual threat. This act of "surrogation" in which the foreigner Manuel comes to stand in for the American reader therefore serves a subversive purpose by blurring the national, racial hierarchies and distinctions frequently reinforced in the pages of the very paper in which the story appeared.

As I suggested in my earlier reading of Melville's "The Fiddler," the participatory aesthetic of the short story papers was often seen in terms of street theatre, yet they troubled the distinctions between the public and private spheres by bringing that public art form into the bourgeois house and parlor. The presumably white, male reader of *Leslie's* effectively becomes the "swarthy" (113) Spaniard Manuel and only in so doing is given access to the inner life of, and, as the narrative proceeds, sexual rights over, the white European Pauline. Alcott further stretches this transgressive act of association in rendering Manuel as essentially feminine with a "slumberous softness" to his eyes and "lips, sensitive as any woman" (113). In effect, to "know" Pauline, the reader is forced to abandon their personal assumptions about their own race and gender. Even as it hangs on to certain populist racial stereotypes, in this scene Alcott creates a version of the operation of sympathy that relies upon the reader's willing participation in a process of "queering" that challenges the traditional position of the white, heterosexual, male observer whose scopophilic desires had often shaped the treatment of women in popular print and on the American stage.

After a long description of the scene and setting Manuel once again serves as a conduit through which the reader is given access to events. When in the narrative he asks to read the letter that is the presumed source of Pauline's suffering, the fourth wall is broken and the reader is presented with the text in full, demarcated from main body of the narrative by the use of italics. As with the documents and papers that were frequently used as props on the nineteenth-century stage (and which I discussed in chapter 3), the text of the letter here serves a dramatic, performative function in revealing the source of Pauline's desire for revenge against her former lover Gilbert, while reinforcing the story's broader aesthetic of exposure. The narrative of the story plays out the nineteenth-century behaviorist concerns that one's actions in the world would come to shape the inner character of the individual, which would be galvanized in the later nineteenth century through the institutionalization of American psychology in universities. In Pauline's case, her desire for vengeance against the man who rejected her, Gilbert Redmond, ultimately turns her into a "baleful spirit . . . crushing all generous impulses, withering all gentle charities, and making her the saddest spectacle this world can show—one human soul rebelling against Providence" (137). Additionally, however, in performing marriage to Manuel in order to make Gilbert jealous, Pauline also comes to love him. Her performance becomes inseparable from her developing character—for good and for ill. This makes the conclusion of the tale (in which Manuel is pushed off a cliff by Gilbert) all the more tragic.

By appearing in *Leslie's*, "Pauline's Passion" deliberately engaged with another performance culture that heightened the story's subversive potential. In addition to utilizing the masculine gaze in its version of nationalism, *Leslie's* magazine was also a well-known component of bourgeois parlor culture and childhood play. In all likelihood the tale would have served as the source material for one of the many parlor theatricals that were a common feature of nineteenth-century domestic culture. On the cover of each issue of *Leslie's* was printed an admonition to "Open this Paper Before Cutting it," indicating that the editors were well aware that the literary content of the paper was perceived as of secondary importance to the rich visual material. Indeed, as Ellen Gruber Garvey has outlined in *Writing with Scissors* (2012), producing scrapbooks by clipping material and illustrations from newspapers and journals like *Leslie's* and *Godey's* constituted a dominant middle-class pastime in the antebellum and postbellum eras—an activity often conducted by children and their mothers. The illustrations to "Pauline's Passion" possess a "staginess" that is suggestive of popular *tableaux vivants*. Around the time that the story was printed in New York there was a boom in books dedicated to the successful performance of *tableaux* in one's home. Works such as Sarah Annie Frost's *The Book of Tableaux and Shadow Pantomine* (1869) and James Head's *Home Pastimes and Tableaux Vivants* (1864) either provided short stories and fairy tales accompanied by illustrations to be read aloud and recreated or advised actors to draw inspiration from popular print periodicals. These works contributed to the meaning of the short story as a theatrical form that I have discussed across this book, from Irving's deliberate use of the magazine form in his New York printing of *The Sketch-Book* in seven parts, through Lippard's *White Banner*, to Poe's play with ritual exposés and Hawthorne's reworking of the Eucharist. From childhood Alcott herself had been a great advocate of tableaux and parlor theatricals, even making such activities an aspect of her education at the hands of her transcendentalist father, Bronson Alcott, whose own brand of behaviorism and disciplinary self-fashioning was overly theatrical in nature. Performance was increasingly being seen in the nineteenth century as a formative influence upon one's character and habit of being, which made the fact that "Pauline's Passion and Punishment" enacted a two-way process in which the reader was embodied by Manuel and then reperformed that character in their private domicile all the more dangerous, subversive, and progressive.

In highlighting the connection between theatrical embodiment or performance and the development of subjectivity, Alcott's story contributed to a developing consensus in the latter half of the nineteenth century around the effect of behavior on identity. In the hands of professional academics such as William James and Charles Sanders Peirce, the question of embodied consciousness that had been a dominant element in magazine and newspaper fiction across the century became a critical meditation upon the question of habit in psychology. By the time of James's publication of *The Principles of Psychology* in 1890, he could argue with considerable confidence that the age in which one could believe in a romantic conception of subjectivity as private, essential, and coherent was well and truly over. Instead, James suggested that "Our nervous system grows to the modes in which it has been exercised" (117) and that our attention to the behavior of our bodies, our performance in the world, was crucial to mental health—an attitude that put him very much at odds with European Freudian psychology and its focus on internality and the individual subconscious.

To historicize Louisa May Alcott's relationship to the idea of embodied consciousness and performance further, it is important to consider the role played by her father, the transcendentalist Bronson Alcott, in her formative development. Bronson Alcott's thought marks him out as an early pioneer of the tradition of American psychology that became institutionalized under James. As a pedagogue and thinker Bronson Alcott's philosophy relied upon the assumption that "character" (or in his own words, "the discipline of human culture") was shaped by means of both repeated performances, or training, and the collective discussion and interpretation of symbols from the material world. Unlike his friend Emerson, whose individualist philosophy frequently questioned the validity of intersubjective experience, favoring some form of internal motivation or romantic subjectivism that implied "character" was innate in the individual and merely required expression, Bronson Alcott's pedagogy suggested the alternative hypothesis that "character" could be shaped or learned. For Bronson Alcott, character was expressive, leading to his central focus upon play and performance in the raising of children—as habits of behavior helped the individual develop individual characteristics and personality. Louisa May Alcott's frequent allusions to drama in her work potentially emerge from this alternative interpretation of transcendental thinking that rejected Emersonian internality and his antiperformative bias. Indeed, Bronson Alcott's classrooms (and his own home) were spaces filled with stimulation and impetuses towards inquiring play (what he called "emblems") that were prompts to moral lessons and instruction. At heart, Alcott valued forms of creativity that Emerson never countenanced, especially imitation, which his friend regarded as the very epitome of self-hate and self-destruction. In "Self-Reliance" Emerson had written, "imitation is suicide." For Bronson Alcott though, material things and other people were there to be learned from. Through discussion in the public sphere and the development of consensus they could give up their lessons, which one could imitate in their own lives. As the Alcott family biographer John Matteson writes:

> In preparation for opening the [Temple] school [at the Masonic Lodge on Tremont Street in Boston] in September 1834, Alcott set about creating the optimal environment for learning. Bronson had recently written to Peabody that he found emblems—his word for what we would call symbols—"extremely attractive and instructive to children." The modern age, he thought had done education a grave disservice by stripping truth of its symbolic garments and making instruction "prosaic, literal, worldly". With these thoughts in mind, he created a schoolroom rich in symbolic associations. The four-story Masonic Temple that housed the school was something of a symbol in itself. . . . The main room was twenty yards long, and the high ceiling supplied an apt visual emblem for Alcott's lofty ambitions . . . As to furnishings and decorations, Alcott spared no expense . . . paintings, maps, assorted statuary, and a copious library added still more splendor. (58)

That Alcott used a Masonic temple as the site of his school further alludes to the kinds of performative, theatrical, creative, and collective cultural forms he favored in his teaching. Like the Masons, Alcott believed that moral instruction came through shared participation in a kind of ritual practice that challenged the egocentrism of Emersonian transcendental liberalism. Additionally, in opposition to a focus on utilitarian rote learning or lecturing, Bronson Alcott favored public "conversations" and even found the writing of essays too closed off from debate and subjective an experience, instead developing forms of writing that resembled playscripts (such as "Conversations with Children on the Gospels" and the obscure, fragmentary, and much parodied "Orphic Sayings").

As with her experiences at the Boston Theatre, Louisa May Alcott developed from her father a sense of the world as a site of play and constant change, in which almost all culture had some lesson to impart. This manifested itself in a form of writing that drew inspiration from carnivalesque popular print and drama as much as from the dominant, middle-class, New England traditions of women's writing (which often favored the gendered essentialisms of sentimental culture) and transcendentalism. Indeed, for Alcott, sensationalism and theatricality, and the culture of display that characterized the short story in the popular press, could be used as resources for the positive development of human character. Like Poe before her, Alcott's short story aesthetic did not turn away from the pleasures of an audience, even courting the excesses of melodrama, but developed in response to them, incorporating them in its overall political vision. At the same time, Alcott was acutely aware of the dangers of pursuing purely selfish passions. "Pauline's Passion and Punishment" (the name says it all, really) is a tale about the blurred lines between performance and identity that courts the pure sensationalism of market-oriented fictions yet also demonstrates how pure cupidity or unfettered desire might result in tragedy for the individual's soul: in Pauline's case, the death of the man she ultimately comes to love. Consequently, the story is engaged in a complex attraction and repulsion to the logic of the sensational marketplace that closely resembles Melville, Poe, and Hawthorne's own authorial dilemmas. But more than this, Alcott would also share with her forebear Washington Irving a sense that sentimentalism was, ironically, always inherently performative.[4] One could not define femininity or national culture against theatricality, Alcott's work often suggests, because in order to be an American woman successfully—including immersing oneself within the bourgeois culture of the parlor—one was required to repress internality in favor of expressions of virtue and duty that might not be sincere but were yet deemed appropriate by the culture. Glenn Hendler has noted that Alcott's work is often characterized by its tendency to satirize the antitheatrical assumptions of sentimental culture by highlighting how "its representations of even the most authentic sympathy are often indistinguishable from theatricality" (695). Alcott's short works for the new national magazines and story papers like *Leslie's Illustrated* and the *Flag of Our Union* made her part of the culture of the parlor, a space where "one received guests who might participate in *tableaux vivants*, guessing or card games . . . musical interludes, or communal readings" (Williams, 42), allowing her to demonstrate the role played by female creativity and performance in modern middle-class, national culture.

It is Alcott's capacity to reconcile a newly emergent public sphere of women's writing with an older tradition of sensational short prose narrative that makes her such an important contributor to the American short story. Indeed, Alcott's magazine work is radical because it bridges the gap between the stage melodrama (a genre of performance that still remained largely closed off to middle-class women) and the sentimental culture of the bourgeois parlor—destabilizing the gendered and class-based logics of both simultaneously. Alcott knew this and even attempted to rewrite one of her early stories, "The Rival Prima Donnas," as a play for the Boston Theatre. Through Manuel's voyeurism in "Pauline's Passion," male readers are called out for their scopophilic, even pornographic, desire to observe the female body in moments of stress and debasement, while the magazine also allowed Alcott access to the domestic spaces of the middle-class household, which challenged the sanctity of the gendered essentialism upon which sentimental home life was often based. Read in this way, the suggestion made by Brodhead and Haltunen that Alcott's work constitutes an acceptance of repressive Victorian codes of morality and social etiquette reveals the influence of a Foucauldian paradigm in placing too great an emphasis on the disciplinary function of culture in the nineteenth century and largely ignoring the powerfully liberatory potential for theatrical self-fashioning organized around the relationship between text and the body that shaped the short story form in the period.

"Behind a Mask: or, A Woman's Power" (which appeared in four parts in the *Flag of Our Union* in 1866) demonstrates Alcott's critique of repressive morality and gendered essentialism quite aptly. The story dramatizes the theatricality inherent in, though frequently suppressed by, the "Cult of True Womanhood" through the protagonist Jean Muir, who is appointed as the new governess to the aristocratic Coventry family. In the narrative, Jean artfully deploys the expectations of ideal womanhood and sentimental culture against itself. More than this though, "Behind a Mask" is also a reflection on the short story form and constitutes a critique of the repressive logics of sentimental novel by bringing the carnivalesque embodiments of the popular stage to bear against the domestic realm of the novel. This is especially evident in the novel's rejection of family as the main source of democratic feeling. Indeed, the family is secondary in the novel to the important, and transformative, function of cross-class affiliation. Jean, it turns out, is a trained actress who "plays" at the various roles marked out for her by Victorian and antebellum sentimental fiction. Each of the "Chapters" is organized around one or more of Jean Muir's theatrical subversions of traditional womanhood. As Sara Hackenberg has observed, Jean deploys "many poses—noble but destitute orphan, world traveller, horse-tamer, accomplished nurse, wronged victim, humble servant, romantic heroine, and, in an evening of tableaux vivants entertainment, alternately a damsel in distress and the Virgin Queen . . ." (435). Each of these performances has the effect of destabilizing the aristocratic household in one way or another, turning Jean Muir's pursuit of personal success into a republican exercise in class politics. Like Richelieu in Bulwer-Lytton's popular play, Jean Muir is Machiavellian in her actions yet also contains the seeds of a more democratic future.

What makes Alcott's story so subversive is that rather than being punished for her transgressions against sentimental codes of behavior, authenticity, and morality—or exposed as a lower-class interloper into the sanctified realms of the aristocratic manor—Alcott actually praises her for it as she is ultimately a "materially and spiritually transformative force" (451). In Jean Muir's Machiavellian performances are Alcott's vision of the ideal republican citizen, who teaches the elites a crucial lesson in acceptance and democratic participation but does so through playful manipulation of deferential gestures and social behaviors coded by the liberal tradition as essential and natural. In this way, "Behind a Mask" plays out the burlesque logic of the American short story tradition I have outlined throughout this book by implying that a form of power can lie in behaviors that conform to the republican celebration of deference. The British setting of the tale even vectors its republican logic through a transatlantic form of affiliation, "paying respects to the symbolic value of England" (Tamarkin, xxiii) as a repository of democratic manners.

Jean Muir, then, is an allegory of magazine fiction itself (theatrical, diverse, heterogeneous, and public) who not only motivates the "smugly complacent, enervated and rather useless" (Hackenberg, 437) Coventry household towards socially useful forms of thought and action, such as marrying outside of their class and bloodline, but also energizes the young heir Gerard Coventry (introduced as lazy, bored, and privileged), bringing an atomized household together by serving as a focus of collective intrigue and speculation. Indeed, despite her machinations, Jean actually serves as a very useful tutor to their daughter Bella, achieving feats of pedagogy that had eluded her previous teachers. Literary styles often regarded as debased or immoral and prohibited by sentimental, liberal culture, Alcott argues, contain valuable lessons of benefit to the wider society—even if they comes at the expense of a purely personal morality.

To illustrate this point and demonstrate Alcott's utilization of the body/mind and performance/text synthesis, I will now turn to a tale that was composed at the same moment as the gothic tales yet is often read as a polite, middle-class diversion with none of the radicalism of those pieces: "The King of Clubs and the Queen of Hearts: A Story for Young America," which shows the shared characteristics of Alcott's style across genres.

"King of Clubs" appeared in Alcott's collection *On Picket Duty* (1864).

This book primarily concerns the effects of martial and educative discipline upon young Americans. Yet the tale also clearly exemplifies the light, humorous spirit of popular local color realism. Additionally, as with "Pauline's Passion," the tale constitutes a challenge to the limits of the logic of disciplinary self-fashioning and bodily reform. It is the tale of a pair of twins, Dick and Dolly Ward, who live in a small New England village well known to readers of midcentury women's fiction. The twins engage in a battle of wits because of the attentions paid to Dolly by a young German professor and local gymnastics instructor, August Bopp. Essentially, the story replays the folktale narrative of Washington Irving's "The Legend of Sleepy Hollow" by dramatizing the attempts of a young, educated interloper to a closed community to win the hand of that society's favored belle and the attempts of another young man (in this instance, her twin brother, Dick) to foil him. The story opens with the people of the village in a gymnasium and adopts a tone reminiscent of a nursery rhyme to break down the distinction between moral reform and play. Alcott writes, "Five and twenty ladies, all in a row, looking very much as if they felt like the little old woman who fell asleep on the king's highway, and awoke with abbreviated drapery, for they were all arrayed in grey tunics with Turkish continuations . . . Five and twenty men, all in a row sat on the opposite side of the hall . . ." (Alcott, *On Picket Duty*, 42). Alcott's satirical tone transforms the setting from a space of bodily reform and discipline into a space of carnivalesque whimsy, blurring the lines as had Bronson Alcott's own schooling of his children. The reader is introduced to August Bopp as a utopian dreamer who wishes to bring Germanic, cosmopolitan modernity to rural Connecticut so as to "strengthen the world's spine, and convert it to a belief in air and exercise" (43) through an extensive unisex regime of weightlifting.

As a response to her cultural moment, Alcott channels the popular interest in the importance of performance to the molding of psychological and physical health described by figures such as William James and the popular muscle builder William Blaikie. Blaikie's guide *How to Get Strong and Stay So* was part of a distinctive post–Civil War valorization of exercise and "popularised a program of weightlifting that undercut some of the most entrenched assumptions regarding the intersections of masculine strength, race, class, and muscularity" (Salazar, 143). This trend towards developing the body was the latest development of Alcott's father's own focus on the importance of physical health, exercise, and diet in his pedagogic practices. This focus on vitality would certainly come to shape the work of such post-transcendentalist thinkers as Charlotte Perkins Gilman, who would use the culture of muscle building to challenge traditional understandings of feminine weakness and submissiveness. Yet the story also subtly subverts the basic logic underlying moral bodily reform. In the plot, despite their differences of gender, the two twins come to resemble one another sufficiently for Dick to play a trick on August Bopp in which he dresses up as his sister and gets the German to declare his love for him during the school fête. This act of queering (at a carnival no less) recalls the "linked surrogations," performances, and network of gazes that structured "Pauline's Passion" within the circum-Atlantic theatrical space of Cuba, but in doing this the New England writer also draws on popular fears concerning the effect of discipline and exercise upon the female body. As with Manuel in the earlier story, Dick is made sufficiently "womanly" to pass as a girl, while Dolly's body is also sufficiently toned to pass for male. As with "Pauline's Passion," Alcott uses the traditions of popular narrative against themselves to show how a didactic, moralizing story of courtship and marriage that sought to perpetuate repressive nineteenth-century mores can be troubled within performative textual spaces of the short story.

Alcott's success as a writer of short fiction depended on her understanding of the genre as Irving, Poe, Melville, and Hawthorne first used it, as the premier site for the presentation of a transnational world of identities in flux. The brevity of the short story helped to abridge identities sufficiently to allow writers to conceive of selfhood as primarily expressive in nature and led to the development of a more playful, carnivalesque form of prose narrative that deployed immanence in ways that challenged the fixed categories of gender, race, and class reified by much nineteenth-century art and culture. By inviting participation and dispute through its circulation in the new public sphere created by newspapers, magazines, and other so-called "ephemeral" forms of print media, the short story dramatized emergent transatlantic modernity in ways that traditional scholars of "the book" have been slow to appreciate. Alcott's extension of this short story tradition into the realm of women's experience occurred at a time when women themselves were beginning to carve out more and more spaces, or "platforms" as Margaret Fuller had called them, for the articulation of their own experience, including oratory, print media, and, increasingly after the Civil War, the stage itself. The play of identities and use of embodied expressivity that Hawthorne, Melville, Poe, and Irving had wedded to the short story tradition in America in the early republic and antebellum eras was deployed by Alcott in generating critiques of racialized, gendered, national culture in the Gilded Age–critiques that went much further politically than the white men that preceded her, and which paved the way for a new generation of feminist, realist short story writers to exceed the essentialisms and class positions sentimental and romantic fiction sutured to the female body. Alcott's short story writing is an important moment in the American short story tradition because it provides a link between the antebellum era and the new aesthetics of figures as diverse as Kate Chopin, Charlotte Gilman, and Sui Sin Far. In finding in short story a site for the navigation of popular print culture and performance, Alcott also located resources for the reinvigoration of American political culture through radical republicanism. In effect, in borrowing from Hawthorne, Poe, and Melville the genre's formal negotiations between market forces and individualism, Alcott preempted the development of modernist subjectivities that embraced bodily sensations and the performativity of all forms of identity. It is beyond the reach of this book, but one need look no further than Chopin's attraction to the thrill of spectacular modernity in tales such as "A Pair of Silk Stockings," or Charlotte Perkins Gilman's consideration of embodied consciousness in "The Yellow Wallpaper," for evidence of the kind of positions Alcott foresaw in her own short work. Hawthorne and Poe, perhaps especially among the writers considered here, may have been surprised to learn that their embrace of the body as a site of communicative power, couched as a rejection of the essentialism and egocentrism of romanticism, would lay the groundwork for an eventual feminist aesthetic in American literary culture, but it nonetheless did. What remained a crucial inheritance in the form from its inception in America was its capacity to mobilize a resistance to the assumption that forms of essentialism, whether nationalistic, racial, gendered, or classed, provided the only basis for the establishment of collectivities. Instead, I have attempted to show that through its engagement with performance, the short story tradition always had embedded within it a fundamental awareness of the audience, an assumption that American individualism inclined towards a socially irresponsible libertarianism, and a predisposition to reject speculation in favor of action in the social world, which makes it an important genre in American literary and political history. As such, it is my hope that this book might help future scholars provide new political readings of the short story that consider its position as an aesthetic practice designed to precipitate forms of democratic participation.

Notes

INTRODUCTION

1. The name was also certainly intended as a satire of the Oliver Oldschool letters written by known Federalist supporter and the Irving brothers' literary rival Joseph Dennie for his *Port Folio* magazine. In sending up Federalist elites, Irving was also attacking Dennie behind the mask of Jonathan Oldstyle. For more, see Dowling, *Literary Federalism in America* (1999).

2. The project of interpreting the anecdotal and gestural idioms of everyday life as counterhistories to teleological narratives of historical development has, at least since the 1970s, become a major element of postmodern and new historicist critical practice. Works such as Catherine Gallagher and Stephen Greenblatt's *Practicing New Historicism* (Chicago: University of Chicago Press, 2000), as well as those of Michel de Certeau and Jean-François Lyotard, have been paradigm shifting. For more on Benjamin's vision of modern life as theatre, see Susan Buck-Morss, *The Dialectics of Seeing: Walter Benjamin and the Arcades Project* (Cambridge, Mass., and London: MIT Press, 1989).

3. Hicks was also one of the subscribers whose funds helped establish William Dunlap's Park Theatre in New York after the closure of the John Street Theatre in 1798. As a critic, then, he had much invested in the success of New York theatre. His case is special, as many Quakers, particularly those in nearby Philadelphia, were opposed to the establishment of permanent theatre in the United States. Additionally, as a Democratic-Republican his support for the Park was out of keeping with the political affiliations of most of the rest of the subscribers, who owed patronage to the Federalist Tontine Coffeehouse political machine.

4. On the necessity of maintaining cultural ties to Britain in the early United States in spite of the revolutionary breach dividing them, see David Waldstreicher, *In the Midst of Perpetual Fetes: The Making of American Nationalism, 1776–1820* (Chapel Hill: University of North Carolina Press, 1997); Elisa Tamarkin, *Anglophilia: Deference, Devotion, and Antebellum America* (Chicago: University of Chicago Press, 2008); Leonard Tennenhouse, *The Importance of Feeling English: American Literature and the British Diaspora, 1750–1850* (Princeton and Oxford: Princeton University Press, 2007).

5. I use the terms "republican" and "liberal" throughout this book. Definitions vary widely, but essentially I suggest that "republicanism" is defined by traditions of "civil rights" against a liberal position that is characterized by "natural rights" discourse. The distinction rests on the role of performance and law in civic life. A republican position suggests that rights are only established through recourse to the logic of the collective—leading to a focus on expressive acts in shaping law and appeals to tradition (republic coming from *res publica*, meaning public concern). Liberal positions I characterize as more committed to a natural-rights position in which one is imbued with rights by virtue of their birth (they do not need to be performed or claimed publically). Republicanism is therefore more *performative* than liberalism, which tends to focus on internality (subjectivity) rather than collectivity or communitarianism in shaping citizenship. In situating the short story tradition in America within the terms of republicanism and performativity, in this book I frequently undercut the traditionally prominent position critics have given to John Locke in framing American attitudes and literatures, emphasizing instead the Machiavellian legacy (including Bentham and Madison) defined by J. G. A. Pocock.

6. For more on the eighteenth-century genre of "burlesque," see Giles, *Transatlantic Insurrections* (2001).

7. This partly rests on how the "New England Mind" has been seen as predominant in the making of US literary culture. The Puritan inheritance shows through in classic works of American literary history, from Vernon Parrington through Perry Miller to Lawrence Buell, in the focus upon forms of republican simplicity, antiperformative bias, and intellectualism.

8. Isabel Lehuu's *Carnival on the Page* describes in detail how from the gargantuan weekly newspapers to the opulence and choice of the Christmas gift books, abundance became a key trope of antebellum print culture that generated a backlash against print from conservatives who felt that such overconsumption was ironically producing a less "literate" or discerning public.

9. This claim is partly a response to Michael Warner's suggestion in *Letters of the Republic* that the emergence of a national political culture in the United States was rooted in the authority of printed materials, which when widely disseminated could abstract ideas sufficiently from the embodied individual of the author to allow them to appear as though they had emerged, without the "mediation of particular persons," from the collective will of "the people."

10. It is slightly beyond the purview of this book but worth noting nonetheless that Brander Matthews, one of the first major academics to take seriously the short story as a separate genre, was, like Poe, a playwright, critic, and the first chair of dramatic literature at Columbia.

11. Jared Gardner has made a similar claim in *The Rise and Fall of Early American Magazine Culture* in relation to the magazine form more generally, arguing that the early American magazine seldom had a nationalist intention in mind and was often highly critical of the political logic of the novel.

12. See Sandra Gustafson, *Eloquence Is Power: Oratory and Performance in Early America* (Chapel Hill: University of North Carolina Press, 2000), and Christopher

Looby, *Voicing America: Language, Literary Form, and the Origins of the United States* (Chicago: University of Chicago Press, 1996).

CHAPTER 1

1. See Burstein.
2. See Busch, "Bowery B'Hoys and Matinee Ladies" (1994), and Faye E. Dudden, *Women in the American Theater* (1994).
3. "L'Envoy" only appeared in the London edition that was published as two separate books. For American readers *The Sketch-Book* would have ended with "The Legend of Sleepy Hollow."
4. Robert Hughes, "Sleepy Hollow: Fearful Pleasures and the Nightmare of History."
5. See Caleb Crain, *American Sympathy* (2001).
6. See John Seelye, "Root and Branch: Washington Irving and American Humor" (1984).

CHAPTER 2

1. Poe had delivered different versions of this lecture at different locations from 1843 to July 1849, at which time the last version was stolen from his valise in Philadelphia. The text of the lecture appeared in an altered form under the title "American Poetry" in the *Aristidean*, November 1845.
2. "Degree" is a term used by most fraternal groups to denote the position of the member within the hierarchy of the lodge. Scottish Rite Freemasonry contains degrees with such astonishing names as Knight of the Royal Ax, or Prince of Libanus, and Sublime Master Elected.
3. Karen Haltunnen's *Confidence Men and Painted Women: A Study of Middle-Class Culture in America, 1830–1870* (New Haven: Yale University Press, 1982) offers a rich and detailed account of how the development of the market economy drove a corresponding theatricalization of the American public sphere. Haltunnen posits that the move from early republican simplicity to a high "Victorian-American" theatricality can be explained as an attempt to find improved forms of social behavior to deal with a public world that was perceived as increasingly dangerous and insincere.
4. Patrician Okker corroborates this claim to Sarah Hale's Masonic connections in *Our Sister Editors: Sarah J. Hale and the Tradition of Nineteenth-Century American Women Editors* (Athens: University of Georgia Press, 2008). Okker quotes Elizabeth Oakes Smith's autobiographical reminiscences of the Masons' support for Hale in the publication of her first work of poetry, *The Genius of Oblivion* (1823).
5. Nathaniel Hawthorne would also reference the Mischianza in his story "Howe's Masquerade" (1837), a work included in *Twice-Told Tales*—a work Poe reviewed in 1842 and knew extremely well.

6. The foot is an unusual charge and appears on only one notable coat of arms, that of the Millars, a clan of Scottish descent. This may account for the motto Poe suggests is the Montressor family motto, which is also the official national motto of Scotland—*Nemo me impune lacessit*, or "None Wound Me With Impunity," effectively "I Take Revenge."

7. In many fraternal rituals ashes and nitre are used to anoint the heads of new initiates. In Egyptian magic, which provides much of the occult tenor in Western Masonic ritual, nitre was a symbol of death and rebirth. In the Bible the ashes spread by Moses to bring the plagues to Egypt were ashes of nitre. Nitre therefore also refers to the destruction of earthly monarchies in Judeo-Christian culture and the arrival of the Lord.

8. Karen Haltunnen's *Confidence Men and Painted Women* is a classic study of how significant antebellum publications like *Godey's* cultivated an interest in the importance of external performances, the "emergence of genteel social form," gesture, and a certain theatricality to middle-class culture.

9. It is interesting to note that amontillado sherry is always aged in American oak casks, making it a commodity that depended upon the circum-Atlantic trade networks of the modern era for its distinctive character.

10. Roughly translated, the epigraph reads: Here the wicked mob, unappeased, long cherished a hatred of innocent blood. Now that the fatherland has been saved and the cave of death demolished, where grim death has been, so life and vitality appear.

11. The Jacobin Club was a political club of left-wing revolutionaries tied to the Freemasonry in Revolutionary France. The Jacobin Club dissolved soon after Robespierre's demise. "Jacobin" was an insult levelled at left-wing bohemians in nineteenth-century America and Europe.

12. Many of the important thinkers that inspired the French Revolution, including Jean-Jacques Rousseau, were Freemasons. Rousseau's own thought concerning liberty, equality, and the importance of social, contractual bonds owes much to the Masonic conception of brotherhood.

13. In Masonic terminology this handshake is called a "token" or a "grip" depending on the degree of the Mason who receives it.

14. In the mid- to late nineteenth century an entire genre of books and magazines emerged designed to assist men and women in copying stage effects in their own amateur parlor theatricals. One such text, *The Book of Tableaux and Shadow Pantomimes* (New York: Dick & Fitzgerald Publishers, 1869), included detailed instructions on which chemicals to mix with gunpowder to produce colored fires and flares.

15. In the absence of the full ritual book and only fragments from which to work we are left to speculate the real meaning of this "H.F." The letters are often depicted beneath a burning chalice on Brotherhood of the Union material culture, suggesting "Holy Fire" or "Holy Flame" as a possibility. This would be commensurate with the notion of "passing the torch" or the flame seen in many ritual cultures. The other option is the "Holy Father" of the Trinity; however, Lippard often speaks of the urge to "reclaim" the "H.F." in a way that suggests something material that has been lost. "Holy Flame" therefore makes the most sense, syntactically.

16. In fact, the Brotherhood of the Union actually had two major publications. The second, a two-hundred-page book of copyrighted rites and rituals called *The BGC* has, regrettably, been lost to history.

CHAPTER 3

1. Melville actually dedicated "The Two Temples" to Sheridan Knowles, a famous Irish playwright that devoted the latter half of his life to the ministry.
2. For further discussion of the twinned roles played by performance and print in the operations of the nineteenth-century British and American government, see Oz Frankel, *States of Inquiry: Social Investigations and Print Culture in Nineteenth-Century Britain and the United States* (Baltimore: Johns Hopkins University Press, 2006).

CHAPTER 4

1. As John M. J. Gretchko has noted, this led to the historical misattribution of "The Fiddler" to Fitz-James O'Brien. This was remedied in the 1960s when the Newbury Library and Northwestern University Press undertook to produce "authoritative" editions of Melville's works. See "Fiddling with Melville's 'The Fiddler,'" *Melville Society Extracts* (1996): 104.
2. See Lawrence W. Levine, *Highbrow/Lowbrow: The Emergence of Cultural Hierarchy in America* (Cambridge, Mass., and London: Harvard University Press, 1988).
3. The irony of the Astor Place Riot was that the Young America group, associated with Duyckinck and famed for their defense of radical democracy, found itself on the side of the Whig elites because of their collective dislike of Forrest's performance style.
4. The first broad group includes Lewis Mumford in "Melville's Miserable Years" and Leo Marx, "Melville's Parable of the Walls," in *Bartleby the Inscrutable: A Collection of Commentary on Herman Melville's Tale "Bartleby, the Scrivener,"* ed. M. Thomas Inge (Hamden, Conn.: Archon, 1979), and Merlin Bowen, *The Long Encounter: Self and Experience in the Writings of Herman Melville* (Chicago: Chicago University Press, 1960). The second group is numerous but includes Michael T. Gilmore, *American Romanticism and the Marketplace* (Chicago: University of Chicago Press, 1985), Naomi C. Reed, "The Specter of Wall Street: 'Bartleby, the Scrivener' and the Language of Commodities" (*American Literature*, 76, no. 2, June 2004), and P. C. Solomon, *Dickens and Melville in Their Time* (London: Columbia University Press, 1975).
5. This is similar to the use of the voice in Poe's "Hop-Frog," where the king, essentially invisible to the majority of his subjects, controls his kingdom with his commanding voice. It is the clownish body of his jester that then becomes the tool of dissent against his rule.

CHAPTER 5

1. In this respect Hawthorne resembles Lippard (a writer with whom he shared much aesthetically but little politically). Lippard's own critique of Calvinism rested upon similar premises to Hawthorne; it either used the doctrine of predestination as a mask of class status or resulted in a version of reform culture that essentially patronized the working classes by imposing alien values upon them.
2. Hawthorne's descriptions of Edith and Edgar closely resemble the image from

"The Lovers" card in a conventional tarot deck. Often the two lovers look similar enough as to be almost unrecognizable from one another save for the phallic symbol of the staff held in the hand of the male lover. Tarot cards first appeared in mid-fifteenth-century Italy and were most often used for a card game that closely resembles modern bridge. However, during the eighteenth and nineteenth centuries the cards became connected with occult religious practices and divination, for which they are now most commonly used. In suggesting a connection with the tarot, Hawthorne is ironically restating the Manichean distinction in "The Maypole of Merry Mount" between the austere Puritans and the mysticism of the Old World.

EPILOGUE

1. In *Louisa May Alcott: Her Life, Letters, and Journals*, ed. Ednah D. Cheney (London: Sampson Low, Marston, Searle, and Rivington, 1889), 87–89.

2. See Brad Evans, *Before Cultures: The Ethnographic Imagination in American Literature, 1865–1920*.

3. Keith Gandall makes the point in *The Virtues of the Vicious* (1997) that whereas antebellum fiction, whether sentimental or not, often dramatized the attempts of an individual (frequently a member of the mechanic class or working poor) to overcome the effects of their environment, by the late nineteenth century environment often dominated and shaped the individual. This was especially evident in popular movements from realism to naturalism, which raised significant questions about the relationship between literary representation and social mobility in the Gilded Age and relegating tales of transcendence and transformation to the realm of children's fiction (e.g., Horatio Alger and Alcott herself).

4. I discussed this tendency in Irving's work in chapter 1, with specific reference to the story "The Wife," which I suggested when read in the context of *The Sketch-Book* as a whole demonstrates the author's burlesque of the sentimental ideologies of true womanhood and domestic duty.

Bibliography

Abrams, N. H. *Natural Supernaturalism: Tradition and Revolution in Romantic Literature.* New York: W. W. Norton, 1971.

Ackerman, Alan L. *The Portable Theater: American Literature and the Nineteenth-Century Stage.* London: Johns Hopkins University Press, 1999.

Adams, John Quincy. *Lectures on Rhetoric and Oratory.* Cambridge, Mass.: Hillard and Metcalf, 1810.

Agamben, Giorgio. *Homo Sacer: Sovereign Power and Bare Life.* Trans. Daniel Heller-Roazen. Stanford: Stanford University Press, 1998.

Agamben, Giorgio. *Potentialities: Collected Essays in Philosophy.* Trans. Daniel Heller-Roazen. Stanford: Stanford University Press, 1999.

Agnew, Jean-Christophe. *Worlds Apart: The Market and the Theater in Anglo American Thought, 1550–1750.* Cambridge: Cambridge University Press, 1993.

Alcott, L. M. *On Picket Duty.* Readhowyouwant.com, 2008.

Alcott, L. M. *Louisa May Alcott: Her Life, Letters, and Journals.* Ed. Ednah D. Cheney. London: Sampson Low, Marston, Searle, and Rivington Ltd., 1889.

Alighieri, Dante. *The Divine Comedy.* Trans. Allen Mandelbaum. London: Everyman's Library, 1995.

Anon. *The Young Roscius: Being Biographical Memoirs of William Hen. West Betty; from the Earliest Period of His Infancy. Including the History of His Irish, Scotch, and English Engagements with Analytical Structures on His Acting at the London Theatres.* New York: Robert M'Dermut, 1806.

Arac, Jonathan. *Commissioned Spirits: The Shaping of Social Motion in Dickens, Carlyle, Melville, and Hawthorne.* New Brunswick, N.J.: Rutgers University Press, 1979.

Arendt, Hannah. *On Revolution.* London: Penguin, 1990.

Assael, Brenda. *The Circus and Victorian Society.* Charlottesville: University of Virginia Press, 2005.

Bakhtin, Mikhail. *Rabelais and His World.* Trans. Helene Iswolsky. Cambridge, Mass.: MIT Press, 1968.

Bank, Rosemarie K. *Theatre Culture in America, 1825–1860.* Cambridge: Cambridge University Press, 1997.

Barnes, Elizabeth. *States of Sympathy: Seduction and Democracy in the American Novel.* New York: Columbia University Press, 1997.

Barrett, Lawrence. *Edwin Forrest.* Boston: James R. Osgood and Co., 1881.

Barrish, Phillip. *The Cambridge Introduction to American Literary Realism.* Cambridge: Cambridge University Press, 2011.

Beecher, Henry Ward. *Seven Lectures to Young Men on Various Important Subjects.* Cincinnati: William H. Moore and Co., 1844.

Bell, Catherine. *Ritual: Perspectives and Dimensions.* Oxford: Oxford University Press, 1997.

Bell, Catherine. *Ritual Theory, Ritual Practice.* Oxford: Oxford University Press, 1992.

Bell, Michael Davitt. *The Problem of American Realism.* Chicago: University of Chicago Press, 1996.

Benjamin, Walter. *Illuminations.* London: Pimlico, 1999.

Bennett, Bridget. *Transatlantic Spiritualism and Nineteenth-Century American Literature.* New York: Palgrave Macmillan, 2007.

Bentham, Jeremy, and J. S. Mill. *Utilitarianism and Other Essays.* Ed. Alan Ryan. London: Penguin Books, 2004.

Bentley, Nancy. *The Ethnography of Manners: Hawthorne, James, Wharton.* Cambridge: Cambridge University Press, 1995.

Bercovitch, Sacvan. *The American Jeremiad.* London: University of Wisconsin Press, 1978.

Bercovitch, Sacvan. *The Puritan Origins of the American Self.* New Haven: Yale University Press, 1975.

Bercovitch, Sacvan. *The Rites of Assent: Transformations in the Symbolic Construction of America.* London: Routledge, 1993.

Berlant, Lauren. *The Anatomy of National Fantasy: Hawthorne, Utopia, and Everyday Life.* Chicago: University of Chicago Press, 1991.

Berlant, Lauren. *The Female Complaint: The Unfinished Business of Sentimentality in American Culture.* London: Duke University Press, 2008.

Berthold, Dennis. "Class Acts: The Astor Place Riots and Melville's 'The Two Temples.'" *American Literature* 71, no. 3 (Sept. 1999).

Bingham, Caleb. *The Columbian Orator.* Boston: Manning and Coring, 1797.

Boddy, Kasia. *The American Short Story Since 1950.* Edinburgh: Edinburgh University Press, 2010.

Boever, Arne De. "Overhearing Bartleby: Agamben, Melville, and Inoperative Power." *Parrhesia: A Journal of Critical Philosophy*, no. 1 (2006).

Boucicault, Dion. *The Poor of New York: A Drama in Five Acts.* New York: Samuel French, 1857.

Bourdieu, Pierre. *Distinction: A Social Critique of the Judgement of Taste.* London: Routledge, 1984.

Bowen, Merlin. *The Long Encounter: Self and Experience in the Writings of Herman Melville.* Chicago: University of Chicago Press, 1960.

Brand, Dana. *The Spectator and the City in Nineteenth-Century American Literature.* Cambridge: Cambridge University Press, 1991.

Brodwin, Stanley, ed. *The Old and New World Romanticism of Washington Irving*. London: Greenwood Press, 1986.
Brooks, Peter. *The Melodramatic Imagination: Balzac, Henry James, Melodrama, and the Mode of Excess*. London: Yale University Press, 1979.
Brown, William Hill, and Hannah Webster Foster. *The Power of Sympathy* and *The Coquette*. London: Penguin Books, 1996.
Bryant, John. *Melville and Repose: The Rhetoric of Humor in the American Renaissance*. Oxford: Oxford University Press, 1993.
Bryant, John. "Poe's Ape of UnReason: Humor, Ritual, and Culture." *Nineteenth-Century Literature* 51, no. 1 (June 1996).
Bulwer-Lytton, Edward. *The Dramatic Works*. Boston: Elibron Classics, 2006.
Bulwer-Lytton, Edward. *England & the English*. Ed. Standish Meacham. Chicago: University of Chicago Press, 1970.
Burke, Edmund. *A Philosophical Enquiry into the Sublime and Beautiful*. London: Penguin Books, 1998.
Burstein, Andrew. *The Original Knickerbocker: The Life of Washington Irving*. New York: Basic Books, 2007.
Butsch, Richard. "Bowery B'Hoys and Matinee Ladies: The Re-Gendering of Nineteenth-Century American Theater Audiences." *American Quarterly* 46, no. 3 (Sept. 1994).
Carlson, Marvin. *The Haunted Stage: The Theatre as a Memory Machine*. Ann Arbor: University of Michigan Press, 2001.
Carlyle, Thomas. *Sartor Resartus*. Oxford: Oxford University Press, 1987.
Carlyle, Thomas. *On Heroes, Heroworship, and the Heroic in History*. New York: Wiley and Halsted, 1859.
Carnes, Mark C. *Secret Ritual and Manhood in Victorian America*. New Haven: Yale University Press, 1989.
Castronovo, Russ. *Necro Citizenship: Death, Eroticism, and the Public Sphere in the Nineteenth-Century United States*. London: Duke University Press, 2001.
Chapman, Mary. *Making Noise, Making News: Suffrage Print Culture and US Modernism*. Oxford and New York: Oxford University Press, 2014.
Chapman, Mary. "Gender and Influence in Louisa May Alcott's *A Modern Mephistopheles*." *Legacy* 13, no. 1 (1996).
Chase, Richard. *The American Novel and Its Tradition*. Baltimore: Johns Hopkins University Press, 1980.
Cicero, Marcus Tullius. *On Government*. Trans. Michael Grant. London: Penguin Books, 1993.
Cicero, Marcus Tullius. *On the Good Life*. Trans. Michael Grant. London: Penguin Books, 1971.
Cicero, Marcus Tullius. *On the State*. Trans. Michael Grant. London: Penguin Books, 1993.
Cicero, Marcus Tullius. *Political Speeches*. Trans. D. H. Berry. Oxford: Oxford University Press, 2006.
Clark, Gregory, and Michael Halloran, eds. *Oratorical Culture in the Nineteenth Cen-

tury: *Transformation in the Theory and Practice of Rhetoric.* Carbondale: Southern Illinois University Press, 1993.
Colacurcio, Michael. *The Province of Piety: Moral History in Hawthorne's Early Tales.* Durham and London: Duke University Press, 1995.
Cooke, Alexander. "Resistance, Potentiality, and the Law: Deleuze and Agamben on 'Bartleby.'" *Angelaki* 10, no. 3 (Dec. 2005).
Crain, Caleb. *American Sympathy: Men, Friendship, and Literature in the New Nation.* New Haven: Yale University Press, 2001.
Crews, Frederick. *The Sins of the Fathers.* New York: Oxford University Press, 1966.
Crews, Frederick. "Whose American Renaissance?" *New York Review of Books*, Oct. 27, 1988.
Davis, Jim, and Victor Emeljanow. *Reflecting the Audience: London Theatregoing, 1840–1880.* Hatfield, Herts: University of Hertfordshire Press, 2001.
Denning, Michael. *Mechanic Accents: Dime Novels and Working-Class Culture in America.* London and New York: Verso, 1998.
Dickens, Charles. *Bleak House.* New York: Alfred A. Knopf, 1991.
Dickens, Charles. *Hard Times.* London: Penguin Books, 1994.
Dickens, Charles. *Memoirs of Joseph Grimaldi.* London: Pushkin Press, 2008.
Dill, Elizabeth. "That Damned Mob of Scribbling Siblings: The American Romance as Anti Novel in *The Power of Sympathy* and *Pierre*." *American Literature* 80, no. 4 (Dec. 2008).
Dimock, Wai-Chee. *Through Other Continents: American Literature Across Deep Time.* Princeton: Princeton University Press, 2006.
Dimock, Wai-Chee. *Empire for Liberty: Melville and the Politics of Individualism.* Princeton: Princeton University Press, 1989.
Douglass, Frederick. *Autobiographies.* Ed. Henry Louis Gates Jr. New York: Library of America, 1994.
Dowling, William C. *Literary Federalism in the Age of Jefferson: Joseph Dennie and the Port Folio, 1801–1811.* Columbia: University of South Carolina Press, 1999.
Doyle, Laura. "Toward a Philosophy of Transnationalism." *Journal of Transnational American Studies* 1, no. 1 (2009).
Dunlap, William. *A History of the American Theatre.* New York: J & J Harper, 1832.
During, Simon. *Modern Enchantments: The Cultural Power of Secular Magic.* London: Harvard University Press, 2002.
Eastwood, David R. "O'Brien's Fiddler—Or Melville's?" *American Transcendental Quarterly* 29 (1976).
Eisler, Benita, ed. *The Lowell Offering: Writings by New England Mill Women (1840–1945).* New York: W. W. Norton, 1998.
Elliott, Michael A. *The Culture Concept: Writing and Difference in the Age of Realism.* Minneapolis: University of Minnesota Press, 2002.
Elmer, Jonathan. *Reading at the Social Limit: Affect, Mass Culture, and Edgar Allan Poe.* Stanford: Stanford University Press, 1995.
Emerson, R. W. *Essays and Poems.* London: Everyman, 2002.
Emerson, R. W. *Nature and Selected Essays.* New York: Penguin Books, 2003.
Evans, Brad. *Before Cultures: The Ethnographic Imagination in American Literature, 1865–1920.* Chicago: University of Chicago Press, 2005.

Fiedler, Leslie A. *Love and Death in the American Novel: Revised Edition*. New York: Stein and Day Publishers, 1975.

Fliegelman, Jay. *Declaring Independence: Jefferson, Natural Language, and the Culture of Performance*. Stanford: Stanford University Press, 1993.

Fogle, Richard Harter. *Melville's Shorter Tales*. Norman: University of Oklahoma Press, 1960.

Foley, Barbara. "From Wall Street to Astor Place: Historicizing Melville's 'Bartleby.'" *American Literature* 72, no. 1 (March 2000).

Frankel, Oz. *States of Inquiry: Social Investigations and Print Culture in Nineteenth-Century Britain and the United States*. Baltimore: Johns Hopkins University Press, 2006.

Fredricks, Nancy. *Melville's Art of Democracy*. Athens: University of Georgia Press, 1995.

Fuller, Margaret. *Art, Literature, and the Drama*. Ed. Arthur B. Fuller. New York: Tribune Association, 1869.

Fuller, Margaret. *Woman in the Nineteenth Century*. Ed. Larry J. Reynolds. New York: Norton and Co., 1998.

Gardner, Jared. *The Rise and Fall of Early American Magazine Culture*. Urbana, Chicago, and Springfield: University of Illinois Press, 2012.

Gandall, Keith. *The Virtues of the Vicious: Jacob Riis, Stephen Crane, and the Spectacle of the Slum*. New York and London: Oxford University Press, 1997.

Garvey, Ellen Gruber. *Writing with Scissors: American Scrapbooks from the Civil War to the Harlem Renaissance*. Oxford: Oxford University Press, 2012.

George, David J., and Christopher J. Gossip, eds. *Studies in Commedia Dell'Arte*. Cardiff: University of Wales Press, 1993.

Giles, Paul. *Atlantic Republic: The American Tradition in English Literature*. Oxford: Oxford University Press, 2006.

Giles, Paul. *Transatlantic Insurrections: British Culture and the Formation of American Literature, 1730–1860*. Philadelphia: University of Pennsylvania Press, 2001.

Giles, Paul. *Virtual Americas: Transnational Fictions and the Transatlantic Imaginary*. London: Duke University Press, 2002.

Gilmore, Michael T. *American Romanticism and the Marketplace*. Chicago: University of Chicago Press, 1985.

Gilmore, Paul. "Romantic Electricity, or the Materiality of Aesthetics." *American Literature* 76, no. 3 (Sept. 2004).

Girard, René. *The Scapegoat*. Trans. Yvonne Freccero. Baltimore: Johns Hopkins University Press, 1986.

Girard, René. *Violence and the Sacred*. Trans. Patrick Gregory. Baltimore: Johns Hopkins University Press, 1977.

Goffman, Erving. *The Goffman Reader*. Ed. Charles Lemert and Ann Branaman. Malden, Mass.: Blackwell Publishers, 1997.

Goldman, Eric. "Explaining Mental Illness: Theology and Pathology in Nathaniel Hawthorne's Short Fiction." *Nineteenth-Century Literature* 59, no.1. (2004).

Graham, George, ed. *Graham's American Monthly Magazine of Literature and Art* 28, (1846).

Gretchko, John M. J. "Fiddling with Melville's Fiddler." *Melville Society Extracts* 104, (1996).

Grimsted, David. *Melodrama Unveiled: American Theatre and Culture, 1800–1850.* London: University of California Press, 1968.
Gunn, Simon. *The Public Culture of the Victorian Middle Class: Ritual and Authority and the English Industrial City, 1840–1914.* Manchester: Manchester University Press, 2000.
Gupta, R. K. "Hautboy and Plinlimmon: A Reinterpretation of Melville's 'The Fiddler.'" *American Literature* 43, no. 3 (Nov. 1971).
Gura, Philip. *American Transcendentalism: A History.* New York: Hill and Wang, 2007.
Gustafson, Sandra, and Caroline F. Sloat, eds. *Cultural Narratives: Textuality and Performance in American Culture before 1900.* Notre Dame: University of Notre Dame Press, 2011.
Gustafson, Sandra, and Caroline F. Sloat, eds. *Eloquence Is Power: Oratory and Performance in Early America.* Chapel Hill: University of North Caroline Press, 2000.
Habermas, Jürgen. *The Structural Transformation of the Bourgeois Public Sphere: An Inquiry into a Category of Bourgeois Society.* Trans. Thomas Berger. Cambridge: Polity Press, 1999.
Heckenberg, Sara. "Plots and Counterplots: The Defense of Sensational Fiction in Louisa May Alcott's 'Behind a Mask.'" *American Transcendental Quarterly* 22, no. 2 (June 2008).
Hadley, Elaine. *Melodramatic Tactics: Theatricalized Dissent in the English Market Place 1800–1885.* Stanford: Stanford University Press, 1995.
Halttunen, Karen. *Confidence Men and Painted Women: A Study of Middle-Class Culture in America, 1830–1870.* New Haven: Yale University Press, 1982.
Halttunen, Karen. "The Domestic Drama of Louisa May Alcott." *Feminist Studies* 10, no. 2 (Summer 1984).
Hamilton, Kristie. *America's Sketchbook: The Cultural Life of a Nineteenth-Century Literary Genre.* Athens: Ohio University Press, 1998.
Harrison, Les. *The Temple and the Forum: The American Museum and Cultural Authority in Hawthorne, Melville, Stowe, and Whitman.* Tuscaloosa: University of Alabama Press, 2007.
Hawthorne, Nathaniel. *French & Italian Notebooks.* Boston: Houghton & Mifflin, 1886.
Hawthorne, Nathaniel. *Mosses from an Old Manse.* New York: Modern Library, 2003.
Hawthorne, Nathaniel. *The House of the Seven Gables.* New York: Heritage Press, 1935.
Hawthorne, Nathaniel. *The Letters, 1843–1853.* Ed. Thomas Woodson, et al. Columbus: Ohio State University Press, 1987.
Hawthorne, Nathaniel. *The Marble Faun: Or, The Romance of Monte Beni.* London: Penguin Books, 1990.
Hawthorne, Nathaniel. *The Scarlet Letter.* London: Penguin Books, 1994.
Hawthorne, Nathaniel. *The Snow-Image and Other Twice-Told Tales.* Hollywood, CA: Aegypan Press, 2006.
Hawthorne, Nathaniel. *Twice-Told Tales.* London: Hard Press, 2008
Hazlitt, William. *Selected Writings.* Ed. Jon Cook. Oxford: Oxford University Press, 1998.
Hendler, Glenn. "The Limits of Sympathy: Louisa May Alcott and the Sentimental Novel." *American Literary History* 3, no. 4 (Winter 1991).

Herbert, T. Walter. *Dearest Beloved: The Hawthornes and the Making of the Middle-Class Family.* Oxford: University of California Press, 1993.

Hewitt, Elizabeth. *Correspondence and American Literature, 1770–1865.* Cambridge: Cambridge University Press, 2004.

Hickey, Donald R. *The War of 1812: A Forgotten Conflict.* Chicago: University of Illinois Press, 1989.

Hobsbawm, Eric, and Terence Ranger, eds. *The Invention of Tradition.* Cambridge: Cambridge University Press, 1983.

Hoffman, Daniel. *Form and Fable in American Fiction.* New York: Oxford University Press, 1965.

Hollinger, David A., and Charles Capper, eds. *The American Intellectual Tradition.* Vol. I, *1630–1865.* 5th ed. Oxford: Oxford University Press, 2006.

Howe, Daniel Walker. *What Hath God Wrought: The Transformation of America, 1815–1848.* Oxford: Oxford University Press, 2007.

Hughes, Amy E. *Spectacles of Reform: Theater and Activism in Nineteenth-Century America.* Ann Arbor: University of Michigan Press, 2012.

Hughes, Robert. "Sleepy Hollow: Fearful Pleasures and the Nightmare of History." *Arizona Quarterly* 61, no. 3 (Autumn 2005).

Hunt, Leigh. *Selected Writings.* Ed. David Jesson-Dibley. Manchester: Carcarnet Press, 2003.

Irving, Pierre. *The Life and Letters of Washington Irving.* 4 vols. New York: G. P. Putnam, 1864.

Irving, Washington. *History, Tales, and Sketches.* New York: Library of America, 1983.

Irving, Washington. *Bracebridge Hall, Tales of a Traveller, The Alhambra.* New York: Library of America, 1983.

Jackson, Leon. *The Business of Letters: Authorial Economies in Antebellum America.* Stanford: Stanford University Press, 2008.

James, C. L. R. *Mariners, Renegades, and Castaways: The Story of Herman Melville and the World We Live In.* Hanover: University Press of New England, 2001.

James, William. *The Principles of Psychology.* Cambridge, Mass.: Harvard University Press, 1983.

Jefferson, Thomas. *The Portable Thomas Jefferson.* Ed. Merril D. Peterson. London: Penguin Books, 1977.

Johnson, Odai. *Absence and Memory in Colonial American Theatre: Fiorelli's Plaster.* New York and Basingstoke: Palgrave Macmillan, 2006.

Kaplan, Amy. *The Social Construction of American Realism.* Chicago: University of Chicago Press, 1988.

Kete, Mary Louise. *Sentimental Collaborations: Mourning and Middle-Class Identity in Nineteenth-Century America.* Durham and London: Duke University Press, 2000.

Kilde, Jeanne Halgren. *When Church Became Theatre: The Transformation of Evangelical Architecture and Worship in Nineteenth-Century America.* Oxford: Oxford University Press, 2002.

Kinlaw, C. J. "Determinism and the Hiddenness of God in Calvin's Theology." *Religious Studies* 24, no. 4 (1988).

Kruger, Loren. *The National Stage: Theatre and Cultural Legitimation in England, France, and America.* London: University of Chicago Press, 1992.

Ladurie, Le Roy Emmanuel. *Carnival: A People's Uprising at Romans 1579–1580*. Trans. Mary Fenney. London: Scolar Press, 1980.
Lang, Amy Schrager. *The Syntax of Class: Writing Inequality in Nineteenth-Century America*. Princeton: Princeton University Press, 2003.
Lawrence, David Herbert. *Studies in Classic American Literature*. London: Penguin Books, 1977.
Lawson, Andrew. *Walt Whitman and the Class Struggle*. Iowa City: University of Iowa Press, 2006.
Leavis, F. R. *"Anna Karenina" and Other Essays*. London: Chatto and Windus, 1967.
Lehuu, Isabelle. *Carnival on the Page: Popular Print Culture in Antebellum America*. Chapel Hill: University of North Carolina Press, 2000.
Levine, Lawrence W. *Highbrow/Lowbrow: The Emergence of Cultural Hierarchy in America*. Cambridge, Mass.: Harvard University Press, 1988.
Levine, Robert S. *Conspiracy and Romance: Studies in Brockden Brown, Cooper, Hawthorne, and Melville*. Cambridge: Cambridge University Press, 1989.
Levinson, Marjorie. "What Is New Formalism?" *PMLA* 122, no. 2 (March 2007): 558–69.
Lewis, R. W. B. *The American Adam: Innocence, Tragedy, and Tradition in the Nineteenth Century*. Chicago: University of Chicago Press, 1955.
Lippard, George. *The Quaker City, or The Monks of Monks' Hall*. Ed. David S. Reynolds. Boston: University of Massachusetts Press, 1995.
Lippard, George. *The White Banner*. Vol. 1. Philadelphia: George Lippard, 1851.
Lippard, George. "Constitution and By-Laws of Progress Circle No. 9 of the Brotherhood of the Union, District of Northern Liberties, County of Philadelphia." Philadelphia: Jos. Severns and Company, 1850.
Lippard, George. *The B.G.C.I. Of the Circles of the Order*. Philadelphia, 1850. [fragment].
Locke, John. *An Essay Concerning Human Understanding*. London: Penguin Books, 1997.
Lohafer, Susan, and Jo Ellyn Clarey, eds. *Short Story Theory at a Crossroads*. Baton Rouge: Louisiana State University Press, 1989.
Looby, Christopher. *Voicing America: Language, Literary Form, and the Origins of the United States*. Chicago: University of Chicago Press, 1996.
Lott, Eric. *Love and Theft: Blackface Minstrelsy and the American Working Class*. New York: Oxford University Press, 1993.
Loughran, Trish. *The Republic of Print: Print Culture in the Age of U.S. Nation Building, 1770–1870*. New York: Columbia University Press, 2007.
Macready, William Charles. *The Journal of William Charles Macready 1832–1851*. Ed. J. C. Trewin. London: Longman, Green, and Co., 1967.
McLamore, Richard V. "The Dutchman in the Attic: Claiming an Inheritance in *The Sketch Book of Geoffrey Crayon*." *American Literature* 72, no. 1 (March 2000).
Mah, Harold. "Phantasies of the Public Sphere: Rethinking the Habermas of Historians." *Journal of Modern History* 72, no. 1 (March 2000).
Matteson, John. *Eden's Outcasts: The Story of Louisa May Alcott and Her Father*. New York and London: Norton and Co., 2007.

Matthiessen, F. O. *American Renaissance: Art and Expression in the Age of Emerson and Whitman*. London: Oxford University Press, 1941.

McConachie, Bruce A. *Melodramatic Formations, American Theatre and Society 1820–1870*. Iowa City: University of Iowa Press, 1992.

McGill, Meredith L. *American Literature and the Culture of Reprinting, 1834–1853*. Philadelphia: University of Pennsylvania Press, 2003.

McWilliams, Wilson Carey. *The Idea of Fraternity in America*. London: University of California Press, 1973.

Melville, Gansevoort. *1846 London Journal*. Ed. Herschel Parker. New York: Astor, Lenox, and Tilden Foundation, 1966.

Melville, Herman. *The Complete Short Fiction*. London: Everyman's Library, 1997.

Melville, Herman. *Pierre, Israel Potter, The Piazza Tales, The Confidence Man, Uncollected Prose, Billy Budd*. New York: Library of America, 1984.

Merrill, Lisa. *When Romeo Was a Woman: Charlotte Cushman and Her Circle of Female Spectators*. Ann Arbor: University of Michigan Press, 2002.

Michaels, Walter Benn. *Our America: Nativism, Modernism, and Pluralism*. Durham: Duke University Press, 1995.

Milder, Robert. "The Other Hawthorne." *The New England Quarterly* 81, no. 4 (Dec. 2008).

Miller, J. Hillis. *Hawthorne and History: Defacing It*. Oxford: Basil Blackwell, 1991.

Mills, Bruce. *Poe, Fuller, and the Mesmeric Arts: Transitions in the American Renaissance*. Columbia: University of Missouri Press, 2005.

Moody, Jane. *Illegitimate Theatre in London, 1770–1840*. Cambridge: Cambridge University Press, 2000.

Moody, Richard. *The Astor Place Riot*. Bloomington: Indiana University Press, 1958.

Moore, Thomas R. *A Thick and Darksome Veil: The Rhetoric of Hawthorne's Sketches, Prefaces, and Essays*. Boston: Northeastern University Press, 1994.

Murray, Laura J. "The Aesthetic of Dispossession: Washington Irving and Ideologies of (De)Colonization in the Early Republic." *American Literary History* 8, no. 2 (Summer 1996).

Nathans, Heather S. *Early American Theatre from the Revolution to Thomas Jefferson: Into the Hands of the People*. Cambridge: Cambridge University Press, 2003.

Nelson, Dana D. "The Haunting of White Manhood: Poe, Fraternal Ritual, and Polygenesis." *American Literature* 69, no. 3 (Sept. 1997).

Nelson, Dana D. *National Manhood: Capitalist Citizenship and the Imagined Fraternity of White Men*. London: Duke University Press, 1998.

Newman, Judie. *Fictions of America: Narratives of Global Empire*. Oxford: Routledge, 2007.

Newman, Simon P. *Embodied History: The Lives of the Poor in Early Philadelphia*. Philadelphia: University of Pennsylvania Press, 2003.

O'Connor, Frank. *The Lonely Voice: A Study of the Short Story*. London: Macmillan and Co. Ltd., 1963.

Ostrowski, Carl. "Inside the Temple of Ravoni: George Lippard's Anti-Exposé." *ESQ: A Journal of the American Renaissance* 55, no. 1 (2009).

Pease, Donald E. *Visionary Compacts: American Renaissance Writings in Cultural Context*. Madison: University of Wisconsin Press, 1987.

Pethers, Matthew J. "Transatlantic Migration and the Politics of the Picturesque in Washington Irving's *Sketch Book*." *Symbiosis* 9, no. 2 (Oct. 2005).

Pixérécourt, René-Charles Guilbert de. *Four Melodramas*. Trans. Daniel Gerould and Marvin Carlsson. New York: Martin E. Segal Theatre Center Publications, 2002.

Playfair, Giles. *The Prodigy: The Strange Life of Master Betty*. London: Secker and Warburg Ltd., 1967.

Plotz, Judith. *Romanticism and the Vocation on Childhood*. New York: Palgrave, 2001.

Plummer, Laura, and Michael Nelson. "Girls Can Take Care of Themselves: Gender and Storytelling in Washington Irving's 'The Legend of Sleepy Hollow.'" *Studies in Short Fiction* 30, no. 2 (Spring 1993).

Pocock, J. G. A. *The Machiavellian Moment: Florentine Political Thought and the Atlantic Republican Tradition*. Princeton and Oxford: Princeton University Press, 1975.

Poe, Edgar Allan. *The Complete Tales and Poems*. London: Penguin Books, 1982.

Poe, Edgar Allan. *The Letters of Edgar Allan Poe*. Ed. John Ostrom. New York: Gordian Press Inc., 1966.

Poe, Edgar Allan. *Essays and Reviews*. Ed. John Ingram. Cambridge: Library of America, 1984.

Pollard, Finn. *The Literary Quest for an American National Character*. Oxford: Routledge, 2009.

Reed, Naomi C. "The Specter of Wall Street: 'Bartleby, the Scrivener' and the Language of Commodities." *American Literature* 76, no. 2 (June 2004).

Reising, Russell. *The Unusable Past: Theory and the Study of American Literature*. London: Routledge, 1987.

Reynolds. David S. *Beneath the American Renaissance: The Subversive Imagination in the Age of Emerson and Melville*. Cambridge, Mass.: Harvard University Press, 1988.

Reynolds, David S. *George Lippard: Prophet of Progress (Anthology)*. New York and Berne: Peter Lang, 1986.

Reynolds, David S. *George Lippard*. Boston: Twayne Publishers, 1982.

Richards, Jeffrey H. *Theater Enough: American Culture and the Metaphor of the World Stage, 1607–1789*. London: Duke University Press, 1991.

Richards, Jeffrey H. *Drama, Theatre, and Identity in the American New Republic*. Cambridge: Cambridge University Press, 2005.

Ringe, Donald A. *The Pictorial Mode: Space & Time in the Art of Bryant, Irving, and Cooper*. Louisville: University Press of Kentucky, 1971.

Roach, Joseph. *Cities of the Dead: Circum-Atlantic Performance*. New York: Columbia University Press, 1996.

Rodgers, Daniel T. *Contested Truths: Keywords in American Politics Since Independence*. London: Harvard University Press, 1987.

Rogin, Michael Paul. *Subversive Genealogy: The Politics and Art of Herman Melville*. New York: Alfred A. Knopf, 1983.

Roth, Martin. *Comedy and America: The Lost World of Washington Irving*. London: Kennikat Press, 1976.

Rousseau, Jean Jacques. *Emile*. Trans. William Boyd. New York: Teachers College Press, 1960.

Rousseau, Jean Jacques. *The Social Contract*. Trans. Maurice Cranston. London: Penguin Books, 1968.

Rousseau, Jean Jacques. *The Confessions*. Trans. J. M. Cohen. London: Penguin Books, 1953.
Rowland, Beryl. "Grace Church and Melville's Story of 'The Two Temples.'" *Nineteenth-Century Fiction* 28, no. 3 (Dec. 1973).
Rubin-Dorsky, Jeffrey. "Washington Irving: Sketches of Anxiety." *American Literature* 58, no. 4 (December 1986).
Rudnicki, Robert W. *Percyscapes: The Fugue State in Twentieth-Century Southern Fiction*. Baton Rouge: Louisiana State University Press, 1999.
Said, Edward W. *Beginnings: Intention and Method*. London: Granta, 1997.
Salazar, James B. *Bodies of Reform: The Rhetoric of Character in Gilded Age America*. New York and London: New York University Press, 2010.
Sánchez-Eppler, Karen. *Dependent States: The Child's Part in Nineteenth-Century American Culture*. Chicago: University of Chicago Press, 2005.
Sarkela, Sandra J. "Freedom's Call: The Persuasive Power of Mercy Otis Warren's Dramatic Sketches, 1772–1775." *Early American Literature* 44, no. 3 (2009).
Seelye, John. "Root and Branch: Washington Irving and American Humor." *Nineteenth-Century Fiction* 38, no. 4 (March 1984).
Shattuck, Charles H., ed. *Bulwer and Macready: A Chronicle of the Early Victorian Theatre*. Urbana: University of Illinois Press, 1958.
Shils, Edward. *Tradition*. London and Boston: Faber and Faber, 1981.
Singleton, Marvin. "Melville's Bartleby: Over the Republic, a Ciceronian Shadow." *Canadian Review of American Studies* 6 (1975).
Smith, Adam. *The Theory of Moral Sentiments*. Ed. Knut Haakonssen. Cambridge: Cambridge University Press, 2002.
Smith, Ryan K. *Gothic Arches, Latin Crosses: Anti-Catholicism and American Church Designs in the Nineteenth Century*. Chapel Hill: University of North Carolina Press, 2006.
Sollors, Werner. *Beyond Ethnicity: Consent and Descent in American Culture*. New York: Oxford University Press, 1986.
Solomon, P. C. *Dickens and Melville in Their Time*. London: Columbia University Press, 1975.
Southworth, E. D. E. N. *The Wife's Victory; and Other Nouvellettes*. Philadelphia: T. B. Peterson and Brothers, 1875.
Sponsler, Clare. *Ritual Imports: Performing Medieval Drama in America*. Ithaca and London: Cornell University Press, 2004.
Stallybrass, Peter, and Allon White. *The Politics and Poetics of Transgression*. New York: Cornell University Press, 1986.
Stephens, John Russell. *The Censorship of English Drama, 1824–1901*. Cambridge: Cambridge University Press, 1980.
Stern, Madeleine. *Behind a Mask: The Unknown Thrillers of Louisa May Alcott*. New York: William Morrow, 1975.
Streeby, Shelley. *American Sensations: Class, Empire, and the Production of Popular Culture*. Berkeley: University of California Press, 2002.
Swann, Charles. *Nathaniel Hawthorne: Tradition and Revolution*. Cambridge: Cambridge University Press, 1991.
Tallack, Douglas. *The Nineteenth-Century American Short Story: Language, Form, and Ideology*. London: Routledge, 1993.

Tamarkin, Elisa. *Anglophilia: Deference, Devotion, and Antebellum America.* Chicago: University of Chicago Press, 2008.
Taubman, Howard. *The Making of the American Theatre.* London: Longmans, Green, and Co. Ltd., 1965.
Thomas, Brook. *Cross-Examinations of Law and Literature: Cooper, Hawthorne, Stowe, and Melville.* Cambridge: Cambridge University Press, 1987.
Thompson, G. R. *The Art of Authorial Presence: Hawthorne's Provincial Tales.* London: Duke University Press, 1993.
Thompson, G. R. "Literary Politics and the 'Legitimate Sphere': Poe, Hawthorne, and the 'Tale Proper.'" *Nineteenth-Century Literature* 49, no. 2 (Sept. 1994).
Thompson, Graham. *Male Sexuality Under Surveillance: The Office in American Literature.* Iowa City: University of Iowa Press, 2003.
Tocqueville, Alexis de. *Democracy in America.* Trans. Henry Reeve. Stilwell, Kans.: Digireads, 2007.
Tomkins, Jane. *Sensational Designs: The Cultural Work of American Fiction, 1790s–1860s.* Oxford and New York: Oxford University Press, 1985.
Turner, Victor. *From Ritual to Theatre.* New York: PAJ Publications, 1982.
Turner, Victor. *The Anthropology of Performance.* New York: PAJ Publications, 1988.
Turner, Victor. *The Ritual Process: Structure and Antistructure.* London: University of Chicago Press, 1969.
Varty, Anne. *Children and Theatre in Victorian Britain: "All Work, No Play."* Basingstoke, Hampshire: Palgrave Macmillan, 2008.
Voegelin, Eric. *The New Science of Politics: An Introduction.* Chicago: University of Chicago Press, 1952.
von Frank, Albert J. *The Sacred Game: Provincialism and Frontier Consciousness in American Literature, 1630–1860.* London: Cambridge University Press, 1985.
Waldstreicher, David. *In the Midst of Perpetual Fetes: The Making of American Nationalism, 1776–1820.* Chapel Hill: University of North Carolina Press, 1997.
Ward, Henry Dana. *Freemasonry: Its Pretensions Exposed.* New York: N.p., 1828.
Warner, Michael. *Letters of the Republic: Publication and the Public Sphere in Eighteenth-Century America.* Cambridge, Mass.: Harvard University Press, 1990.
Warner, Michael. "Irving's Posterity." *ELH* 67, no. 3 (Fall 2000).
Waterman, Bryan. *The Republic of Intellect: The Friendly Club of New York and the Making of American Literature.* Baltimore: Johns Hopkins University Press, 2007.
Watts, Steven. "The Idiocy of American Studies: Poststructuralism, Language, and Politics in the Age of Self-Fulfillment." *American Quarterly* 43, no. 4 (Dec. 1991).
Weisbuch, Robert. *Atlantic Double-Cross: American Literature and British Influence in the Age of Emerson.* Chicago: University of Chicago Press, 1986.
West, Peter. *The Arbiters of Reality: Hawthorne, Melville, and the Rise of Mass Information Culture.* Columbus: Ohio State University Press, 2008.
Weston, Jessie L. *From Ritual to Romance.* Princeton: Princeton University Press, 1993.
Whalen, Terence. *Edgar Allan Poe & The Masses: The Political Economy of Literature in Antebellum America.* Princeton: Princeton University Press, 1999.
Williams, Susan S. *Reclaiming Authorship: Literary Women in America, 1850–1900.* Philadelphia: University of Pennsylvania Press, 2006.

Winter, Per, Jakob Lothe, and Hans H. Skei, eds. *The Art of Brevity: Excursions in Short Fiction Theory and Analysis*. Columbia: University of South Carolina Press, 2004.
Wordsworth, William. *The Prelude: The Four Texts*. London: Penguin Books, 1995.
Wordsworth, William. *The Major Works*. Oxford: Oxford University Press, 2008.
Young, Philip. "The Machine in Tartarus: Melville's Inferno." *American Literature* 63, no. 2 (June 1991).
Young, Philip. *American Fiction, American Myth*. Philadelphia: Pennsylvania State University Press, 2000.
Ziff, Larzer. *Literary Democracy: The Declaration of Cultural Independence in America*. New York: Viking Press, 1981.

Index

Abolitionism, 4, 51, 132, 172, 173, 229
Adams, John, 4, 10
Addison, Joseph, and Richard Steele, 1, 2, 18, 34–38, 42–43, 46, 49
Cato, 89
Africa and Africans, 2, 82, 173
Agamben, Giorgio, 176, 187
Agnew, Jean-Christophe, 165, 201
Agrarianism, 36, 125
Alcott, Bronson, 230
   and the Temple School, 235–37
Alcott, Louisa May, 30
   "Behind A Mask," 228, 231, 239–40
   Journal, 227
   "King of Clubs and the Queen of Hearts," 240–43
   "Letter to Her Father," 227
   Little Women, 17
   On Picket Duty, 231, 240
   "Pauline's Passion and Punishment," 231–35
Alien and Sedition Acts, 10
André, John (soldier and spy), 13, 71, 73
   André: A Tragedy (Dunlap), 12–17, 104
   and *The Mischianza*, 85
Anti-Federalist, 11, 57
Anti-theatricalism, 5, 11, 30, 78, 198
Arnold, Benedict, 13, 71
Astor Place Riot, 117–29, 157, 168–69, 186, 249n3
   "Account of the Terrific and Fatal Riot," 166–67

Audiences
   and "Bettymania," 158–62, 179
   and class, 9, 14–15, 93, 115, 121, 122, 132, 140, 141, 153, 157, 167, 203, 206, 217, 219, 220, 224, 228, 230, 232, 238, 243
   and gender, 30, 66, 70
   and race, 172–73
   See also Davis, Jim, and Victor Emeljanow
Automata. *See* During, Simon

Baker, Benjamin (playwright), *A Glance at New York*, 169
Bakhtin, Mikhail, and carnivalesque, 164
Barnes, Elizabeth, on sentimentalism, 28, 52, 183
Barrish, Phillip, and realism, 224
Bell, Catherine, on forms of ritual, 58, 67, 128
Benjamin, Walter, 2, 100, 245
Bentham, Jeremy (philosopher), 36, 246n5
   and Benthamism, 115, 122
   and the middle class, 125–26
   panopticon, 125, 167, 138
   welfare state, 140
Berthold, Dennis, on Melville and individualism, 118, 119
Betty, William Henry West, 151, 155–62
Bingham, Caleb (educator), *Columbian Orator*, 89

Blaikie, William (author and bodybuilder), 241
Boddy, Kasia, short story form, 30
Bonaparte, Napoleon, 135, 158, 160
Boucicault, Dion (playwright), 57, 75
  The Poor of New York, 17
Bowery B'Hoys, 167, 169
Brand, Dana, flaneur, 2–3
  and the sketch, 44
Brodhead, Richard, discipline, 230, 239
Brooks, Peter, 101
Brown, Charles Brockden, 105
Brownson, Orestes (author and transcendentalist)
  The Laboring Classes, 145–46
Bulwer-Lytton, Edward (playwright and politician), 17, 107
  Richelieu; Or, The Conspiracy, 117, 120–22, 123–26
Burke, Edmund, and sublime, 45–47
Burr, Aaron (politician), 1, 5–6, 9, 37

Carlyle, Thomas (historian)
  Chartism, 145
  On Heroes, Heroworship, and the Heroic in History, 172
Carnes, Mark, masonic rituals, 79–80, 87, 91, 99, 102–3
Carnival, 25, 40, 90, 94–96, 164, 192, 197, 199–200, 201, 210
  carnivalesque, 155, 165, 174–75, 204, 211, 217, 220, 237, 239, 241, 242
Castronovo, Russ, on necro ideology, 162, 181, 189, 213
Censorship, 121
  and Dunlap, William, 15
  and Theatre Regulation Act, 122
  see also "Alien and Sedition Acts"
Child, Lydia Maria (author and abolitionist)
  "The Black Saxons," 172
  Hobomok, 35
childhood/adolescence, 87, 160–62, 173, 175, 179–80
Cicero, Marcus Tullius (politician and orator), 88, 131, 175, 184

Coffeehouses, "Tontine," 6, 19, 245n3
  as public sphere, 18–19
Colacurcio, Michael, 191, 197, 202–3
Coleridge, Samuel Taylor, 125
Crain, Caleb, on sympathy, 13
Cuba, 232, 242

Dante (poet)
  Divine Comedy, 146–49
Davis, Jim, and Victor Emeljanow, audiences, 123–24
Democratic-Republican Party, 1, 5–6, 38–40, 44, 47
Denning, Michael, on "accents," 157
Deference, politics of, 19, 89, 97, 118, 129–30, 134–36, 177
Dickens, Charles (author), 107, 154, 177
Dimock, Wai Chee, and imperialism, 144
diptych form, and Melville's "The Two Temples," 135–37
Douglass, Frederick (author and abolitionist)
  The Heroic Slave, 172–73
Dunlap, William (playwright and historian)
  Andre: A Tragedy, 12–17, 104
  The History of the American Theater, 4, 8, 140
  Park Theatre manager, 4, 56, 245n3
During, Simon, automata, 218

Ekphrasis, 12, 23
Elliott, Michael, and realism, 229
Emerson, Ralph Waldo (author and transcendentalist), 139, 154, 209, 216, 219–20, 222, 230, 236–37
  Essays: First Series, 198–99
  Nature, 21, 170, 192, 198
Evelev, John, and professionalism, 212

Fairy Tales, 80–81
Federalist Party, 1, 4–14, 36, 38, 39, 50, 62, 136, 245n1
Fiedler, Leslie, on homosociality, 64, 205
Fliegelman, Jay, on social performance, 22, 84–88

Foley, Barbara, class politics in Melville, 117–19, 127, 176, 185
Forrest, Edwin (actor), 66, 117–18, 123, 157, 165
  in L. M. Alcott's journal, 227
Fraternal Orders
  Brotherhood of the Union (see Lippard, George)
  Freemasons, 78–79, 84–85, 91, 248n7, 248nn11–13
  Odd Fellows, 77–79, 81–84, 105
Fuller, Margaret (author and transcendentalist)
  Woman in the Nineteenth Century, 149–50, 242

Gardner, Jared, and magazines, 105, 246n11
Geertz, Clifford, and culture, 93
Gesture, 2, 12–19, 26, 28, 48, 55, 58, 63, 65, 72, 85–87, 90, 91, 96, 100–101, 110, 118, 124, 134, 141, 184, 197, 208, 219, 228, 240
Giles, Paul, and transatlanticism, 35, 49, 50, 61, 162, 209, 246n6
Gilmore, Michael, and marketplace, 171, 182, 185–86, 206, 217
Gilmore, Paul, and the aesthetic, 218–19
Girard, René, and the scapegoat, 71, 73
Gnosticism, 193, 195, 198–99, 203, 212
Goffman, Erving, presentation of self, 19
Gothic
  architecture, 110, 132–34
  literary mode, 22, 31, 67, 75, 144, 161, 177, 178, 181, 192, 228, 230, 240
Gustafson, Sandra, performativity, 22

Hackenberg, Sara, theatricality in Alcott, 239–40
Hadley, Elaine, melodramatic mode, 81, 90, 163–64, 192–93, 196, 200
Haltunnen, Karen, social performance, 93, 197, 213, 232, 239, 247n3, 248n8
Hamilton, Alexander (politician), 8, 35–36
Hamilton, Kristie, sketch tradition, 34, 37, 143

Harrison, Les, cultural hierarchy, 223, 225
Hawthorne, Nathaniel (author)
  "The Christmas Banquet" 214–17
  "Main Street," 217–26
  "The Maypole of Merry Mount," 191–209
  "The Procession of Life," 211–14
Hazlitt, William (critic), 158, 189
Heraldry, 89–90
Hicks, Elias, 4, 245n3
Hobsbawm, Eric, nationalism as performance, 83
Home, John (playwright), *Douglas*, 125

Imperialism
  American, 47, 69, 145, 232
  British, 2, 13, 27, 35, 37, 115, 118, 120, 134, 136, 138
  Transnational, 80
Irving, Peter (journalist and businessman), 1, 2, 4, 6
Irving, Pierre, *Life and Letters of Washington Irving*, 3, 39
Irving, Washington
  Bracebridge Hall, 37
  A History of New York, 41, 60
  The Morning Chronicle "Oldstyle Sketches," 1–6
  The Sketch-Book of Geoffrey Crayon, 33–75

Jackson, Andrew, 14, 36, 76, 83, 125–26, 167–68, 180, 230
James, C. L. R., 126
James, Henry (author), 203, 228, 229, 231
James, William (psychologist)
  Principles of Psychology, 231, 235, 241
Jefferson, Thomas, 5, 36, 37, 40, 43, 44, 47, 54, 60–62, 68
  "Jeffersonian," 8, 36, 59, 62, 137
  Notes on the State of Virginia, 61
Johnson, Odai, and antitheatricalism, 11, 78, 198

Kaplan, Amy, and realism, 229
Kete, Mary-Louise, mourning rituals, 212–13

Kilde, Jeanne Halgren, church architecture, 132–33
Knowles, Sheridan (playwright and clergyman), 17, 249n1
Virginius, 125

Ladurie, Emmanuel Le Roy
Carnival: A People's Uprising at Romans, 1579–1580, 94–95
Lawson, Andrew, and Walt Whitman, 166, 169, 204, 220
Leavis, F. R., "Americanness of American Literature," 21
Lehuu, Isabelle, print culture, 17, 20, 155, 164, 199–200, 246n8
Levine, Lawrence, cultural hierarchy, 9, 16, 157, 229
Liberalism, 99, 125, 139, 140, 180, 231, 237, 246n1
Lippard, George
"Adonai: The Pilgrim of Eternity," 81, 108, 110–12, 114
"Brotherhood of the Union," 77, 102, 104–10, 112, 248nn15–16
The White Banner, 104, 107–10, 114
Locke, John, 36, 57, 89, 246n1
Looby, Christopher, 22–23, 36
logocracy, 23
The Lowell Offering (periodical), 150

Macready, William, 117–27, 136, 157, 165
Mah, Harold. *See* Coffeeshops
Marx, Leo
and myth and symbol, 21
Mather, Cotton (politician and clergyman), 70, 73
Matthews, Brander, 246n10
May, Charles, short story form, 22, 27
McConachie, Bruce, on theatre culture, 56, 66, 125
McGill, Meredith, reprinting, 27–28
Melodrama
genre, 17, 56, 66, 80, 93, 101, 122, 125–26, 143, 169, 172, 238
as mode, 25, 91, 101, 111, 114, 121, 138, 146, 163, 177, 220, 228, 229, 232

See also Pixérécourt, René-Charles Guilbert de
Melville, Herman
"Bartleby, the Scrivener," 22, 130, 176–89, 249n4
"Benito Cereno," 173, 182, 184–85
and Bulwer-Lytton, Astor Place Riot, 119–21
criticism of Irving, 36
"The Fiddler," 153–76
"Hawthorne and His Mosses," 21
Moby-Dick, 4
Omoo, 119
"The Paradise of Bachelors and the Tartarus of Maids," 137–51
Pierre: Or, the Ambiguities, 119, 153, 155
"Poor Man's Pudding and Rich Man's Crumbs," 139–41
"The Two Temples," 117–37
Typee, 119
Mill, John Stuart, on Bentham and Coleridge, 125
Mormonism, 82–83
Murray, Judith Sargent, 8

Nathans, Heather, on theatre culture, 5
Neal, John
Logan, 35
"Unpublished Preface to the North American Stories," 35
Nelson, Dana, fraternity, 78, 206, 215

O'Connor, Frank, and short story theory, 26–27, 228
O'Sullivan, James, Young America, 194
Olson, Charles, on Melville and Shakespeare, 16, 117, 155
Oratory, 110, 139, 167, 242. *See also* Bingham, Caleb
Orature. *See* Roach, Joseph; wa Thiong'o, Ngugi
Ostrowski, Carl, exposé, 82

Pantomime, 90, 91, 135
Peabody, Elizabeth Palmer

Aesthetic Papers, 218
Pethers, Matthew, on *The Sketch-Book of Geoffrey Crayon*, 41, 45, 46
Pixérécourt, René-Charles Guilbert de (playwright), 56
"Melodrama," 93
Playfair, Giles, on Master Betty, 158
Plotz, Judith, romantic childhood, 158, 161
Plummer, Laura, on Sleepy Hollow, 70–73
Poe, Edgar Allan
 "The American Drama," 92–93
 "The Cask of Amontillado," 85–97
 "The Masque of the Red Death," 23
 "The Philosophy of Composition," 25
 "The Pit and the Pendulum," 97–104
Post-Lauria, Sheila, Melville and literary marketplace, 154, 168, 170
Public sphere, 2, 8, 10–11, 19, 30, 66, 82, 115, 119, 141, 142, 145, 147, 171, 199, 206–9, 218, 219, 225, 231, 233, 238, 242

Realism
 and Alcott, 227–31
 and anthropology, 226
 and drama, 11, 226
 and "local color," 225
 in "Main Street," 224
 and the short story, 22
 and social mobility, 250n3
 and technology, 225
 See also Barrish, Phillip
Reform Act of 1832, 123
Reising, Russell, allegory, 194
Republicanism, 246n5
Reynolds, David, on Lippard's politics, 102, 105 109
Richards, Jeffrey, theatre culture, 9, 15
Ritual
 forms of, 58, 67, 128
 gesture as, 2, 12–19, 26, 28, 48, 55, 58, 63, 65, 72, 85–87, 90, 91, 96, 100–101, 110, 118, 124, 134, 141, 184, 197, 208, 219, 228, 240

 and mourning, 30, 209–17
 and nationalism, 34, 50, 62, 84, 104–15, 128, 130, 232
 and social performance, 22, 84–88, 93, 197, 213, 232, 239, 247n3, 248n8
 theory, 28, 58, 93, 129 (*see also* Roach, Joseph; Turner, Victor; wa Thiong'o, Ngugi)
 See also Carnival
Roach, Joseph
 "expressive movements," 19
 "social boundaries," 22
 definition of "orature," 24
 surrogacy, 63
 "living memory," 214
Robespierre, Maximilien, 98
Rohrberger, Mary, short story theory, 58
Roscoe, William, 49, 51
Rousseau, Jean-Jacques
 "social contract," 10, 177
 as Freemason, 248n12

Sánchez-Eppler, Karen, childhood, 180–81
Sarkela, Sandra J., on Mercy Warren's dramatic sketches, 7
Sentimentalism
 and gender, 51–52, 114, 229, 237–40, 243
 as literary mode, 41, 85, 111, 176, 177, 185, 189, 208, 220, 224, 226
 as social imaginary, 13, 28, 54, 62, 65, 115, 169, 180, 184, 214–15, 229
Shakespeare, William, performances of, 157
Short story
 and allegory, 176, 194–96, 240
 form, 23, 47, 194
 and the literary sketch, 2–6, 34–38, 43–47, 51, 54, 57, 60–69, 72–75, 108, 109–11, 135, 143, 214–18, 222
 and "Lyric effects," 26, 58, 201
 See also Diptych; May, Charles; Rohrberger, Mary; Tallack, Douglas

Sincerity, 134, 215–17
  and performance, 154, 157, 161, 174, 175, 208, 218
Smith, Adam
  Theory of Moral Sentiments, 129
Southworth, E. D. E. N.
  "The Wife's Victory," 52–54
Sponsler, Claire, on medievalism, 130
Stephens, John Russell, on censorship, 120, 122
Streeby, Shelley
  story papers, 107–8
  racial hierarchies, 233
Sublime, 28, 37, 40, 51, 54, 161, 165, 166, 179, 181–89, 195, 197–99, 213, 217, 222
  in "The Author's Account of Himself," 42, 44
  in *The Laboring Classes*, 146
  See also Burke, Edmund
Swann, Charles, Hawthorne as romantic, 222

tableaux vivants, in Alcott, 235, 238–39
Tallack, Douglas
  lyric effects, 26
  short story form, 23
Tamarkin, Elisa
  "Anglophilia," 120
  deference and power, definitions of, 129
Tammany Society, 6, 19, 165, 167, 169
Tappan, Lewis (abolitionist, evangelical)
  and Broadway Tabernacle Church, 132
Tarrytown
  as female space, 70
  as site of trauma, 71
Theatre boxes
  cause of Astor Place Riot, 166
  and power, 167
Theatre culture, 5, 8, 9, 15, 56, 66, 125
Thompson, G. R.
  on "The Hawthorne Question," 202
  on short story form, 194

Thompson, Graham
  desire in "Bartleby," 180, 183
  spatiality in "Bartleby," 177
Tocqueville, Alexis de
  theatre culture, 8
  tyranny, 15
Tontines. *See* Coffeehouses
Transcendentalism
  and Puritanism, 198
  and embodiment, 218
Transatlanticism, 11, 14
  and memory, 29, 36, 37, 73, 82, 128, 136
  and performance, 90–91, 93, 98
  and sympathy, 85, 86, 104, 147–48, 206, 240
  and republicanism, 58 , 79, 130, 137, 177
  theory, 22, 50, 118, 157, 209
Turner, Victor
  "liminars," 22, 101
  "social drama," 23, 62–63
  structure/anti-structure, 93

Varty, Anne, childhood, 161, 179
Voegelin, Eric. *See* Gnosticism

wa Thiong'o, Ngugi, 24, 82
Walsh, Mike (protester, politician), 167, 185
Ward, Henry Dana (polemicist)
  Freemasonry; Its Pretensions Exposed, 80, 103
Warren, Mercy Otis (journalist and playwright)
  "dramatic sketches" (*The Adulateur; The Defeat*), 7–8
Whitman, Walt (poet), 166
Wordsworth, William
  The Prelude, 153
  and Master Betty, 189

Young, Philip, 61
  on Melville and Dante, 146–47
Young America, 35, 36, 115, 118, 195